TOLERANCE
AND
INTOLERANCE

The Proof of Fire Before the Sultan. Giotto di Bondone (1266–1336). Cappella
Bardi, S. Croce, Florence, Italy. Courtesy of Scala/Art Resource.

TOLERANCE
AND
INTOLERANCE

Social Conflict in the Age of the Crusades

Edited by MICHAEL GERVERS
and JAMES M. POWELL

 SYRACUSE UNIVERSITY PRESS

Library of Congress Cataloging-in-Publicatin Data

Tolerance and intolerance : social conflict in the age of the crusades / edited by Michael Gervers and James M. Powell.
    p. cm.—(Medieval studies)
  Includes bibliographical references and index.
  ISBN 0-8156-2869-2 (alk. paper)—ISBN 0-8156-2870-6 (pbk. : alk. paper)
    1. Toleration—History—To 1500. 2. Social conflict—History—To 1500. 3. Religious tolerance—History—To 1500. 4. Crusades. I. Gervers, Michael, 1942– II. Powell, James M. III. Medieval studies (Syracuse, N.Y.)
HM1271.T65 2001
303.3'85—dc21

                                                           00-030780

Manufactured in the United States of America

In memoriam

LEONARD E. BOYLE, O.P.

Contents

Acknowledgments

The editors would like to thank all who contributed to this project, in particular, Michael Powell, who served as assistant editor in charge of the computer files. Special thanks go to Gillian Long and Ghada Jayyusi Lehn for proofreading. We also wish to thank Cynthia Maude-Gembler of the Syracuse University Press for her patience with us.

Introduction

Although it may not be susceptible of proof, it is probable that more wars have been fought out of a desire to obtain justice than as a result of intolerance. Difficult as it may be for us to regard the Crusades in this light, it is important that historians recognize that the concepts of tolerance and intolerance, which are among the common coin of the modern age, are themselves fitting objects of scrutiny. They did not emerge suddenly or fully formed; they have a prehistory that has not received sufficient attention.[1] Not surprisingly, and for reasons rooted in our own agonized past, historians of the recent past have put great stress on the study of tolerance and intolerance but have based their views largely on an image of its medieval roots seen, at least among the cultural elites, as a product of religious intolerance and superstition that was overthrown only by the triumph of reason in the Age of the Enlightenment.[2] As is well known, historians of the premodern period, and especially historians of the Middle Ages, undertook a revision of this view earlier in this century.[3] Without spending excessive time on this much-discussed issue, we should note that contemporary trends in scholarship—often characterized as postmodernist—have also begun to take up this work of revision. The essays that follow clearly reflect medieval revisionism but also echo other current research. They do not present a single, unified view of tolerance and intolerance in the age of crusades but share many common concerns. Like all good research, they are part of an ongoing dialogue.

Various aspects of that dialogue are reflected in the divisions that group the twelve essays in this collection, which had its origins in the sessions of the Society for the Study of the Crusades and the Latin East at the Eighteenth International Congress of Historical Sciences, held in Montreal in late August and early September 1995. The papers presented there formed such an interesting and coherent body of material, thanks in large part to the efforts of Michael Gervers, that it seemed desirable to try to preserve as many of them as possible in a single volume of essays. The papers here are, therefore, a selection of those delivered at the conference, to which has been added one other, that by James Brodman, which is included in the first part.[4] Their authors are all leading experts in the field.

As a whole, the papers are quite coherent and lend themselves easily to a number of subthemes. The authors provide context and definition for aspects of the history of tolerance that have been little understood and often badly neglected. The result, we hope, demonstrates the importance of a deeper knowledge of particular circumstances and environments to a better understanding of tolerance. The papers here avoid the kind of ethnic and religious stereotyping that, in our opinion, contributes little to the discussions of these issues. Moreover, these essays deal little with the issue of victimization. It is unfortunately true that a sense of victimization is not limited to oppressed minorities and may also provide a motive for oppressors. The emphasis on actual circumstances helps us to grasp the varieties of experience that fall under this topic.

Part One is entitled "Confrontation, Captivity, and Redemption." These four essays provide significant insights, many of them the direct product of the research of these authors, into the relationship between Muslims or Christians during military confrontations, into their attitude toward captives, and into the complex of ideas—political, religious, and economic—that motivated their activities. In the opening essay, David Hay raises questions that have long disturbed scholars and contributed to the negative side of the image of the Crusades. How did the crusaders behave in battle? What motivated their actions? What can we believe about accounts even in Western sources of widespread massacre of soldiers and civilians? Clearly, as he argues, we must learn more about how contemporary views on warfare were shaped as well as their limits, He emphasizes concerns among contemporary writers about the influence of Islam on Christians, which not only served to justify violence by crusaders but also led some authors to exaggerate that impact. Yaakov Lev also demonstrates how difficult it is to understand the specific decisions as well as the attitudes and policies that lay behind the treatment of those captured in battle, whether soldiers or civilians. Giulio Cipollone explores the religious roots of humanitarianism that led to the founding of the Trinitarian order and its mission of ransoming captives. He argues that the use of language reveals religious prejudices among both Christians and Muslims. James Brodman shows how, in the case of the Mercedarians, founded for the same purpose, the interplay of crusade ideology and politics had a considerable impact on the direction taken by the order. These essays not only directly challenge older and now largely dated views of the Crusades as manifestations of irrational intolerance, they also help us to understand better where concepts like tolerance and intolerance fit in broader political agendas pursued both by Muslims and crusaders. In no case can we draw simple lines that would establish that the treatment of captives was motivated by ideological hatred or fanatical religious motives, but in many cases we can see that religion, both Muslim and Christian, played various roles, at times fostering mercy and generous treatment of captives and at other times inspiring or, at least, influencing the severest treatment of captives, even to execution. These essays are placed first because they raise questions that we need to keep before us as we proceed to our next section, "Cooperation, Conflict, and Issues of Identity."

What happened when Western Europeans came into direct contact with Eastern Mediterranean peoples about whom they knew very little? Although there had long been contacts with Byzantium and Islam, as well as with Jews, and Westerners had gained some information about the East from their travels as pilgrims or merchants, the Crusades represented something closer to a mass movement and brought virtually every social group in the West into contact with Easterners. James Ryan points up the changing relationships between Latins and Christian Armenians that resulted from these contacts and suggests reasons, both political and religious, for those changes. His essay traces for us the beginnings of antagonisms as well as cooperation that extend from this period to our own day and are reflected throughout the region among many Christian minorities. Paul Sidelko focuses not on religion but on the everyday dealings between Muslims and Latins. He suggests that current views regarding the continuance of Muslim administration of land and taxes under Latin rule need to be reexamined. His essay is especially interesting in light of current research on Latin settlements in the East. The empasis on cooperation between these groups, found in some authors' work, is, in his view, more difficult to trace than previously believed.

In his essay on "Edward of England and Abagha Ilkhan," Reuven Amitai throws additional light on the effort to secure an alliance between the Latin West and the Mongols against Islam. The appearance of the Mongols, who built a great empire in the steppe lands and the Far East in the thirteenth century seemed to promise Latins a hope for victory over the Muslims. In examining the negotiations between Edward and Abagha, Amitai has probed the difficulties and misunderstandings that plagued efforts at cooperation. He demonstrates that impediments to cooperation were not merely cultural but emerged from logistical problems. His concerns are reflected in a very different manner in the following essay. Adam Knobler pursues a topic that has long held a fascination not only for historians of the Crusades but also for those studying the history of discovery. The world of the Crusades was much larger than the battle lines drawn in the western Mediterranean or even in the Levant might suggest. There was an almost invisible line between the real and the unreal, peopled by such figures as Prester John, the Mongols, or the Jewish nation in the East discussed by Knobler that David ha-Reuveni claimed to represent in the early sixteenth century. It was out of the fault line between the real and the mythical that geographical knowledge was slowly emerging. At the same time, the experience of the Crusades prepared people for this new reality. The negative image of the Crusades always had its positive side.

The next two essays, one by the late Annetta Ilieva and the other by Andrew Jotischky, examine much-debated issues involving Latins and the Greek Orthodox communities in Greece, Cyprus, and the Patriarchate of Antioch. While both Byzantine scholarship and many earlier historians of the Crusades have stressed the argument that antipathies that had developed between the Easterners and Westerners in the early Middle Ages were exacerbated by the Crusades, some recent scholars, notably Bernard Hamilton, have found that there was a greater degree of mutual respect and practical cooperation than was previously known.[5] Even though the events of the Fourth Crusade were crucial in forming anti-Latin attitudes in the Byzantine Empire, the emergent picture was far from uniform.[6] Attitudes on the ground were often dictated by practical concerns. Various groups reacted in different ways to the presence of Latins. Likewise, among Latins, there were considerable variations in both attitude and relationships. The lengthy presence of Latins in the eastern Mediterranean forms an important chapter in the history of that region. Anneta Ilieva devotes much of her paper to an analysis of the fourteenth century chronicle of Leontios Machairas entitled *Recital concerning the Sweet Land of Cyprus*. This was a much-vexed period in the history of this strategic island, with its large Greek-speaking population; ruled by the Frankish house of Lusignan since the twelfth century and more recently by the Genoese, it now faced an expanding Ottoman Empire. This chronicle has much to tell us about the efforts of the various parties to maintain their positions. In his essay, Andrew Jotischky looks at the theological disputes that affected relations between Latins and Orthodox, particularly that between the Orthodox priest Sala and Bishop Gerard of Nazareth. This interesting discussion shows how difficult it was to separate major theological differences from minor issues and to what degree differences in theological and ecclesiastical views were grounded in conflicts over authority.

The final section of the book "Historical and Intellectual Perspectives," is composed of two essays: "Tolerance and Intolerance in the Medieval Canon Lawyers" by James Muldoon and "William of Tyre, the Muslim Enemy, and the Problem of Tolerance" by Rainer Schwinges. These probing studies of intellectual attitudes provide us with some very important insights that add further dimensions to the preceding essays. They reveal that the concepts of tolerance and intolerance were not the starting points for ideas about relations among these various groups. Rather, they were a product of the effort to establish legal limits or to define the nature of coexistence. Muldoon shows that canon lawyers were not willing to deny fundamental rights, such as marriage, to Muslim and Jewish spouses who did not convert to Christianity after the conversion of the other party, and indeed tried to craft solutions to protect both parties, though certainly favoring Christianity. He rightly points out how far such thinking is from our own, yet how deeply these ideas are still enmeshed in our thinking. In his important essay Rainer Schwinges examines the thought of the greatest intellectual figure of the Latin kingdom of Jerusalem in the twelfth century: William, archbishop of Tyre and chancellor of the kingdom. Educated in Jerusalem, Paris, Orleans, and Bologna, William was fully conscious of the major intellectual currents of his time and was able, in his great history of the kingdom, to place the experience of the crusader East and the knowledge he had gained from Easterners in a context that emphasized the realities of life amid peoples of different cultures and religions. He did not start with a notion of tolerance, but Schwinges leaves us in no doubt that he contributed to it in his thought.

The present volume does not presume to be a complete study of tolerance and intolerance in the Age of Crusades. Rather it constitutes a contribution to the discussion of the way in which the broadening of knowledge and the often disturbing experiences of the Latins in the Crusade era raised issues that would not go away. The path to modern ideas of tolerance emerged from the effort to reconcile conflicts within their experience as well as from their political needs and their religious and cultural values. The modern idea of tolerance was a product of European culture because of the unique features of European experience. But it was not the result of a triumph of superior virtue. That view misses the point that is so evident in these essays. It was as much or more a result of the conflicts that occurred among Europeans themselves as a result of competing agendas that were seeking accommodation: for example, the practical concerns of politicians, feudal lords, and merchants, and the religious concerns of the papacy, the hierarchy, and ordinary clergy. It was precisely because of the internal divisions and built-in diversity of European culture that a struggle for toleration became necessary. But much of that story goes beyond the topics dealt with here and belongs to the sixteenth and seventeenth centuries.

Contributors

Reuven Amitai is senior lecturer and department head in the Department of Islamic and Middle Eastern Studies, Hebrew University of Jerusalem. He is the author of *Mongols and Mamluks: The Mamluk-Ilkhanid War, 1260–1281* (1995) and coeditor (with David Morgan) of *The Mongol Empire and its Legacy* (1998).

James W. Brodman is professor of history at the University of Central Arkansas. He is the author of *Ransoming Captives in Crusader Spain: The Order of Merced on the Christian-Islamic Frontier* (1986) and *Charity and Welfare: Hospitals and the Poor in Medieval Catalonia* (1998).

Giulio Cipollone, O.SS.T., is professor at the Università Urbaniana, Rome, and the author of *Cristianità-Islam: Cattività e Liberazione in Nome di Dio: Il Tempo di Innocenzo III dopo "il 1187"* (1992).

Michael Gervers is professor of history at the University of Toronto, Scarborough. He edited *The Cartulary of the Knights of St. John of Jerusalem in England*. pts. 1 and 2. (1982–1996). He has also edited (with Ramzi Bikhazi) *Conversion and Continuity: Indigenous Christian Communities in Islamic Lands, Eighth to Eighteenth Century* (1990) and *The Second Crusade and the Cistercians* (1992).

David Hay is assistant professor of history at the University of Lethbridge (Alberta).

The late **Annetta Ilieva** held a Fulbright Fellowship at Dumbarton Oaks (1990–1991) and a Philip Whitting Grant at the Centre for Byzantine, Ottoman, and Modern Greek Studies in Birmingham, England (1993–1994).

She was author of *Frankish Morea: 1205–1262: Socio-Cultural Interaction between the Franks and the Local Population* (1991) and more than thirty articles in various journals and collected essays.

Andrew Jotischky is lecturer in history at the University of Lancaster, England. He is author of *The Perfection of Solitude: Hermits and Monks in the Crusader States* as well as of essays on Latin-Orthodox relations in the crusader period.

Adam Knobler is associate professor of history at the College of New Jersey, with a primary research interest in the relationships between Western and Non-Western peoples in the later Middle Ages and the early modern period. His articles have appeared in the *Journal of World History* and the *Journal of the Royal Asiatic Society,* among others.

Yaacov Lev, is senior lecturer at Bar Ilan University, Israel. His publications include *State and Society in Fatimid Egypt* (1991) and *Saladin in Egypt* (1998).

James Muldoon, professor emeritus of history, Rutgers University, is a research fellow at the John Carter Brown Library of Brown University. He is the author of several books, including *Popes, Lawyers, and Infidels,* and *The Americas in the Spanish World Order,* and has edited volumes including *Varieties of Religious Conversion in the Middle Ages.*

James M. Powell, RHS (Corresponding Fellow), is professor emeritus of medieval history at Syracuse University.

James D. Ryan is professor of history at the City University of New York, Bronx Community College. His long-term research interest is the history of missionary activities in the High Middle Ages.

Rainer Christoph Schwinges is professor of medieval history at the Historical Institute of the University of Bern, Switzerland.

Paul L. Sidelko is assistant professor of history at Louisville. He has published articles on cross-cultural contacts between Europe, the eastern Mediterranean, and central Asia.

PART ONE

Confrontation, Captivity,
and Redemption

1

Gender Bias and Religious Intolerance in Accounts of the "Massacres" of the First Crusade

DAVID HAY

I t is indeed ironic that this paper was initially delivered in a session entitled "Killing in the Name of God," for its primary purpose is to show that
the killing that took place during the sieges of the First Crusade was never as
massive nor as indiscriminate as certain medieval historians have alleged—
nor as most modern historians, following them, have assumed. In his recently published *Victory in the East: A Military History of the First Crusade*,
John France speaks with an uncommonly sober voice of dissent when he
warns against exaggerating the massacre that followed the crusaders' capture of Jerusalem in 1099 and urges historians to resist the temptation to
portray crusader conduct purely in terms of bloodthirsty religious intolerance; in reality, he argues, the treatment of the defenders and inhabitants of
the city was not far removed from the standard practices of contemporary
warfare in the Latin West.[1] While France rightfully directs attention to the
events at Jerusalem, he does not extend his comments to cover the alleged
"massacres" at the sieges of Antioch and Albara—to which his comments
are even more directly relevant—nor does he fully explain why this tendency
towards exaggeration has been so consistently powerful. In the following
paper I suggest some reasons why modern historians have fallen into the trap
of greatly overestimating the extent and especially the indiscriminateness of
the violence at these sieges, and I suggest how a more realistic appraisal of
events can be achieved. Because the trap of exaggeration was in some ways
prepared for the modern historians by the medieval chroniclers' idiosyn-
crasies and ideological allegiances—most notably their tendency to exaggerate, their desire to promote the crusade and the reforming papacy, and their

gendered focus and language—it is to a discussion of these three factors and their influence on perceptions of the First Crusade that I now turn.

That the medieval chroniclers were liable to exaggerate is obvious enough from the fantastic figures given for the size of the armies of the First Crusade;[2] Fulcher of Chartres himself remarked that the predilection for extravagance was a disease lamentably common among his contemporaries.[3] Nevertheless, while modern historians are well aware of the exaggerations in the chroniclers' estimates of army sizes and battle casualties, there does not appear to be a corresponding awareness of the frequency with which the medieval chroniclers overstated the extent (and even more importantly the indiscriminateness) of the bloodshed that occurred after the climax of the fighting had passed. A case in point concerns the siege of Albara, a small town southeast of Antioch that was seized by Raymond of Toulouse in late September of 1098, a few months after the crusaders' defeat of Kerboga. The most detailed and trustworthy account of events at Albara is provided by Raymond of Aguilers, who, as chaplain to the count of Toulouse was almost certainly present at the siege. His chronicle states that although many "Saracens" were killed, others were enslaved and later sold at Antioch, while those who surrendered before the town fell were set free.[4] In contrast, the other crusaders' accounts do not describe the taking of prisoners or the honoring of terms: Fulcher writes that the city was completely depopulated by the massacre of the citizens,[5] and the Anonymous explicitly states that the crusaders killed all the Saracens they found there, male and female, great and small.[6] Given the certain absence of Fulcher and the probable absence of the Anonymous from the siege,[7] the comparison of these three sources serves to illustrate the truism that the further authors were removed spatially or temporally from a siege, the greater their tendency to embellish their accounts with extravagant tales of capricious cruelty and massive bloodshed.[8]

This point would scarcely need to be made were it not for the fact that modern historians have overlooked it. For example, Runciman, apparently relying on the more hyperbolic accounts of the Anonymous and Fulcher, states that "The inhabitants [of Albara], who were all Moslem, capitulated, but were either massacred or sold as slaves at Antioch."[9] Thus, whereas Raymond of Aguilers depicts the crusaders conducting themselves according to the usual customs of war in the West, Runciman portrays them as treacherous butchers. If we accept Raymond's testimony as the most valid—as I feel we must, given the fact that he was a chaplain to the leader of the expedition and is the only eyewitness chronicler whom we can place at the siege with any degree of certainty—then the crusaders' conduct at Albara can be understood as quite conventional by the standards of contemporary Western warfare. In Latin Europe the initial breaching of a town's defenses was often an extremely bloody affair, and terms given after a breach had been made usually allowed the defenders and inhabitants to leave the city with nothing but their lives;[10] if the defenders did not immediately surrender it was assumed that these too were forfeit.[11]

Of course, there were important differences between crusading warfare and war in the West, and these should not be overlooked. The vast size, extreme poverty, and divided leadership of the crusading army not only made it difficult to control but also made an orderly and equitable division of booty all but impossible, as the confused climax to the siege of Ma'arra clearly shows. By nightfall of December 11, 1098, the crusaders had just managed to fight their way onto Ma'arra's walls, but the leaders of the crusade decided to wait until dawn before continuing into the town proper. At some point Bohemond discussed terms with some of the citizens.[12] During the night, however, the poorer crusaders, made desperate by lack of money and supplies, broke into the city in search of plunder. Somewhat later on, certain Christians, disappointed with their spoils, began torturing and executing prisoners in order to force them to reveal the wealth they were rumored to be concealing.[13] In the West, commanders were usually able to take steps to avert such tragedies: when William the Conqueror received the surrender of the citizens of Exeter, for example, he posted a guard at the city gates so that his soldiers could not "break in suddenly and violently plunder the wealth of the citizens."[14] Another general difference between war in the West and East was that enslavement as a consequence of defeat in battle remained a regular feature in Outremer long after it had fallen out of general use in the internal wars of Latin Christendom.[15] That non-Christian captives were more readily enslaved than Christian ones, however, did not necessarily mean better treatment for prisoners in the West than in the East; on the contrary, in the East even the poorest Jewish or Muslim captives retained some economic value to the crusaders as slaves and so were often spared, whereas in the West those Christians who were of no economic value because they were too poor to pay ransoms were often executed.[16] And whatever these general patterns may have been, at Albara at least it seems clear that terms of surrender were respected and prisoners were taken, the rhetoric of the Anonymous and Runciman notwithstanding.

The medieval chroniclers' natural tendency to exaggerate—whether due to misinformation or to their own desire to praise the crusaders or captivate an audience—was exacerbated by the fact that most of the chronicles were written from ideological perspectives whose proponents would have benefited significantly if the bloodshed were to be widely perceived as massive and indiscriminate. Just as the hyperbole of Christian accounts of the conduct of the Turkish armies in the East fueled the preaching of the First Crusade,[17] so too the equally inflated accounts of Christian atrocities at Jerusalem served the interests of countercrusading propaganda.[18] But while it has been well established that these ideological considerations tended to encourage distortions in reports of the violence perpetrated by adherents of other religions, the extent to which these same considerations could at the very same time foster extravagant accounts of the conduct of those of the same religion has not yet been fully appreciated. Taking a step in the right direction, Penny Cole has shown[19] how the ideology of religious pollution and purification pervades the writings of most of the Christian historians. Cole documents the general tendency among the Latin chroniclers to view any Muslim presence in the Holy Land (and in Jerusalem in particular) as "a violation of the places sacred to Christ," and to see the crusade as a war "mandated by God for the purification of his sacred places from Muslim defilement."[20] To authors such as these, massacres were not to be abhorred but were instead divinely ordained rites of purification, and consequently these writers sought to convey the impression that non-Christian populations were completely annihilated. Hence Fulcher relates how Jerusalem was "restored to its pristine dignity" and cleansed of the contagion of its pagan inhabitants by the triumphant crusaders,[21] while Raymond invokes imagery from the Old Testament and Revelation to show how the fall of Jerusalem not only confirmed Christianity and restored the Faith but "ended all paganism" (i.e., Islam).[22]

While Cole notes that the theme of religious pollution served to justify the crusaders' violence,[23] it must be acknowledged that as a literary motif it tended to distort it as well. The taking of prisoners and the survival of many inhabitants are facts easily obscured by Raymond and Fulcher's bloated rhetoric, although it is clear that such things did occur even at Jerusalem itself. The Anonymous, who unlike Raymond and Fulcher did not attempt to justify the crusaders' violence through the pollution/purification motif[24] (and who is not, coincidentally, usually the most sober in his reports of conflict),[25] mentions that prisoners (both male and female) were taken at the building that the crusaders believed to be the Temple of Solomon.[26] Again unlike Raymond and Fulcher, the Anonymous adds that it was the surviving inhabitants who cleared the bodies of the dead from the city after the fighting had ceased.[27] The Anonymous's testimony that prisoners were taken and some inhabitants survived is corroborated by a number of sources: by a document from the Jewish community at Ascalon indicating that prisoners were so abundant that the normal ransom price was lowered; by a letter describing how captive Jews had been dispersed throughout the Eastern Mediterranean; and by the fact that many Muslim refugees from Jerusalem were later to be found at Damascus; and even by Ibn al Athir's uncharacteristically restrained statement that although the men were killed, the women and children were taken prisoner.[28] The most atrocious treatment of noncombatants at Jerusalem did not occur on the "day that ended all paganism," but (if we are to believe Albert of Aix) three days later, when the imminent approach of the Fatimid army resulted in the order to execute all remaining prisoners;[29] and the documented existence of all the aforementioned survivors and ransom agreements casts some doubt on the rigidity with which this order was carried out.

Unfortunately, most modern historians have bought into the pollution/purification ideology and have followed Raymond and Fulcher rather than the Anonymous. Prawer, apparently confusing the bloodshed at the climax of the siege of Jerusalem with the executions three days later, describes a three-day-long slaughter with 20,000 to 30,000 dead.[30] Runciman states that "The Crusaders rushed through the streets and into the houses slaying everyone that they saw, man, woman, and child," and that "the only survivors" were the few hundred troops of the garrison who surrendered to Raymond St. Gilles;[31] even when noting that the city was cleared of corpses after the siege, he fails to mention that this task was performed by the surviving inhabitants![32] Less scholarly histories, following Runciman's lead, have popularized these inaccuracies. Jones and Ereira describe how the crusaders' "fanatical blood-lust" ensured that the troops of the garrison "were the only Moslems in Jerusalem to escape with their lives"—while on the very next page, and apparently unaware of any contradiction, quoting the Anonymous's description of how the surviving inhabitants cleared the city of the dead![33]

The ideology of Church reform, which at this time was producing more and more aggressive justifications for pious violence,[34] appears to have functioned in a manner similar to that of the ideology of religious pollution/purification. The distorting effect of reforming ideology is suggested by the fact that, of the earliest eyewitness accounts of the First Crusade, the two sources that tend to exaggerate the most are also those written by men most firmly entrenched in the reforming camp: Raymond d'Aguilers's patron, the count of Toulouse, was a prominent *fidelis sancti Petri*,[35] while Fulcher, the son of yet another *fidelis*,[36] devoted an entire chapter of his history to defending Urban II and Matilda of Tuscany against the antipope Wibert.[37] In an age in which victory in battle was widely seen as a sign of divine favor and defeat as the punishment for sin,[38] exaggeration served the purposes of both reform and crusade. Raymond's and Fulcher's accounts of great crusading victories and Old Testament–style massacres of infidels not only served to defend their specific enterprise from its critics[39] but also added the aura of divine approbation to the reformers' more general claim that the papacy could legitimately raise armies and direct them to war.[40] Given that this claim was still vigorously opposed by the imperial party,[41] nothing short of total, pagan-annihilating massacres would suffice, and so such massacres were described in all their gory detail—even when they did not actually happen.

Adding to the confusion created by such ideological considerations is the gendered nature of the language used by the Christian chroniclers and the difficulties involved in translating their Latin into modern languages. Apparent contradictions arise when the chroniclers' biases are not identified. In describing the fall of Caesarea in 1101, for example, Ryan's translation of Fulcher reads that the crusaders "slew with their swords everyone whom they encountered,"[42] and that although the "Saracens," seeing that their city was captured, tried to flee, "they were unable to hide anywhere and instead were slain in a death that was well deserved"; but it then goes on to state that "a great many of the women were spared because they could always be used to turn the hand mills," and describes how after the siege the Franks bought and sold prisoners, both male and female, among themselves.[43] Fulcher seems to be contradicting himself: was everyone killed, or were prisoners taken?

Such passages become comprehensible only if one acknowledges that, when describing the climax of a battle or siege, these sources are primarily and often exclusively concerned with describing the fates of the male combatants. Christian and Muslim chroniclers are alike in this regard: Ibn al-Qalanisi, describing the crusaders' attack on Ascalon, reveals this bias quite clearly when he states that, "It is said that the number of the people of Ascalon who were killed in this campaign—that is to say of the witnesses [who could testify in court], men of substance, merchants, and youths, exclusive of the regular levies—amounted to two thousand seven hundred souls."[44]

Thus, when Fulcher and others use words in the masculine, such as *Saraceni, Turci,* and *defensores civitatis*—and even more neutral words like *cives* or *omnes*—in such contexts, they refer only to adult male citizens, not to the women, children, and male noncombatants.[45] Able-bodied men—all of whom, both soldiers and civilians, would normally be armed and organized for the defense of their cities—suffered the highest casualties because they were all seen as combatants and hence as military threats. Women, children, and male noncombatants, on the other hand, who comprised the majority of the population, were seen not as threats but as spoils. When mentioned at all, they are not discussed in the context of the actual fighting but in the search for plunder and the cataloguing of the loot, where they are grouped with the booty rather than with the defenders. Thus, for example, in his description of the fall of Antioch, Ralph of Caen states that the crusaders seized boys, girls, gold, and women, but that the citizens *(cives)* fled to the citadel; he goes on to relate that, of these citizens, father did not wait for son, nor son for grandfather.[46]

Obviously, the crusaders did modify their treatment of the inhabitants of Antioch according to distinctions of age and gender, and one must be careful not to project the fate of the able-bodied men of the captured cities onto the rest of the inhabitants by translating terms used to describe male combatants with words denoting the population as a whole. The fact that the Latin writers sometimes used masculine endings when describing groups of mixed gender can sometimes be confusing, but a comparative analysis of the context makes their gendered perspective clear. What truly complicates the matter is when modern historians perpetuate the gender biases of their sources. Runciman states that at Antioch the Christians massacred "all the Turks that they saw, women as well as men", and that "By nightfall on 3 June there was no Turk left alive in Antioch"; more popular histories peddle the fiction that the crusaders "spared neither sex nor condition and paid no respect to age . . . They killed the servants, . . .mothers of families and the children of nobles."[47] All this despite the very words of the leaders of the crusade themselves, who in a letter to Pope Urban II, which is preserved in Fulcher"s narrative, described the capture of Antioch in the following terms: "We slew Cassianus [Yaghisiyan], the tyrant of the city, and many of his soldiers, and kept their wives, children, and families, together with their gold, silver, and all their possessions."[48]

Thus, beneath the hyperbole of the misinformed, beneath the rhetoric of crusade and religious pollution, and beneath the confusions created by gender biases and the gendered focus of the historians, we find evidence for the continued (if troubled) survival of the noncombatant inhabitants of the cities of the East.

To be aware of the factors contributing to exaggeration is not to deny that massacres did happen on the First Crusade, nor to apologize for them.[49] Many noncombatants did indeed perish in the course of the sieges, especially at Ma'arra and Jerusalem, and the crusaders certainly had a lot of blood on their hands; but by the same token their killing was seldom indiscriminate. On the contrary, being desperate for money and supplies, they selectively utilized violence and the threat of it as means of acquiring the greatest amount of money and booty. When this could be done by torturing and executing prisoners who were believed to be hiding their wealth (as at Ma'arra), then things could certainly be very bad for the inhabitants;[50] but when it could more easily be achieved by taking non-Christians prisoner for ransom or enslavement (as was usually the case), the crusaders simply ignored the chroniclers who railed against them for associating with "loose pagan women."[51]

The idea that the crusaders would wantonly destroy the only sources of wealth keeping most of them alive should be relegated to the realm of historical fiction.[52]

Where terms of surrender were honored—as at Albara—and where large numbers of prisoners were taken—as at Antioch and Caesarea—it would be stretching the truth to characterize events as treacherous and indiscriminate massacres, as Runciman and others have done; these were simply hard-fought military victories in which the crusaders adhered to the laws of war as they knew them. This is why it is so dangerous to fail to acknowledge the chroniclers' gendered focus or to accept at face value their portraits of the final moments of the sieges as "purifying" orgies of religious intolerance. Indeed, when we do so, we merely perpetuate the very mythology by which so much of the violence and religious intolerance of subsequent centuries was (and continues to be) justified.

2

Prisoners of War During the Fatimid-Ayyubid Wars with the Crusaders

YAACOV LEV

War was endemic in the medieval Muslim Middle East. The human cost of warfare was immense, and the danger of being captured by enemies or brigands was a very real one. The study of how prisoners of war were treated touches upon central aspects of human life and attitudes—religion, politics, propaganda, and economics, although, in the context of this paper, the last aspect is the most elusive one. We shall proceed by examining how prisoners were actually treated and then discussing the political, communal, individual, and religious dimensions of the topic.

Treatment of Prisoners of War

The wars of the First Crusade were marked by atrocities and large-scale massacres of civilian populations committed by the crusaders. However, it appears that this intensification of warfare had no direct consequences on the wars between regular Muslim armies and the crusaders. Usually, prisoners were taken by both sides.[1] But execution of captured prisoners took place, too. In fact, in the wars between Muslim armies and the crusaders, the two tendencies coexisted. The killing of prisoners of war should not be interpreted as an attempt to annihilate the enemy completely. Total war was rare in the Middle Ages. Ibn al-Qalanisi (1072–1160), the renowned historian of Damascus, characterizes war as marked by killing, taking of prisoners, and looting.[2] However, our ability to understand under which circumstances and for which reasons prisoners were kept alive or summarily executed is rather limited. One of the reasons is the terse way that incidents of warfare are re-

11

ported in Arabic sources. The other reason is inherent in the act of war itself. War is savage and hazardous. When violence is unleashed, the difference between human and inhuman treatment of the defeated enemy, even under the best of intentions, is precarious.

A few well-known incidents of war illustrate these two coexisting tendencies. On 18 May 1102, the Fatimids captured the fortress of Ramla and took, according to Arabic sources, 700 prisoners, of whom 300 were brought to Cairo and 400 were put to death.[3] In this case, as in many others, we are in the dark in regard to the motives of the winning side. Why were some of the prisoners executed while the lives of others were spared? In winter 1105, Tughtakin, the ruler of Damascus, conquered the fortress of Al'al, lying southwest of the Sea of Galilee, and took many prisoners. A year later, the stronghold of Toron was attacked by the army of Damascus; the fighting was fierce, and no prisoners were taken.[4] In 1108, Tughtakin was very successful in his war against the crusaders, capturing, in a battle outside Tiberias, Gervase of Basoches and many of his men. Gervase turned down Tughtakin's proposal to set the prisoners free in exchange for three towns in Palestine. On his part, Tughtakin refused Gervase's offer to provide ransom and instead put him and some of the captives to death and sent others to Baghdad for display.[5]

The dispatch of captives to Baghdad was done for propagandistic reasons. Although lacking any real political power, the Abbasid caliph still enjoyed tremendous prestige within the Sunni world, and Sunni rulers sought from the caliph recognition of their rule. Later, Saladin did the same; he sent to Baghdad for display Frankish knights captured at Hittin. As on earlier occasions, it was a purely propagandistic move, serving as a live illustration of Saladin's greatest victory and demonstrating in Baghdad his might and achievements in the Holy War.[6] He, like other Sunni rulers, constantly approached the Abbasid caliphate seeking recognition of his rule and authorization for holding territories he had seized from other Muslim rulers and the Franks.

Saladin's wars against the crusaders were more frequent, extensive, and violent than those of the Fatimids. In spite of his reputation for magnanimity, Saladin's treatment of prisoners of war was quite callous. A certain pattern in his behavior is evident. At times of military successes, Saladin's behavior toward conquered populations and captured leaders of the crusaders was generous. However, at times of no military successes or in periods of military setbacks, Saladin's behavior toward prisoners was savage, and they were quite systematically put to death. The killing of prisoners was not regarded as sinful or even shameful behavior. Under certain conditions, Muslim law permits the execution of prisoners of war. The Muslim jurists rely on the authority of the Prophet, who ordered the execution of two prisoners captured at the battle of Badr (624).[7] Historians such as 'Imad al-Din al-Isfahani, al-Qadi al-Fadil, and Ibn Shaddad, who admired Saladin and served as his close administrative aids, report the execution of prisoners in a matter-of-fact way. Although 'Imad al-Din in his writings expresses no condemnation of the killing of prisoners, he personally shunned taking part in the butchery. Al-Qadi al-Fadil unequivocally denounced the killing of prisoners.[8]

During campaigns conducted in the late 1170s, Saladin put to death prisoners of war. For example, in 573/1177–1178, during a raid on southern Palestine, captured prisoners were brought to Saladin's camp and executed there.[9] By no means was this action an isolated event; rather, it was a matter of policy. In 574/1178–1179, Saladin ordered put to death Frankish and Christian prisoners (meaning apparently crusaders and Christian civilians) captured in a war with the crusaders in the vicinity of Hama and during a raid on villages in that area. The killing of prisoners was carried out by men of religion.[10] Militarily, these campaigns were insignificant. But through them Saladin was trying to establish his position and reputation as a warrior of the Holy War. It appears that in the absence of any real military successes, the killing of prisoners seemed to Saladin instrumental for achieving his aims. During the Third Crusade, especially following the fall of Acre, prisoners were frequently executed by Saladin.[11] Saladin's conduct reflects his frustration in face of constant military setbacks as well as his desire for vengeance for the execution by the crusaders of 3,000 of his soldiers captured at Acre.[12]

On other occasions Saladin's killing of prisoners was more selective. For instance, Saladin ordered put to death the surviving prisoners of the crusaders' incursion into the Red Sea that had aimed to reach Mecca. Saladin insisted on the killing of these prisoners in spite an objection by his brother al-'Adil who, in absence of Saladin, was in charge of affairs in Egypt. Apparently these prisoners surrendered themselves and were promised quarter. Saladin explained his decision to put these captives to death by the need to keep the routes of the Red Sea secret and to deter any further attempts in that direction.[13] The killing of the captured Hospitallers and Templars following the victory at Hittin was motivated by the desire to purify the land from those who had defiled it. This is an unprecedented explanation, which accords to execution of prisoners the status of a religious duty, and the executions were carried out by people of religion.[14] The origin of this approach should be sought in the concept of the Holy War as it had evolved in the twelfth century. The ideology of the Holy War maintained that the lands were made impure by the presence of the Franks and that the aim of the Holy War was to reconquer and purify these lands.[15] In 1179, following a victory at the battle of Jacob's Ford, Saladin put to death captured apostates from Islam and crossbowmen. The execution of apostates from Islam is permitted by Muslim law and was a standard practice in such cases. Thus in this case Saladin behaved within the boundaries of his religion and moral values.[16] These examples do not mean that Saladin conducted a systematic policy of killing prisoners of war. On many occasions the lives of the captives were spared.[17] Saladin was a man of complex personality. He was capable of calculated acts of killings, but he was well aware of the danger of sliding into pathological cruelty.[18]

Nonetheless, Saladin's behavior stands in contrast with his fame as a person who treated defeated enemies kindly. Saladin earned his reputation by some highly publicized deeds. One of these, reported also by William of Tyre, took place during the war for Acre. A Christian mother came to Saladin to plead for the life of her baby, who had been snatched from her by Muslim raiders. Saladin bought the baby from the soldiers who had captured it and returned it to the mother. This was a quite unusual act of human pity and generosity. Usually private people, not foreigners, were involved in the ransoming of their coreligionists. Other acts of generosity by Saladin were more calculated and politically motivated.[19]

Although Saladin, like other men of his age, had no scruples about killing prisoners of war, he did recognize the potential "commercial value" of captured enemy prisoners. His behavior following the Muslim victory at the battle of Marj 'Uyun, 10 June 1179, exemplifies this point. Saladin captured a number of high-ranking prisoners, whom he imprisoned in Damascus. The highest ransom, 150,000 *dinars* of Tyre, was demanded for Baldwin of Ibelin, who agreed as a part of the deal for his release to set free 1,000 Muslim prisoners. Another prisoner, Hugh of Tiberias, was ransomed by his mother for 55,000 *dinars*. Odo of Saint-Amand, the master of the Templars, died in a prison in Damascus, and the fate of many other high-ranking prisoners remains unknown.[20] We must distinguish between ransom of prisoners from captivity and sale of prisoners by their captors. Sale of prisoners was not very common but did occur. In such cases prisoners were bought from captivity by their enemies.[21]

Naval warfare constituted a different category. Full-scale battles between enemy war fleets were very rare. On the other hand, naval raids on enemy shipping and coasts were very common. In this type of warfare, enslaving people and looting were the main goals. But the results of naval warfare were even more unpredictable than those of war on land. Therefore, many naval raids ended in the killing of people on board enemy ships although that was not the initial aim. In the Fatimid period, the spoils of naval raids were shared between the ruler, who received the captured people and weapons, and the crews of the warships, who received the rest of the booty. Some events of 504/1110–1111 exemplify a successful naval raid. In that year merchants who sailed from Egypt were captured by the Franks and their goods worth 100,000 *dinars* looted. They remained in captivity until they ransomed themselves.[22] The same is true for the naval raids in 550/1155–1156 and in 552/1157–1158; in these two incidents pilgrims captured on the high seas were brought alive to Cairo. On the other hand, in 546/1151–1152 none of the Christian pilgrims attacked on the sea by the Fatimid navy survived.[23]

Although enslavement of people and looting were the main motives for naval raids, other factors were at work, too. Occasionally these factors were more powerful than those mentioned above. For instance, in 517/1123–1124, the Fatimids captured a great number of men and women during a naval raid on Christian shipping. The ransom value of these prisoners was in excess of 20,000 *dinars*. Nonetheless, the vizier, Ma'mun al-Bata'ihi, ordered them put to death, explaining that it was in retaliation for the execution of five hundred Muslim prisoners whose ransom value was 100,000 *dinars*. The execution of the Christian prisoners took place in Cairo in a great public spectacle after their offer to ransom themselves for 30,000 *dinars* was refused.[24] We have no information on the Muslim prisoners allegedly executed by the crusaders, but it must be taken into account that the ransom value of 20,000 or even 30,000 *dinars* for the Christian prisoners captured in 1123–1124 represented only a theoretical estimate. Ransoming was a long and tedious affair, and the sums achieved could have been much lower than estimated. This is especially true in respect to the pilgrims. A lack of any concrete "commercial value" of these prisoners was undoubtedly a factor behind al-Ma'mun's savage treatment of them. On another occasion the same vizier behaved differently. He exchanged with the crusaders prisoners who belonged to the military class.

The execution of prisoners of war was not a practice limited to wars between Christendom and Islam. Such killings took place in intra-Islamic wars, too. Three examples taken from Fatimid history illustrate this point. The anti-Fatimid rebellion of Abu Yazid in North Africa (944–947) was marked by large-scale atrocities committed by both sides. Civilians were not spared, and five hundred rebel prisoners who had been brought to the Fatimid capital city of al-Mahdia were butchered by the population. In February 920, the Fatimid navy, which participated in an attack on Egypt, then under Abbasid rule, was destroyed off Rosetta, and hundreds of captives were taken. The prisoners were separated into three groups: naval officers were put on public display; captives whose origin was from Sicily and the North African coastal towns of Barqa and Tripoli were set free; but hundreds of Kutama and

Zuwayla prisoners were massacred by soldiers and the civilian population. The Kutama were Berbers and staunch Fatimid supporters. The Zuwayla were most probably blacks, and they, like the Kutama, comprised the backbone of the Fatimid army. We have here a case of selective killing of prisoners. Prisoners who belonged to sociomilitary groups known as Fatimid supporters were put to death, while prisoners who were not regarded as such were unconditionally set free. The Fatimids did the same with their enemy prisoners. In 972 they executed 1,500 Qarmatian prisoners of war.[25]

Types of Prisoners

When speaking about prisoners of war, we must distinguish between two groups: people belonging to the military class and ordinary civilians. The treatment of high-ranking prisoners of the military class oscillated between the desire to make use of them and savagery. High-ranking prisoners of the enemy were regarded as an economic asset and as a bargaining card for the release of one's own prisoners from enemy captivity. In contrast to high-ranking people of the military class, simple soldiers were treated badly. On many occasions they were butchered or sold as slaves. Among the civilians only wealthy merchants were regarded by their captors as having a "commercial value." Other civilians were treated as chattel. Nonetheless, in the Constantinople of the High Middle Ages, there lived a large population of Muslim prisoners, some of whom spent long years in captivity. They enjoyed freedom of religion and prayed in a special mosque. The composition of this rather large prisoner population must have been quite diversified, including high-ranking military men and wealthy merchants as well as simple soldiers and civilians. Occasionally some of the more important persons among these prisoners were invited to the court, and others acquired a fair knowledge of Byzantine institutions.[26] The treatment of Muslim prisoners in Constantinople was sometimes a subject of diplomatic contacts and acrimony between Baghdad and Byzantium. Christian prisoners (Rum) captured in raids on Byzantine territories lived in the Christian quarter of Baghdad.[27] On the conditions in which Frankish prisoners were kept in Fatimid and Ayyubid Cairo little is known. When Saladin abolished the Fatimid state in 1171, he found that Christian prisoners were imprisoned in al-Hakim's mosque, where they had established a church for themselves. He put an end to this, but the mosque was not restored for service; it became a stable, which was removed only by the Ayyubid sultan al-Salih Ayyub (1240–1249). It seems that during the Ayyubid-Mamluk period high-ranking Christian prisoners with their wives and children were kept in a jail known as *kha'zina al-bunud*.[28]

Perhaps the best illustration of the fate of civilians who fell into enemy hands is provided by Ibn al-Tuwayr's (1130–1220) description of the results of a successful Fatimid naval raid on Christian shipping to the Levant. Following this raid over one thousand people were brought alive to Cairo. A thousand men were sent to work at the stores and mills of the royal palace. A group of women and children among the captives was given to the vizier and the others were brought to the palace. Some were assigned for service in the palace, and others sent to work at the workshops of the palace. The very young boys were sent for training as military slaves while elderly prisoners and some others were put to death. The use of prisoners as a work force at the stores and mills of the palace continued under the Ayyubid rulers. And Saladin allotted captured Christian women as slave girls among his closest aides.[29]

This information, as well as other accounts, points out the employment of a servile work force in the Fatimid and Ayyubid periods. During the North African period of the Fatimid state (909–969), slaves were used in the production of textiles for the needs of the court.[30] But the most telling report is that of the famous North African traveler Ibn Jubayr, who visited Egypt in 1182–1183. He says that Christian prisoners were used by Saladin for the construction of the citadel of Cairo. According to him, there were so many prisoners that on other construction projects carried out by Saladin there was no need for a free work force.[31] This information is exaggerated by later historians who say that 50,000 prisoners were employed by Saladin in the building of the citadel.[32] The use of prisoners of war on construction projects was not limited to Cairo. The fortification of Acre, conquered by Saladin after his victory at Hittin, was done with servile labor, and the same is true for Jerusalem, fortified by Saladin during the late stages of the Third Crusade. The use of prisoners of war on construction sites continued under Ayyubid and Mamluk rulers. For example, the sultan al-Salih Ayyub employed prisoners captured in a battle fought in 1240–1241 for building the citadel on the Rawda island and other religious monuments in Cairo.[33] Nonetheless, for the period under study, it is very difficult to determine to what extent captive labor was of importance to the economies of the Muslim state, Byzantium or the crusader kingdom of Jerusalem.

In regard to later centuries, the evidence for the employment of prisoners of war as a slave work force in the Mamluk period is very scant.[34] But in seventeenth-century Muslim North Africa, captive labor was of great importance, and Spanish prisoners of war were employed in a wide range of tasks.[35] From earlier centuries there are three examples of wide use of servile work forces in agriculture. The most notorious case is the employment of African slaves (zanj) on plantations in ninth-century southern Iraq. Slaves were also important in the agriculture of ninth-century Tunisia and in the agriculture of the mid-eleventh-century Ismai'ili state at al-Ahsa' in the Bahrain region of Arabia.[36] Outside agriculture and large-scale construction projects carried out by the state, the employment of slaves in urban economy is not attested to in the sources.

The Plight of Women

In periods of war the plight of women was especially bitter. Separation of families, flight of husbands from war-infested areas, and rape were common calamities that befell women in such times. The fate of women who belonged to a defeated ruler was not much better than that of common women caught in hostilities beyond their control. From biblical times the possession of the royal harem was regarded as a highly prized trophy of war, symbolizing the demise of a dynasty and the transfer of power to a new claimant. This ancient Near Eastern tradition was very much alive in the Middle Ages. For example, when the Fatimid propagandist 'Abd Allah al-Shi'i overthrew the Aghlabid regime, he also took the slave-girls of Ziyad Allah III, the last ruler of the dynasty. But he kept and provided for them until the arrival and the coronation of his master, 'Abd Allah al-Mahdi, the first Fatimid ruling imam. Only he took possession of those slave-girls, leaving some for himself and dividing the rest among his son and the leaders of the Kutama Berbers.[37] When Saladin removed the Fatimid dynasty, he found himself in a situation not much different from that of 'Abd Allah al-Shi'i. He could not take possession of the Fatimid royal women, because he was not a ruler in his own right, and formally the overthrow of the Fatimids was done on behalf of Nur al-Din and in his name; therefore, Fatimid women were in fact Nur al-Din's booty. But Saladin did not send them to Damascus, preferring to imprison them and the male members of the Fatimid family in Cairo. Saladin's policy toward the Fatimid family must be seen in light of his reluctance to acknowledge his formal subordination to Nur al-Din with whom, by 1171, his relations had already been strained.[38] In other cases, a respectful treatment of women and children of the enemy signaled an attempt at reconciliation.[39]

When towns were conquered and the population massacred, women were not spared. Such atrocities were committed in intra-Islamic wars as well as during the Crusades.[40] On other occasions, for instance, in bedouin raids on towns and villages women and children were captured and taken away. From the point of view of a bedouin tribe, those were very valuable captives. Children could be raised as members of the tribe, augmenting its membership and fighting manpower. Women were used as concubines and as a work force or even married; in that way new females not related were absorbed into the tribe. But bedouin warfare was diversified and flexible, lacking rigid patterns of behavior, and conquest of a town by bedouins exposed women to the danger of rape. On the other hand, when Muslim regular armies fought the bedouins, the capture of bedouin women was an important aspect of the campaign. For the tribe it was not only a human tragedy but also a loss threatening its reproductive ability.[41] Similar policies were adopted by the Byzantines, who in their raids on Muslim towns and territories enslaved and carried away women and children.[42] Imperial policy in its scope and motives greatly differed from the warfare practiced by the bedouins. Women and children fetched high prices on slave markets in the Byzantine empire and could enrich the military leaders and troops involved in the raids. For example, the emperor John I Tzimiskes (969–976) issued an imperial decree regulating the taxes owed to the state by soldiers who acquired prisoners of war after a campaign. In other cases, Muslim prisoners captured in the warfare along the frontier with Islam were, as a matter of policy, forcibly converted to Christianity and settled on land.[43]

Women dreaded the possible consequences of captivity. Rape during captivity had bitter consequences for a woman for the rest of her life. Evidence from Jewish sources indicates that women who had been raped and later ransomed were ready to enter into polygamous marriages as second wives—or, more precisely, were left with little choice but to do so.[44] The ransom price demanded for women who were not sexually abused during captivity far exceeded the standard ransom price of 33.3 *dinars*, and those engaged in ransoming found it difficult to raise such excessive sums of money.[45]

Exchange of Prisoners of War

In the Middle Ages, through many centuries of an almost constant state of belligerency and warfare between Islam and Byzantium, procedures for the ransom of prisoners became institutionalized. Redemption of prisoners from enemy captivity involved two levels of activity: that of states and that of individuals and communities.

Islam does prescribe the exchange of prisoners. The Qur'an, in fact, sanctions the release of enemy prisoners by exchange or as an act of grace. The most important Qur'anic verses on this subject say: "When you meet the unbelievers, smite their necks, then, when you have made wide slaughter among them, tie fast the bonds; then set them free, either by grace or ransom, till the war lays down its loads" (47:4–5). The same attitude, namely, that prisoners can be taken following the defeat of the enemy, is revealed also in other verses: "It is not for any Prophet to have prisoners until he made wide slaughter in the land" (8:66–67), and "O Prophet say to the prisoners in your hand" (8:71).[46] In addition, the Qur'an says that a portion of the alms-tax is to be allotted for ransom of slaves (9:60). Commentators on the Qur'an and jurists interpreted this verse as an obligation to help prisoners and slaves get themselves freed.[47] The Qur'anic dictum (47:4–5) tallies with the norms of warfare in pre-Islamic Arabia. In tribal wars the taking of prisoners among the male and the female population of a defeated tribe was very common, and the prisoners were held for ransom or enslaved. The same is true for early Islamic warfare, the wars of *ridda,* in which prisoners taken by the Muslims eventually were returned to their tribes.[48] However, the Muslim wars of conquest of the Middle East in the seventh century were marked by the killing of the fighting men of the Persian and Arab opponents of the Muslims and the enslaving of the women and children of the defeated enemies.[49] Nonetheless, when whole regiments of the Persian army surrendered to the Muslims, they were given quarter and were incorporated into the Muslim armies.[50]

Tenth-century Arabic sources make mention of twelve organized ransoms of Muslim prisoners *(fida')* from Byzantine captivity in the period between 805 and 946. These events took place on the Lamas-Su river in southern Anatolia.[51] The historian Tabari (839–923) provides two detailed accounts of how exchanges of prisoners were conducted between the Abbasids and Byzantines. In 231/845–846, several thousand Muslim prisoners were ransomed from Byzantine captivity. They included men, women, children and even *dhimmis* (i.e., Christians and Jews who, apparently, were captured during raids on Muslim territories or shipping). Tabari's account is made up of different versions of this event. According to one of these versions, thirty Muslims who had converted to Christianity in Byzantine captivity were released, too. If this account is true, these prisoners, upon their liberation from captivity, could have been accused of apostasy; however Tabari does not elaborate on their fate. He does note that the caliph ordered the officials in charge of the *fida'* to subject the released captives to *mihna,* that is, to ask them whether they professed that the Qur'an was created. Whoever denied the creation of the Qur'an was to be left in captivity. It must have been one of the last cases of *mihna,* for it was abolished by the caliph al-Mutawakkil (847–861). During the *fida'* of 241/855–856, the Muslim prisoners released from Byzantine captivity were no longer subjected to *mihna.*[52]

Other Muslim rulers were also involved in ransom of Muslim prisoners from Byzantine captivity. On several occasions the Muslim rulers of Egypt were approached by the Byzantines in regard to exchange of prisoners. According to the Coptic-Arabic chronicle, such a request was made by the two emperors Leo VI and Alexander to Ahmad ibn Tulun. Muhammad ibn

Tughj, the Ikhshidid ruler of Egypt, dealt with the issue of exchange of prisoners with Byzantium quite frequently, committing considerable resources. In 325/936–937 an exchange of prisoners was arranged after long diplomatic exchanges between Byzantium and Ibn Tughj. In 355/965–966, Ibn Tughj was approached in Damascus by a delegation from the frontier zone of Northern Syria and a Byzantine envoy and was asked to agree to a *fida'*. Ibn Tughj died shortly afterwards in Damascus, but his general and the future ruler of Egypt, Kafur, provided a large sum of money, 30,000 *dinars,* to pay for the release of Muslim prisoners from Byzantine imprisonment. Another participant in this *fida'* was Sayf al-Dawla al-Hamdani, a local Arab ruler of northern Syria.[53]

The Arabic sources clearly indicates that the rulers of the Muslim world saw the release of Muslim prisoners held by Byzantium as their duty. The Fatimids, for instance, during their rule in North Africa and later in Egypt (969–1171), were much involved in efforts to release Muslim prisoners from Byzantine captivity. During the North African phase of their history, the Fatimids were engaged in many land and naval wars with Byzantium in Sicily and southern Italy. But warfare was only one side of Fatimid-Byzantine relations. Political contacts between the two states were no less extensive, and Byzantine diplomats often came to the Fatimid court. Among the various Fatimid political demands from Byzantium, two issues figure prominently: a request to release Muslim prisoners and the demand to pronounce the Friday sermons at the mosque of Muslim prisoners in Constantinople in the name of the Fatimid rulers.

During the rule of al-Mu'izz in Tunisia, the Fatimids found themselves in a war with the Umayyads of Spain and the Byzantines who cooperated with them. In 346/957–958 both the Umayyads and the Byzantines offered a truce to al-Mu'izz. According to Qadi al-Nu'man, the foremost Fatimid jurist and a man of al-Mu'izz's inner circle, the Fatimids demanded from Byzantium the release of Muslim prisoners captured by the Byzantines in their wars with the rulers of the eastern Muslim world (apparently meaning the Middle East and the Abbasid territories in general).[54]

Al-Mu'izz's peculiar demand must be understood in light of his efforts to win from the Muslim world a legitimization for the Fatimid rule. He was keen to demonstrate to the Abbasids that the Fatimids were capable of winning from Byzantium concessions that they and other Muslim rulers of the Middle East failed to achieve. But winning concessions from Byzantium was only one facet of al-Mu'izz's political efforts aimed to impress Muslim rulers and to gain recognition for Fatimid rule. On other occasions al-Mu'izz, eager to demonstrate to the rulers of the Muslim East that he was the true champion of the Holy War against Byzantium, contrasted his zeal with their slackness. In reality, however, al-Mu'izz's approach to Byzantium was entirely pragmatic and not governed by the precepts of the Holy War.[55]

After the transfer of the Fatimid state to Egypt (962), and an expansion into Palestine and Syria, the Fatimids and Byzantium became entangled in hostilities in northern Syria. As during the North African period, war and diplomacy went hand in hand, and the Fatimid political demands on Byzantium did not change. In 377/987–988, Byzantine diplomats arrived in Cairo. They tried to end a round of bitter fighting sparked by a Fatimid attempt to conquer Aleppo (992–995). Among the Fatimid conditions for signing a seven-year truce were stipulations for the release of Muslim prisoners, the pronouncement of the Friday sermons at the Constantinople mosque in the name of the Fatimid rulers, and a supply of some unspecified goods.[56]

The release of prisoners held by the Byzantines was demanded by the Fatimids in 429/1037–1038 also. This time there were several outstanding bilateral issues to be settled between the two states. In 1011 the Fatimid ruler al-Hakim destroyed the Church of the Holy Sepulchre in Jerusalem. This was part of al-Hakim's religious policies that included persecutions of Jews and Christians. In 1021, following al-Hakim's demise, the new regime revoked al-Hakim's religious policies and tried to reestablish relations with Byzantium. In 418/1027–1028 a Fatimid-Byzantine agreement was concluded. The Fatimids granted the emperor the right to finance the redecoration of the Church of the Holy Sepulchre and demanded the reopening of the mosque in Constantinople and the pronouncing of Friday sermons in their name. The Byzantines on their part were ready to release 5,000 Muslim prisoners.[57] However, the implementation of this agreement was marked by difficulties that sprang from the continuous clash of interests in north Syria and especially in Aleppo. Only in 429/1037–1038, following a release of 5,000 prisoners by the Byzantines, was the restoration of the Church of the Holy Sepulchre begun and the church opened. In 437/1045-1046, a new truce agreement was signed between the Fatimids and Byzantium. The Fatimid imam and the emperor exchanged splendid gifts, and the Byzantines as a sign of goodwill set some Muslim prisoners free.[58]

In the second half of the eleventh century, Fatimid-Byzantine relations were utterly shattered by the outbreak of an unexpected war. In 447/1055–1056, the Fatimids asked Byzantium for a supply of grain to combat a severe famine caused by insufficient rise of the Nile in the previous year. The Fatimid request had been approved by Constantine IX Monomachus but was revoked by the Empress Theodora, who ruled January 1055-September 1056. Furthermore, during the sojourn in Constantinople of the Fatimid envoy al-Quda'i, a qadi and a renowned historian, the Byzantines changed the sermons in the mosque of the Muslim prisoners in favor of the

Abbasids, archenemies of the Fatimids. This change took place on the demand of Sultan Tughril Beg's delegation that arrived in Constantinople while al-Quda'i was negotiating with the Byzantines. The Fatimid reaction was swift; the Church of the Holy Sepulchre was seized, and the patriarch was removed from the church complex. The deterioration in Fatimid-Byzantine relations sparked a war over the port town of Latakiyya in Syria. Neither the chronology of this war nor the full ramification of the events is clear. Eventually, in the negotiations to resolve this conflict, an exchange of prisoners was discussed by the two states. The Fatimids had to admit that they were unable to secure a release of Byzantine prisoners held by other Muslim states.[59]

It seems that the tradition of exchanging prisoners of war that had evolved between Byzantium and the Muslim states was instrumental for the setting of similar practices during the First Crusade and later between the Fatimids and the crusader kingdom of Jerusalem. The Fatimids and the crusader kingdom of Jerusalem did exchange prisoners of war, especially those belonging to the military class. The clearest attestation of this practice is from 510/1116–1117. In this year the Fatimid emir Shawar was released from the captivity of the crusaders. Shawar was of bedouin origin and his kinsfolk were ready to pay a vast sum of money for his release. However, the crusaders were not interested in money but in the release of their prisoners held by the Fatimids. Their demand was refused by al-Afdal, the vizier and the military dictator of Egypt. He is described as adamantly opposed to the release any prisoners from his jails. Only following his demise and the rise of a new vizier, al-Ma'mun al-Bata'ihi, did a change in policy take place. Al-Ma'mun, the same vizier who was responsible for the public execution of Christian pilgrims, released Frankish prisoners, paving the way for the release of Shawar.[60] But these events do not indicate necessarily that norms of ransom and exchange of prisoners between the Fatimids and crusaders had been firmly established. For instance, in 533/1158–1159 the Fatimids captured some high-ranking military leaders of the crusaders, whom they set free and sent to Byzantium. At that period the Fatimids and the Byzantines were territorially separated and their relations dwindled. There was no immediate reason behind Fatimid goodwill toward Byzantium. It seems that the Fatimids were simply interested in manifesting their might and keeping the option of friendly relations with the empire.[61]

Saladin was quite indifferent about ransoming his own men captured by the crusaders. His most notable failure was to ransom the garrison of Acre. Prior to the fall of Acre on 12 July 1191, Saladin made an attempt to secure a safe departure of the garrison from the besieged town. He offered to surrender the town with its installations, and he was also ready to release a number of Christian prisoners equal to the number of Muslim soldiers who

would leave Acre. In Acre the Muslims held 1,500 Christian prisoners described as commoners and 150 high-ranking persons. However the leaders
of the Crusades were sure of their ability to conquer Acre, and they turned
down Saladin's proposals for the surrender of the town. Following the fall of
Acre, Saladin failed to ransom his captured garrison, of whom 3,000 simple
soldiers were executed by the crusaders in the view of Saladin's army.[62] It was
a monumental failure on the part of Saladin. Neither did Saladin do much
for the release of Baha' al-Din Qaraqush, the commander of Acre, from captivity. On other occasions Saladin was more cooperative in helping his captured comrades-in-arms. For example, in the disorderly retreat from the
battle of Mont Gisard, the jurist Diya al-Din 'Isa with his brother and their
companions were captured by the crusaders. The brothers were ransomed
after two years in captivity for 70,000 *dinars*. Who put up the money is not
referred to in the sources. However some cooperation on the part of Saladin
was needed as Christian prisoners in Saladin's captivity were released as a
part of the deal.[63] Arabic sources are reticent about the fate of the simple soldiers of Saladin's army captured following the defeat at Mont Gisard.

It is very interesting to examine Saladin's behavior when the ransom of
the members of his own family was at stake. Shahansha, the son of Saladin's
nephew, Taqi al-Din, was captured by the Hospitallers as a result of his own
stupidity, if not worse. He was in captivity for seven years, and Saladin paid a
vast sum of money for his release. In addition, he had to set free all of the Hospitallers held in his prison.[64] On the one hand, in this case Saladin behaved in
a very different way in comparison to other cases. On the other hand, it is
very difficult to explain the length of Shahansha's captivity. Was it a result of
objective difficulties in the negotiations and raising the money or a reflection
of lack of adequate goodwill and cooperation on the part of Saladin?

Saladin, like other contemporary rulers, was also fully aware that the
issue of prisoners could be used for political and propagandistic aims. State
efforts to release Muslim prisoners from Christian captivity had a long tradition in the Muslim medieval world, and Saladin maintained that tradition.
Between 1181 and 1192, Saladin maintained extensive diplomatic contacts
with the Byzantines and signed political treaties with Byzantium. As part of
the cordial relations between the two sides, prisoners were set free by both
Saladin and the Byzantines. Also, the mosque of the Muslim prisoners in
Constantinople continued to figure high on the political agenda in the relations between Byzantium and the Muslim rulers of Egypt. In 591/1194, for
instance, Byzantine emissaries informed the Ayyubid sultan al-Malik al-'Aziz
'Uthman that the mosque was reopened for religious services.[65] Usually truce
agreements signed between the Muslims and Franks included stipulations
for the setting free of captives.[66] In 1180, Saladin intended to fight the Ar-

menian ruler Roupen III, whom he accused of treacherous behavior toward Turkmans and mis-treatment of Muslims in general. Roupen III strived to settle the conflict peacefully, and he made a number of offers to Saladin, including the release of Muslim prisoners. Following Saladin's rejection of these proposals, Roupen III made an improved offer by saying that he would pay the Franks for the release of five hundred Muslim prisoners.[67] These negotiations reflect Roupen III's awareness of Saladin's sensitivities. He offered him concessions that Saladin's propaganda could use as a tangible proof of political and moral achievement: the release of Muslim prisoners from Christian captivity. Since the release of prisoners was so highly valued in the Muslim world, it should not come as a surprise that Arabic sources report enthusiastically about the release of Muslim prisoners in towns and strongholds conquered after Saladin's victory at Hittin. The overall number of Muslim prisoners redeemed from Christian captivity is quoted as 20,000 people. In Acre and Jerusalem there were especially large populations of Muslim prisoners (4,000 and 3,000 respectively).[68] The state involvement in the release of Muslim prisoners from enemy captivity continued also under the Mamluks and the Ottomans.[69]

Ransom of Prisoners of War

In Judaism ransom of prisoners *(pidyon shevuyim)* is a religious duty *(mitzva)* of paramount importance. The Jewish law *(halakha)* sets forth in detail the order of priority in the ransoming of captives and what kind of funds can be legally used for that purpose. In medieval times the Jewish communities had to organize the ransom of their coreligionists with their own communal resources and funds, receiving no help from the authorities. Jewish sources of the High and Late Middle Ages bear eloquent testimony to the extensive communal efforts to release captured Jews.[70]

The Jewish communities were much involved in ransoming their coreligionists from enemy captivity. This activity constituted a tremendous strain on their charity services and financial resources. As specified by S. D. Goitein, the total costs involved per captive were much higher than the ransom price of 33.3 *dinars*. The community had subsequently to maintain the ransomed people, provide them with clothes, and pay for their journey back to their native towns and countries. In addition, the poll tax had to be paid for them to the Muslim authorities, as well as port duties.[71] A number of Geniza letters from the late 1020s and early 1030s deal with the ransom of Jewish captives in Alexandria. These people were brought to the city by Muslim pirates who captured them when raiding Byzantine shipping in the Mediterranean. The Jewish community in Alexandria could not deal with the problem alone, and it appealed for help to the Jewish community of Fustat-Cairo, the largest and richest in Egypt. Other Jewish communities in Egypt also became involved in raising money to free Byzantine Jews in Alexandria.[72] Jewish communities along the shores of the Mediterranean were permanently engaged in the redemption of prisoners. The Jewish communities of North Africa, especially Tunisia, used to ransom prisoners captured by pirates on the high seas or in raids conducted by the Muslim rulers of Tunisia on the shores of Sicily and south Italy.[73] Ransom of prisoners was considered a very serious issue, and the leaders of the Jewish communities dealt with it themselves. The collection of the money needed for the ransom could take a long time. On many occasions, however, it was possible to secure in the meantime the release of the prisoners from the hands of their captors, but prominent members of the community had to stand surety for them.[74] In any case, ransom of prisoners was a long, tedious, and costly affair, which required the goodwill and cooperation of many communities, their leaders, and wealthy members. In the twelfth and thirteen centuries most cases of ransom of captives involved the crusaders rather than the Byzantines. The Jewish communities in Egypt made great efforts to redeem Jews captured by the crusaders in Palestine.[75]

Similar attitudes prevailed in the Muslim and Christian worlds.[76] For example, communal efforts to redeem captive prisoners are recorded by the Muslim tenth-century geographer Muqaddasi. He reports that Byzantine ships used to bring Muslim captives to the coastal watch-stations of Palestine where they were ransomed by the local population.[77] In Byzantium redemption of prisoners was part of the Byzantine notion of philanthropy, and churchmen and emperors invested their efforts for that goal.[78] In the Christian world—especially in Spain, as the studies of James W. Brodman and Ellen G. Friedman point out—the ransom of prisoners from Muslim captivity was well organized, involving great efforts and considerable economic resources.[79]

The price of 33.3 *dinars* for the ransom of a prisoner from enemy captivity was an enormous sum of money, more than a year's income of a skilled worker.[80] Accordingly, only very few rich individuals could ransom prisoners by relying solely upon their own wealth. A notable example was a powerful and fabulously rich Egyptian official, Abu Bakr al-Madhara'i, who in 343/954–955 ransomed a number of Muslim prisoners in Alexandria and provided them with clothes and money. He turned the event into a spectacular display of his wealth, magnanimity, and power.[81] Another example comes from the twelfth century: the Arab noble and warrior Usama ibn Munqidh, was personally involved in the ransom of Muslim North African pilgrims to Mecca who had been captured by pirates operating on behalf of the crusaders in Palestine.[82]

Al-Qadi al-Fadil, a leading member of Saladin's inner circle, went a step further, setting up a special pious endowment *(waqf)* for the ransom of prisoners. He devoted to that purpose the revenues of a caravansary *(khan)* that he owned in Cairo.[83] Although pious endowments for the freeing of prisoners were set up also in twelfth-century Syria,[84] in most cases their ransoming was a communal effort, each member of the community contributing according to his ability. It is interesting to note that Muqaddasi does not refer to any involvement of the authorities in the ransom of prisoners in the watch stations of Palestine. It was a voluntary, communal effort of the local population.

Conclusions

When the medieval Mediterranean world is examined as a whole, it is clear that religion permeated the attitudes of individuals, communities, and states toward the ransoming of their prisoners from enemy captivity. Rulers, Muslim and Christian, saw it as their duty to release prisoners from enemy captivity. Their actions reflect a mixture of religious and humanitarian as well as political and propagandistic motives. But religious scruples were not powerful enough to prevent execution of prisoners of war. More humane treatment of captives was influenced by practical and economic considerations and easily gave way to the inhumane, governed by merciless brutality and desire for revenge.

3

From Intolerance to Tolerance

THE HUMANITARIAN WAY, 1187–1216

GIULIO CIPOLLONE, O.SS.T.

In this presentation to the International Congress on "Tolerance versus Intolerance in the Confrontation of Societies during the Crusades," my aim is to emphasize that the dual phenomena of intolerance and tolerance have their basis in the religious belief of Christians and Muslims.[1] Tolerance, when it concretely manifests itself in humanitarian service, becomes the exemplary solution to intolerance.

In the Middle Ages, whether in the realm of Christian culture or that of Muslim culture, the whole of daily life was directly filtered through the word of God. In addition to all the problems of hermeneutics, exegesis, and the transmission of the Bible and the Qur'an, we must emphasize that adherence to the word of God—though not an obtuse adherence—calls for an unending "updating" in the encounter with God's word. It means stimulating this open reading in line with the growth of all humanity. In short, a static, literal, and unchanging reading harms the rights of God and believers. Indeed, in the period we are now examining—as in our own time—one finds the seeds of tolerance in the open reading of God's word according to the essential mutability of the Divine Word. We see in the period we are studying that men and women lived in a situation with little movement, an almost static environment with regard to God's word, that caused a predisposition to intolerance. With regard to the Bible, one thinks of a few interpretative places: the interpretation delegated to the clergy, to the vision of Christianity's life and vitality as the continuation of Israel's history, to the "leap backwards" with the "fulfillment" of the Old Testament that justifies religious hatred and holy war, human choice's clear use and waste of the word of God.

On the Muslim side, there is more consistency. However, because the Qur'an is considered the immutable word of God, the return for tolerance is weaker. On the Muslim side, God, who is most free, can abrogate previously

28

sacred precepts. In the Qur'an, there is bloody recourse to physical force and the *lex talionis;* moreover, there is the duty of Islamization through arms. Nevertheless, one tries to get at the essential: more than intolerance and physical violence, one sees the idea of a God who makes humanity grow. We note that clearly the Bible and the Qur'an offer the certainty that *in God there is no intolerance.*

Biblical references, especially from the New Testament, are plentiful. The follower of Christ is the true and faithful disciple who has the duty of loving the enemy and returning the sword to its scabbard. The following passage from Luke is one among many with value for our topic: "John said in reply: 'Master, we saw someone casting out demons in your name, and we forbade him because he does not follow with us.' But Jesus said to him: 'Do not forbid him; for he that is not against you is for you" (9:49–50). "But the people [the Samaritans] would not receive him, because his face was set toward Jerusalem. And when his disciples James and John saw this, they said: 'Lord, do you want us to bid fire come down from heaven and consume them?' Jesus turned and rebuked them. And they went on to another village" (9:53–56).

We know that the Qur'an admits the plurality of revelation (5:65–66; 42:14) and foresees the Lord's reward for faithful Jews, Christians, and Sabeans (2:62). In addition, it establishes that "there be no compulsion in religion" (2:256;50:45). The Qur'an, more than the New Testament, leaves room for contradictory interpretations, but the Qur'an's references to a merciful and compassionate God—to the unjust and transient result of intolerance—and a reading of the Qur'an that is centered on the essential should lead to tolerance itself. Such a reading was not the common one in our period, when to hypothesize religious freedom was difficult if not improbable.

The time of the Crusades has been interpreted as a time of intolerance. We are trying to clarify this picture by emphasizing the following: the process of identifying the enemy, the pretexts of intolerance up to the war, and the voices that expressed doubts about intolerance as God's will, along with "personal tolerance."

Christianity and Islam were based on the solidity of the Word of God, revealed by the one and only God.

Christianity is nourished by citations from the Old Testament in such a way that it must base and furnish the principle of justice on the concept of enmity and the subsequent practice of enmity. It is this overall belief of the "Old Testament" that places the Christian people in the limits of territorial boundaries that consolidate the certainty of a covenant with God himself.[2]

From the Qur'an one draws the clear impression of great diversity, difference in rules and attitudes.[3] One thinks of tolerance and intolerance in the matter of religious freedom, war, and living together. The relationship with the People of the Book is manifestly changeable: because they are alternatively considered believers and unbelievers, sometimes they are among the saved, other times destined for hell.

Above all else, it is vital to see how the image is created and consolidated. We must, therefore, maintain a universal psychology: the rejection of what is not part of the group and can impede the group's equilibrium, and the reverse, namely, highlighting the esteem of that very group. The process just brought into relief as a *mirror image* is important to examine in the actions, reactions, and hostility of groups. With regard to the enemy, the image and its identification will be said to happen without having knowledge. And that statement finds punctual verification in the whole vocabulary of epithets, adjectives, appositions, and expressions commonly used but applied without having direct knowledge. From this common and risky attitude we can deduce the facility of having images without knowledge.

The West in the Middle Ages was certainly not a crystallized structure, but one of slow movements. Because of illiteracy, which slowed knowledge and relied on a primary and mediated recourse to the Bible as the unchangeable and eternal word, different Christian nations lived for centuries as object-subject of the sedimentation of images. We deal with closed images so deeply rooted that they make it extremely difficult to introduce new data that may be codified in a different way. Christians ran the risk of becoming schismatics or bold innovators, or in some cases, suspects. The images present strong opposition to changes and a strong attachment to what went before. Attempts at comparison and introductions that could have changed the situation were rejected. *Cognitive consistency* rejected *cognitive dissonance.*

The way of describing the enemy and the vocabulary expressing enmity both reveal a fundamental religious intolerance. Among the possible references one can include the following qualifiers of those not in the Christian group: "remote," "barbarians," "gentiles," "idolaters."[4] Regarding skin color, which already shows difference from and identification with the Christian group, the enemy is called "Moor." With reference to black, to a dark color, to the experience of little light, all those outside the group are called "Tartars," recalling the dark depths of hell.

Apart from the biblical certitude, they draw from the Bible the infidel enemies of YHWH, which they fix on the enemy with a religious automatism. Whoever does not belong to the group is an enemy; hence, God is involved in a modern enmity either by faith or as a caution against the unknown force of the enemy. By the result of this process, we see that the Muslims become enemies. They are called *inimici*: enemies of the Catholic faith, enemies of the Church, enemies of our Lord Jesus Christ. Furthermore, they are characterized as infidels: unholy, perfidious servants of evil. Finally, the enemy acquires the designation of aggressor and persecutor. The enemies are called tyrants, persecutors, *sitientes omnium christianorum sanguinem* [thirsting for the blood of all Christians]. Besides these descriptions, the enemy undergoes a metamorphosis and becomes something with a biblical connotation: the beast, the Antichrist.

Both believers, the Christian and Muslim, deal with a God who has "spoken," a God who is revealed and stimulated with his word, a God who directs and gives "form" to human relations. One thinks of the works of charity and benevolence and the works of tolerance and intolerance; one thinks of the practice of friendship or enmity, of pardon or revenge.

The plurality of the word of God and the diversity of the messages are the basis of trouble, of rejection, of intolerance. They form, so to speak, a draft for aggression. In reality, there is an experience of a god who, because he is not ours, is false. These people believe and follow this other god; therefore they are godless. These other people have different interests detrimental to ours. In short, we are dealing with idolaters, pagans, the godless, people to be avoided, enemies, and potential aggressors who are to be eliminated. Furthermore, in God's word one finds that man by himself cannot make war. Whether in the Christian or in the Muslim worlds, human beings base the lawfulness of enmity, of war, of captivity, and of liberation on the word of God.

On the part of Muslims, the current vocabulary with which they express their image and knowledge of the world and designate Christians is a vocabulary that reflects the inverse process with the same upside-down proportions.[5] All this has to do with a process of mirror images applied to the same postulates that were applied to the Christian world. The fluidity and imprecision of image and knowledge continued to grow; in this case, moreover, this development even preceded the systematic knowledge of the enemy. The ideological principles of the Qur'an agree with the idea of enmity; also, everyone who refuses to convert to Islam is *per se* an enemy.

The variegated concept of the pagan, idolater, exploiter, impostor, oppressor, infidel drawn from the faith of the Qur'an is found to be the same definition of the enemy in the person of the Christian. References to the devil and the force of the evil one, the number one enemy to crush, are pushed onto the Christian and applied with the entire theological force that commands enmity and supports it in the case of direct exchange. Basically, this is enmity permitted and legalized by God, solidly maintained, considered upright and for the glory of God.

In Arabic a substantive is often used as a qualifier or adjective with appositive force. Hence, we find the following words applied to Christians: *al-*

kufr (unbelief, infidelity), *ash-shirk* (polytheism, idolatry), *al-haira* (confusion, perplexity, bewilderment), *an-nifaq* (hypocrisy, dissimulation), *al-batil* (vain, futile, groundless, absurd; deception, falsehood), *al-ghaddr* (perfidious, treacherous; faithless), *at-taghiya* (tyrant, oppressor, despot), *tawaghit al-kufr* (tyrants of idolatry).

We also find terms of utter contempt that can be used to mock the Christian religion: *sulban* (crosses, crusaders, darkness, dirt), *a'agim* (pagans), *kafirun* (atheists, unbelievers), *ahl ad-dalal* (the people of error), *musrikun* (idolaters), *tughyan* (oppression, tyranny, terrorization), *a'da' Allah* (the enemies of God). Some of the insults have a particularly religious connotation in order to denigrate the Christian enemy. Some epithets are directed to the theology and worship of Christians, specifically, the Trinity, the Messiah, baptism, the cross, and Sunday: *al-mutallithun* (Trinitarians, those who profess three), *ahl at-tathlit* (Trinitarians), *'abadat as-sulban* (adorers of the crosses), *ahl al-ahad* (the people of Sunday). *Al-Masih* (the Christ), *al-ma'mudiya* (baptism), *Iiman al-Masih* (the faith of the Christ) are concepts applied to indefinite pronouns to designate Christians. Muslims are reminded of *dabbat al-ard* (the beast of the earth) when they refer to Christians. Subject Christians are called *dhimmi* (subject people of the book), *a'agim* (pagans), *a'gam adh-dhimma* (subjected pagans), *nasara adh-dhimma* (subjected Nazarenes), and *musta'rib,* terms that can be called characterizations of a religious nature.

Even qualifications indicating a regional origin are used as synonyms for Christians: e.g., *nasara, nasrani* (Nazarenes, Christians), *rum* (the Byzantines). Similarly, when Christians are designated by geographical origin: *ifrang, farang* (Frank), *al-isban* (Spaniard), *al-inkitir* (English), *al-alman* (German), and so forth.

When one reads the proposed insults as a dictionary of enmity, then it brings to light the unending reciprocity of the two groups of Muslims and Christians. Reciprocity is as endless as the fact of their certitude about their respective just relationships with God, who is allied with the group and is its guardian. The enemy does not deserve confidence, and an alliance cannot be established with him. He remains at the margin and controlled by sight. Certainly this reading has some nuances and exceptions, a certain evolution and growth of enmity according to the current tension or a period of rest in the contest. Even the personal relationships of the actors from the two groups can permit a tolerance that a closed application of the word of God would exclude absolutely.

The endless reciprocity between the two groups or worlds, Muslim and Christian, permits the establishment of descriptions, if fluid and certainly on the elusive side, of the limits between the two worlds themselves, a licit privilege of expansion by each of them. Even here the supposed expansion and thus the pressure and provocation of the enemies are strengthened by the word of God, of their own God. Further, the particular alliances drawn up against the interests of the alliance of the whole people with their God form further motives for friction. The commerce and well-being demanded by the worldliness of the two groups, just as politics, will be blind to both of them and agree to deal with their enemies as friends: idolatry and perfidy not allied.

The missionary calling found in Matthew 28:18–20 and other New Testament passages and in the ninth sura of the Qur'an, "Repentance," offer enough space for the worldliness of the annoying, even if necessary confrontation with intolerance. From this comes a proof of aggression or the need to convince with force. Another way one experiences the strong temptation of endurance and of intolerance is that of feeling as a protected minority and guided by sight or in the enemy's territory.

Some of the measures and countermeasures evidence and accentuate the difference between Muslims and the *dhimmi* by restricting the freedom of the latter, who in fact remain persons outside the group, not allied, and with another God, even allied with another God. Rigorists insist that the following prohibitions be placed on the *dhimmi*: dressing like Arabs, insulting Islam, trying to convert a Muslim, inducing a Muslim to apostatize. Any of the foregoing, regarded as an attempt to destroy religion, is punishable in principle by death.

The convention of 'Umar ibn al-Khattab (634–44), in any case, is a classic in such a juridical definition, and we find it cited as an example. The so-called convention of 'Umar was particularly important because of its written character, even without going further. We have the model of the convention furnished by ash-Shafi'i.[6] The dispositions relative to the great alliance are the following. If any Christian uses an improper expression when speaking of the Prophet Muhammad, the Book of God (the Qur'an), the Commander of the Faithful, or the Muslim community, then all his goods and life are at the mercy of the Commander of the Faithful, just as in the case with the goods and lives of enemies in war. If a Christian draws a Muslim away from his religion, then his goods and life are at the mercy of Muslims. In Muslim cities, Christians must not display the cross, manifest their polytheism, build churches or meeting places for prayer, sound the *naqus* (church bell), or proclaim their polytheistic belief about Jesus the son of Mary in the presence of a Muslim.

A complete juridical process regulates the so-called spiritual freedom of the *dhimmi*. The freedoms considered are the following: teaching, conscience, matters dealing with buildings for worship and religious ceremonies, and finally the relationship of the religious community with the Muslim state.

Daily provocations and disturbing actions initiate a state of intolerance ready to explode. One could say that each side was hypersensitive and itching for a fight. There was a matter of contention that caused unchangeable intransigence: Jerusalem. The biblical and Qur'anic codifications of enmity caused an enduring annoyance that was most especially felt in a regulation of this contention. How can one stick to the facts when the parties involved are both bundles of exposed nerves with an incurable enmity founded on suspicion and radical mistrust?

The most vivid expressions of the latent state of war and of open intolerance are found in the expression of the lawfulness of "holy" enmity. There is an infidelity to alliances because of the group's interests, which manifest the community's strong belief in its God. There are piratical undertakings against the enemy. This is a matter of damage that produces psychological terror. It leads to the capture of people and goods, and more or less consciously expresses a religiosity. Between Christianity and Islam has been pronounced an unending reciprocity between fidelity and infidelity to the work of their God. Between fidelity and infidelity to the covenants with their God. Allurement and torment involves the conscience.

Jerusalem existed. A city thrice holy, in our period a city twice holy. It is this city, a highly contentious city, that is between our two communities of monotheistic believers. In reality, Jerusalem is the holy city for both Christians and Muslims. Because of a holy dispute, it will become a matter for holy competition. Hence, to the holy war for the conquest or reconquest of the holy city. Belligerence will become the act of highest worship. It could open the doors of Paradise for the martyrs fallen in the struggle for their God. It could have been the beginning of Calvary for the captives who fell into the hands of the infidel enemy.[7]

The glorious exploits of Saladin culminated in 1187 with the capitulation of Jerusalem and in 1192 with the humiliation of the crusaders in their third global undertaking. Here we have to summarize the vocabulary used in the chanceries of Saladin and Innocent III to describe the enemy. This vocabulary demonstrates an irreversible religious intolerance.

Above all, from 'Imad ad-Din, secretary of Saladin, we know of a religious vocabulary used to denigrate the Christian enemy.[8] The fiercest and most intolerant insults of the Muslims directed against the Christian enemy touched the very core of the Christian faith: the Trinity. In this context of epithets, the following is simply one example: "I killed thirty Trinitarians and left forty of them unsold on the ground." Among the most "theological" insults, one can mention these: "Trinitarians," "adorers of the Trinity," "sectarians of the Trinity," "adorers of the human nature and the divine nature," "followers of the hypostases," "partisans of Satan," "partisans of the demons," "polytheists," "demons of the cross," "demon [satanic] adorers of the cross," "observers of Sunday," "enemies of God," "idolaters," "doubters," "dissociates." In a more general context, we find the following terms applied to enemies of their God: "evil," "perfidious," "impious," "infidels," "rebels," "criminals," "damned," "unjust," "infernal beings," "deviants," "demons." Both the people and the enemy army are described in the same ways: "people of polytheism," "champions of lies," "impure race," "coreligionists," "people of the Trinity," "partisans of error," "band of the lost," "people destined for the fire of hell," "troops of the cross," "slaves of the cross," "hypocrites." [9]

Innocent III, while he gives a side invoking Christ quasi-physically in the warlike undertaking of the Holy Land's liberation—"a land profaned, dirtied, and in the hands of the impious"—is describing the enemy army, or the intolerance of the strategy of war as "depraved," "a perverse nation," "an inhuman nation," "barbarians battle-lines of Philistines," "battle-lines of Saracens," "Saracen barbarians," "pagan barbarians," and "Saracen persecution of pagans." [10]

With reference to tolerance, read in the present time as "transgression to be suppressed," we want to number the possible alliances with the enemy against the great alliance with their God, and the contradictory and worldly aspect of the infidelity of the faithful toward their God which was automatically conceived as damaging to the interests of their group and thus punishable by any means. The warlike and violent place of the worldly interests permitted alliances, truces, and commercial pacts that required blame and censure on the part of the supreme authority, of the chiefs of the faithful, and also we should say, of the mass of believers faithful to the word of their God. More evidently in the Christian "world," even by the explicit evangelical will, we note the attitudes that demand tolerance up to heresy.

Certainly the powerful chorus of voices that cried *Deus vult*[11] had support from the secular elite, as well as the official guarantee of the *magisterium,* the official theology, and the official law. In any event, it is a most interesting fact that among so many clamorous shouts, there are voices of perplexity or open dissent. These voices often come from the impetus of warlike euphoria.

The reasons for dissent are multiple: reasons absolutely spiritual and reasons of a worldly calculation. Peter the Venerable differs from Bernard. Their discord will make a din. Among the voices that cried *Deus non vult* there was one who was a hothead and disposed to schism, to support infamy and almost linked to heresy.[12] There was also the complaint of the Waldensians, who will become heretical. Immediately before Innocent III, the responses of Alain de Lille to the Waldensians and the thought of Ralph Niger enlightened the dissent of the cry *Deus non vult*. Alain de Lille summarizes in a few lines the text of the followers of Peter Waldo. He states that the aforementioned heretics and enemies of the church even assert that human beings are not to be killed in any situations or circumstances, or for any reason. For they say that God prohibited homicide when he said in the law (Ex 20:13; Dt 5:17; Mt 5:21; 1 Jn 3:15): "you shall not kill." Also, in the Gospel (Mt 26:52): "All who draw the sword shall perish by it." The gospel radicality of *in no situation or circumstance, nor for any reason* had a heretical interpretation.

The aversion to killing Muslims is clearly present in the thought of Ralph Niger. Chapter 2 of his *De re militari et tribus viis ierosolomitanae peregrinationis* is dedicated to the topic "Saracens must not be killed but repelled," and he writes here: "Therefore, whoever seeks to propagate the faith through violence goes beyond the limits of the faith." [13] A very clear light from the New Testament, but the option for the "low light" of the Old Testament prevails. We can retain the great contribution of the perplexity, of the dissent, and the heresy of the cry "God does not will it." In any event, this cry was swept away by the contrary and more deafening cry, an almost universal cry, raised by voices that counted.

A Muslim equivalent to the Christian *Deus non vult* does not exist. That the *jihad* is the will of God and an untouchable prescription of the Qur'an is unquestionable. No Muslim dare oppose such certitudes, at least as a principle. Nevertheless, there are Muslims who do not participate in the *jihad,* or try to get out of it, or are unwilling to participate in it. In a letter to the caliph, a letter handed down to us by Abu Shama, we find a heartfelt appeal for the *jihad.* "What has become of the fire of Muslims, the pride of the faithful, and the zeal of the friends of truth? What amazes us is the zeal to emulate the infidels and the indifference of some believers." When people depart from God's command and enter into alliances other than his, they become infidels and are unable to have victory over the enemy. "How can you have victory, when you drink wine in your own encampment, then listen to the flute and tambourine, and when you circulate other objects equally abhorrent to God?"

We know the contempt that faithful and zealous Muslims had for schoolteachers who opposed the *jihad* and were exempt from the obligation.[14] Nonetheless, the intellectual *jihad* existed and continued to have supporters. The Islamic sources are rich in value because they express moments of meditation, of pause, although they live in an atmosphere of war. Various elements of a synthesis emerge from the urgency of a decision and the gravity of the problem of the strategy to follow in order to stimulate the best of Muslim sensibility. The troubled decision in 1192 concerning the defense of Jerusalem is a good example. Anyway, it dealt with a strategic opportunity and not with criticism of the *jihad* when some of Saladin's counselors disagreed with continuing the war.

Peace between the two enemy groups was greeted with rejoicing: "The day in which the peace was concluded was like a feast day. . . . the joy was so great that only God could measure it."

It is a fact that in the human conscience in an inaccessible way there resides the real adhesion or rejection of that which is done externally and obliged by many factors. Not everyone has the courage to reveal his conscience to the outside, since it is not shared with the heart. It can certainly be held that "religious" persons are the most intolerant; religious intolerance gives glory to God while other men created by the same God are being killed or imprisoned. We have pointed out the voices of dissent that tried to cry out for tolerance as the way forward—they cried out: do not kill.

But it is the very experience of killing and capturing as the outcome of holy war that caused the turn to tolerance from intolerance. The obtuseness of "religious people" and of the clergy in general—together with the strategy of rearming, whether in the Christian camp or in the Muslim—insist more on the necessary practicability of intolerance than on tolerance as an alternative.[15]

In this context of an alternative, the experience of some "Trinitarian" redeemers will be framed. These Trinitarian liberators or redeemers proposed a project of liberation to the pope, who made their project his own and publicized it in the name of all Christians. In fact, a project for the liberation of the holy war's victims did not exist in the Christian world. Innocent III, even if with his tenacious and absolute will to rearm, showed different attitudes toward the Muslims, not only hostility and rejection but tolerance and finally benevolence.[16]

Already in the first year of his pontificate, he had contact with the Trinitarian redeemers.[17] The pope showed his interest in the liberation of captives. From the second year of his pontificate, however, he took the initiative of writing to the "princes of the believers." He dealt with a humanitarian initiative based on merciful charity and the Gospel command. The addressee of the famous letter of March 8, 1199, was a representative of the Muslim world. Abu 'Abd-Allah Muhammad an-Nasir, *amir al-mu'minin*. In the letter of Innocent III, the prince is called "miramolino, *amir al-mu'minin*" and *regi marrochetano*, king of Morocco. In fact, this king was more than a king; he was a sort of emperor and head of the Almohad dynasty, which dominated North Africa from Tunisia to the Atlantic and all of Muslim Spain.

Innocent III makes the project of the Trinitarian liberators his own. He espouses their cause and even presents it as *the* plan of liberation in the name of Christianity. "In reality, some men, one of whom is the bearer of this letter, having been enflamed by God a short while ago, have established a rule and an order according to which they must spend a third of their present and future income for the liberation of captives."

This is a work of mercy. The following is another passage from another letter addressed to the Muslim princes: "In the Gospel, among the works of mercy recommended by our Lord Jesus Christ to his faithful is the liberation of captives. This work has no small place among the works of mercy." Taking a disarmed position as his point of departure, the pope seizes the initiative: mercy as a high and tangible form of tolerance. Moreover, the project of liberation that the pope wants to present to Muslim judgment is not conceived by him, but by a faithful Christian.

A meditative reflection brings us to read the characteristics of another culture, or of a totally disarmed culture in the Christian relationship with Islam. We say "totally disarmed" because besides the blunt instrument of physical arms, there are very evident signs of force and pressure, whether certain political inducements or, finally, certain religious attitudes that try to impose Christianity—to increase the number of the faithful and thus Christian "force"—by means other than arms. In some key elements there seems to be an awareness of the disarmed, expressive gestures of the Trinitarian redemptionists: the name *Trinitarian,* the red and blue cross, the *signum Trinitatis et captivorum.*

Our group of Christian redemptionists will be found in constant contact with Muslims, but without the prejudice that accompanies people who want or must show tolerance. Basically, the way was indicated by the Gospel of Christ, which obliges unconditional tolerance to the point of normative pardon for one's enemy.

The consideration of the phenomenon of intolerance and tolerance, together with the humanitarian alternative as the road to tolerance, allows us to strike a balance starting from "recurring" events, and to make a proposal leading to a more tolerant future. The UN's designation of 1995 as the "Year of Tolerance" was an occasion particularly favorable to the purpose.[18] The religious expression of intolerance is, on one hand, founded on the "limited human constitution" and, on the other hand, the elaboration of the different interpretations of the word of the one and only God. Religious intolerance is a phenomenon among both Christians and Muslims. Further consideration makes us see frequent points of agreement.

At the beginning of the experience of the newborn community of believers, tolerance is understood as a rule of life, and intolerance must be avoided. Later, the more the community of believers acquires power and force, is structured in a hierarchy, and is recognized within territorial boundaries, the more believers become intolerant. We have said that in God there is no intolerance, to the point that the conscience of believers is attributed to the word of God. The vocabulary of intolerance begins to become larger and to express "a system of life." The terms "prejudicial," "alienation," "refusing," "polemics," "diversity," "preconceived approach," "emotional reception," "absolutism," "dogmatism," "fundamentalism," "holy enmity," "fanaticism," and "holy war" are among those that could be taken from the that vocabulary which reveal particular attitudes of an operative intolerance.

The period of holy enmity, the holy intolerance of holy war, whether called a crusade or a *jihad*, inasmuch as it is called such, makes us see these concepts in a properly religious sphere either as purely ideal or pragmatic intolerance. Whether drawn from biblical and Qur'anic interpretations, from the "state" religions, from the clergy, or from the governing class. In addition to the recurrent aspects of the codification of enmity and the ghettoization of minorities, we find "modes of making intolerance," in the context of promoting hostility and even more in the context of the treatment of the conquered religious enemy.

The human consequence of war is death or captivity for the defeated. The enemy killed goes to hell. In both camps there are supports for the worldliness of self-interest, as well as for alliances with the enemy, betrayal, and apostasy. When victorious, Muslims destroy Christian altars, remove church bells and sacred images. Christians transform mosques into churches and cancel all traces of Muslim worship: sacrilegious contempt and profanation is reciprocal.[19]

Understanding the religious element as a provoking element is clearly important. The total exaltation of Islam results in fanaticism, revenge, violence, the total humiliation of the enemy, and the glory of their God. "In mercy" or "in power" is not a euphemistic syntagma. It brought on sexual violence, sexual abuse, lynching, the auction block of the market, sale for the lost "value" of the captive, merchandise taken as booty, commercialized with time and the glory of God to show Islam's strength. Certainly, religious fanaticism or "blind" attachment to Islam is nourished by fundamentalism and ends in radical intolerance and extreme violence.

The same reflections apply to Christians. When there is a truce or peace, they fraternize with Muslims. The desire for brotherhood opens the way for "applied humanity," which is sometimes understood as "schismatic and heretical" by the clergy. We find expressions of tolerance in addition to intolerance; stories of love, marriages, friendships, and the fusion of daily life.

Eight centuries after extreme intolerance leading to fundamentalism and fanaticism, we hold to the modern alternative of tolerance and the practice of mutual, humanitarian service. The heart of each believer can go beyond the declarations of holy war. In spite of irreligion and the rejection of theology, there will be success when God's word in the two monotheisms is connected with disarmament.[20] With the realistic aim and conviction about the good of living together, the two monotheistic traditions can meet in the sphere of reason as well as faith. To want to multiply alliances in view of respect for the word of honor remains a noble attempt, if impractical. Religion still offers hope of disarmament. Disarmament is more in line with God's heart.

Christians and Muslims celebrated together when the war ended. According to Baha ad-Din, "the end of the war was like a feast day: and the joy was so great that only God could measure it."[21] Was this reaction due to a lack of faith or the result of true worship? Certainly the latter, for the best way to give God glory, who alone can measure joy, is living in peace. To the One, Almighty, Creator, compassionate and merciful, the one God in whom there is no intolerance. Intolerance is a sign of human weakness, but tolerance reveals divine omnipotence and human force.

4

The Rhetoric of Ransoming

A CONTRIBUTION TO THE DEBATE
OVER CRUSADING IN MEDIEVAL IBERIA

JAMES W. BRODMAN

Historians of medieval Spain as well as those interested in the Crusades have long debated how the experience of the Iberian Peninsula relates to the broader themes of European expansion, the confrontation with other civilizations, and the whole notion of religious warfare. Were those series of wars that later writers would call the *Reconquista* genuine crusades, which shared in the ideology and motivations that underscored the expeditions to the eastern Mediterranean or to the Baltic? Or are they better explained in terms of the secular and territorial aspirations of those individuals who would establish the dynastic kingdoms of Christian Iberia?

Recent historians of Peninsular history have been sharply divided on this problem. Arrayed on one side of the issue are Bernard Reilly and James Powers. While Reilly acknowledges a crusading fervor among Iberia's Muslim protagonists, whom he is willing to label as fundamentalists, from the Christian side he depicts the conflict in purely secular terms and rarely even employs the term "crusade."[1] Powers, for his part, except by implication, addresses the techniques, not the ideology, of warfare. But by viewing the Reconquest through the prism of municipal legislation, which for the most part ignores issues of religion and ecclesiastical polity, he stresses the competition for land and power and ignores the realm of ideas and culture.[2]

Robert I. Burns, on the other hand, enthusiastically embraces the notion of the Hispanic crusade, which he sees as representing "an encounter between two Mediterranean societies, fellow inheritors of the Hellenic past, drawn together at almost every level, yet simultaneously repelled by their respective ideologies."[3] Angus MacKay echoes this view in his descriptions of Alfonso I and James I of Aragon: the former is possessed of "crusading fervor," and the latter is "a flamboyant crusader for God." In his mind, the Reconquest of the twelfth and thirteenth centuries represented a form of "crusading manifest destiny." [4]

Somewhere in the middle are Derek Lomax and Thomas Bisson. Lomax sees the notion of crusade in its narrow and legalistic sense as a proclamation of the papacy that conferred upon crusaders specific privileges, among them indulgences. He acknowledges that religion, along with friendship, self-defense, greed, and a preexisting sense of Christian solidarity, helped motivate Catalans and Castilians to fight against Muslims. Spaniards had some sense that their wars were part of a larger drama because events in Syria and Palestine were the only non-Iberian happenings to gain the notice of twelfth-century Peninsular chroniclers. Yet, in the final analysis, Lomax believes that a competition for lands and offices superseded all other factors in explaining the dynamic of the Reconquest. [5] Bisson also notices a crusading consciousness and a willingness to utilize papal indulgences, but views the campaigns of James the Conqueror against Majorca and Valencia as cultural, rather than religious, undertakings. [6]

The ransoming of captives is one of those issues that might help us to understand the relative weight that should be given to religious sentiment as a factor in the conflict between the Christian and Islamic states of the medieval Mediterranean. Unlike many other activities associated with these confrontations, ransoming stands at the intersection of the secular and religious. Because it is a reaction to the capture of soldiers and civilians by an enemy, it is prominently treated in those same sources from which James Powers has derived his study of municipal militias. Ransoming thus could be a secular activity, undertaken for profit by *exeas, alfaqueques,* and others who might bid for a royal concession. [7] From this perspective, ransoming—and the trafficking in slaves—was but just one element in the normal commercial connections between the Christian and Islamic coasts of the Mediterranean. [8] As far back as antiquity, however, the act of restoring liberty to a captive or to a slave also had a religious dimension. In the Middle Ages, principally due to the introduction of the idea of indulgence, the moral benefit gained by ransoming captives was extended to anyone who assisted the process in any fashion. Thus, by the twelfth century, episcopal and papal indulgences were issued to those who contributed to the payment of ransoms, and bequests for the ransoming of captives became relatively common benefactions in the wills of Mediterranean Christians. [9] Furthermore, ransoming became incorporated into the formal apostolate of the Church as responsibility for the work was assumed by various new orders that grew out of the Gregorian reform movement.

While the act of liberating captives was practiced along the entire length of the Mediterranean, Iberia provides the ideal vantage point from which to examine European society's perception of the institution. All of the elements of this human drama are present: pitched battles, sieges, hit and run raiding between Christians and Muslims, and from the mid-twelfth century a continuous history of ransoming. Unlike Palestine, where the Western principalities were fragile and in decline, the Christian states here were vigorous and ultimately ascendant. Christianity itself was the dominant religion, and by the thirteenth century it had become the predominant creed in most areas of the Peninsula. Ransomers of all types operated within this arena, including those of ecclesiastical affiliation who will provide the primary focus for this study.

Religious redemptionism—i.e., the liberation of captives by members of religious orders—is our point of departure because this aspect has been more fully documented and studied than the activities of secular ransomers. Within Iberia, ransoming became a concern of three religious orders: the Order of Santiago, the Trinitarians, and the Mercedarians. Santiago was the only military order active in Iberia that devoted much attention to ransoming. Between 1180 and 1227 the order developed a network of seven ransoming hospitals, located along the Castilian frontier in places like Toledo, Cuenca, and its headquarters town of Uclés; two others, at Zamora and Salamanca, were established in the kingdom of Léon. Three additional ransoming houses, at Saragossa, Teruel, and Castiel, were founded within the kingdom of Aragon. Unfortunately, however, we know little about the functioning of these redemptionist shelters, apart from their existence and their apparent disappearance after the Christian conquests of Andalusia and Valencia.[10] If ransoming was never more than an auxiliary activity of the knights in Spain, it became the principal activity of the Trinitarians and Mercedarians. While each of these orders bears organizational similarities to hospitaller groups and other congregations of canons, these two redemptionist orders uniquely centered their energies upon the task of liberating Christians held captive by Muslims.

As Giulio Cipollone has admirably demonstrated in his recent study, the Trinitarian order was created as a response to the catastrophes that had struck Christian forces in the late twelfth century: the fall of Jerusalem in the East and the defeat at Alarcos in Spain. Cipollone argues that in this era when the capture of Christians assumed massive proportions, Pope Innocent III encouraged the Frenchman John de Matha to establish a mechanism for the peaceful and mutual exchange of prisoners with the Muslims. In the process the pontiff emphasized the religious character of ransoming by comparing Christian captives to the suffering Christ and their liberators to crusaders.[11] Trinitarians would go on to establish centers for redemption in Palestine, France, and England, but, with the decline of crusading efforts in the East during the thirteenth century, their most important efforts came to be centered in Iberia. In Spain the Trinitarians were most visible in Castile, where they established ransoming hospices at Toledo, Segovia, and Burgos early in the thirteenth century, and then followed the armies of the Reconquest south into Andalusia, where houses were established at Córdoba and Seville, as well as in Murcia. In Portugal there was a ransoming hospice at Santarem. Within the Crown of Aragon, the Trinitarians were less prominent. Their principal establishments were at Lleida, on the border between Catalonia and Aragon, and at Valencia, where the order seems to have turned its energies more toward sheltering needy Christians than to ransoming captives.[12] But the activities of the Trinitarians in Iberia have only been sketched out, and much remains to be discovered and examined.

The Mercedarian order was in origin a Catalan group that grew out of James I's advance against Majorca in the late 1220s and toward Valencia in the 1230s. Given his dynasty's rivalries with the French, and the death of his father at the battle of Muret, the king and his successors showed greater favor to these local ransomers than they did to the Trinitarians, who had strong ties to forces beyond the Pyrenees.[13] Consequently, the Mercedarians, with houses in Barcelona, Majorca, Valencia, Girona, and Perpignan, came to dominate religious ransoming in the Crown of Aragon during the medieval era. Outside of the Aragonese Crown, on the other hand, the Mercedarians were far less important than the Trinitarians. They held, for example, only a handful of houses in Andalusia and the southern regions of France.[14]

This study will examine how ransoming was perceived by Mercedarians and by their clients and patrons during the thirteenth and fourteenth centuries within the context of the Crown of Aragon. The principal sources are the series of donatary charters, royal and papal privileges, and internal Mercedarian documentation. Because the thirteenth-century brothers were, for the most part, laics and without advanced education, there are no collections of sermons or liturgical documents to illuminate our search. Many, and perhaps most, contemporary references to the Mercedarians in this era are too cryptic to assist our inquiry; typically the organization is called the "order," "house" or "brothers of captives," the "order" or "brothers of mercy," the "house of Santa Eulalia," etc. Other documents, however, through their description of the act of ransoming or their characterization of captives and Muslims, do express a point of view that will help us to understand why and in what context Christians of eastern Spain felt captives ought to be ransomed.

Institutionally, the Mercedarians, as well as the Trinitarians, belong to a broader subset of religious orders that I have in other contexts termed the "caritative orders." These shared in a general sense the characteristics of the new orders that were a product of Gregorian spirituality: namely, service to others, voluntary poverty, and interior spirituality. But these caritative groups can be distinguished from the mendicants and the military orders, the two other principal groupings to be found under this general heading, by the character of their work, which comes to be centered around hospitals and the care of society's needy. Indeed, the early houses of both of the ransoming orders are frequently described in the sources as hospitals. For the Mercedarians, these were shelters specifically for captives, but those pertaining to the Trinitarian order served the local poor as well. Thus, it is not surprising to find that the earliest citations of Mercedarian ransoming describe the work as essentially one of charity. For example, there are references from 1231, 1232, and 1234, all before Pope Gregory IX's initial sanction of the order in 1235, to the "alms of captives" and to the "charity of captives." [15]

This characterization of ransoming as a work of benevolence by the earliest donors and patrons of the Mercedarian order is a persistent theme that can be found throughout the medieval documentation and is expressed by all of Merced's constituencies. Mercedarians themselves clearly regarded ransoming as an activity comparable to the works of sheltering and nurturing that were practiced by the broader hospitaller community. This equation is most clearly expressed in the prologue to the order's first written constitutions, redacted in 1272:

> Thus, on the day of Judgment, through the mercy of Christ they [i.e., the Mercedarians] will be assigned to the right side as being worthy of hearing the sweet words that Jesus Christ will utter from his lips: come, blessed of my father, take the kingdom that has been prepared for you from the beginning of time because when I was in prison, you came to me. When sick, you visited me. I was hungry and you gave me to eat. I was thirsty and you gave me to drink. I was naked and you clothed me. I was homeless and you took me in. All of these things have been ordained by Jesus Christ to be fulfilled in this order—to uphold and increase the important work of mercy implicit in visiting and redeeming Christian captives from the power of the Saracens. [16]

King James I echoes this notion in the *guidaticum,* or safe-conduct, that he extended to Mercedarians in 1251. There he depicts ransoming as chief of all the virtues, and again in 1255 the king calls this "a pious work." His grandson, James II, repeats the designation in a communication of 1310. [17] Pere, from the village of Valls, as executor for Bernat de Gatello in 1251, likewise describes ransoming as "one of the works of mercy and a praiseworthy and pious work." The Aragonese nobleman Fortun de Verga in his donation of 1265 includes ransoming among the corporal works of mercy.[18] In a similar vein, Pope Alexander IV in 1255 recommended Mercedarians to the generosity of all Christians, arguing that "among the works of charity through which to gain heaven, the redemption of captives is commended by God and by the sacred canons."[19]

To the extent that ransoming is regarded as an act of charity, and re-demptive in the same sense as the other corporal works of mercy, it is an in-ternal activity, performed for the benefit of the community and the individual. Just as any other act of kindness, it serves a neighbor and pro-vides an occasion of grace. This association between ransoming and other acts of piety—such as the support of local churches or of the mendicant or-ders, gifts to hospitals, and subsidies to young women of marriageable age—is most clearly seen in written wills. Typically, legacies for captives appear as part of a long list of *pro anima* bequests that are a commonplace in Catalan wills.[20] These are motivated by the notion that society has a moral obligation to aid the poor, who are frequently designated as "Christ's Poor," and that spiritual benefits would accrue to those who provided some form of assis-tance.[21] Pope Alexander IV's privilege of April 9, 1255, placed captives within this broad context of the poor by associating their relief with that of poor pilgrims and the sick. Furthermore, the first extant gift to the Order's founder, Pere Nolasch [Peter Nolasco], describes him in 1226 as "rector of the poor of mercy."[22]

Service to the poor highlights one aspect of Mercedarian work, for in addition to the actual ransoming of captives, the order collected and dis-bursed alms to needy captives, not all of whom were actually redeemed by the brothers. The assumption underlying this activity was that the Mer-cedarians were to help those who lacked the financial and technical means of arranging their own ransoming; consequently, this was a work of charity. This justified the order's effort to raise alms from the Christian population, the ecclesiastical indulgences that were granted to givers as a reward, and the requirement that captives who were liberated with these alms must assist Mercedarians in their solicitation of additional offerings. To the public, Mer-cedarians appeared like any other charitable agency that set up alms boxes around town and dispatched preachers to take up collections in parish churches.[23] Thus, to at least some degree, the justification for the Mercedar-ian apostolate derived from internal values and not from conflict with Mus-lims. Captives were helped because, like lepers and orphans, they were *miserabiles personae,* and thus counted as being among Christ's poor.

On the other hand, the captives who were assisted by Mercedarians were never the prisoners of coreligionists, but always individuals in the hands of

Muslims. This is implicit even in those sources that describe such prisoners as nothing other than captives. The earliest Mercedarian sources indeed make reference only to "captives" or "Christian captives." The earliest specific identifications that I have found of the captor date from 1244 and 1245, just as King James was completing his conquest of southern Valencia. In the first, Bernat de Tonyà, the Mercedarian commander at Tarragona, provided money to free Bernat de Curciano, who is described as being captive at Almería and held by the Saracens. In the second, the Mercedarians of Barcelona are given an endowment to support "the redemption of Christian captives who are held in chains by the Saracens."[24] Both documents refer to Muslims as Saracens, which is one of the vague and generic terms that Europeans used to designate Arabs and Muslims.[25] The citation of "Saracen" or, more pejoratively, of "infidel Saracen" and "perfidious Saracen" becomes common in the Mercedarian documentation; "Moor" and "barbarian" also appear. Papal correspondence also uses "pagan" and "enemy."[26] While papal language is less neutral, the majority of references to Muslims in Mercedarian documents are no more than that and only identify the agents who are holding the captives who require ransom. Thus, in these sources the emphasis remains upon the caritative act of ransoming, and only scant notice is made of those responsible for the act of captivity.

In a minority of documents, however, there is an anti-Muslim rhetoric that is highly suggestive of a crusading ideology. The most consistent source is the series of privileges that the Mercedarians received from the papacy; these granted indulgences to individuals who made financial contributions to the order's work of ransoming. By the thirteenth century the indulgence came to be applied as an incentive toward support of a wide variety of good works, but the idea itself had originated in the twelfth century as a part of the papal program to promote the Crusades. At various times in the thirteenth century, popes promised ransoming benefactors indulgences that ranged between forty days and a plenary indulgence, the dispensation of certain types of vows and of the obligation to say the canonical office, and absolution for crimes of larceny.[27] While these bulls, as we have already seen, acknowledge that ransoming was one of the acts of charity, they also take pains to paint Muslims in a negative light and Mercedarians in one that is heroic. The first example is Pope Innocent IV's indulgence of January 13, 1245, that praises the order "for redeeming captives from the hands of the pagans," a designation for Muslims that is repeated in the privileges of most thirteenth-century pontiffs. Pope Alexander IV, in 1255 and again in 1258, uses stronger language. The latter document, addressed to the clergy, describes Mercedarians as "traveling to lands beyond the sea on behalf of suffering Christians [who are] captive in the hands of the enemies of the Christian faith," and who "do not shrink from subjecting their own bodies to the danger of death, seeing how those captives are afflicted and crucified with harsh and diverse torments." John XX in 1276 asserts that those Muslim captors are "the enemies of Christians," a designation repeated in 1357 by the papal legate to Castile as justification for his privilege to the Mercedarians of Seville.[28] These descriptions become formulae and are reiterated in bulls that come to be reissued as a matter of routine at the onset of each new pontificate. Yet, nonetheless, they move the work of ransoming considerably beyond the realm of the merely caritative. Captives are more than "miserable persons"; they are prisoners of God's enemy and of the enemy of all Christians. Mercedarians consequently become crusaders who risked their safety to complete the work of ransoming. The papacy, of course, had long viewed the confrontation between Christians and Muslims in precisely these religious terms. To what degree did Catalans and others in Iberia share this perspective?

The Mercedarians themselves echo the papal rhetoric in their constitutions of 1272, where they describe Muslims as Saracens who are "enemies of our law" and "enemies of the order of Christ."[29] While other Mercedarian documents are too cryptic in their description of ransoming to shed additional light upon this theme, the obligation of recently ransomed captives to accompany Mercedarian preachers on their rounds of churches suggests that the sufferings of Christians at the hands of Muslims must have formed part of their appeal for alms.[30] The theme of hostility to Islam does have documented expression from three Mercedarian constituencies: captives, contributors, and the crown.

The voice of captives is preserved by just a few charters in which ransomed Christians acknowledged receipt of a cash subsidy that they had received from the order and which they, or their friends, used to gain their liberation; the purpose of the record seems to be the provision of a guarantee that the money was spent for ransoming and not illegitimately diverted to some other purpose. In one of these instances, Bernat Rubio describes his liberation as an act of "God's grace"; in another, Guillem of Blanis states that he "stood in captivity in the power of the perfidious Saracens in the city of Bugia." In 1320 the bailiff, along with the priest and other residents of Jordana, a parish outside Gerona, asked for and received a subsidy with which to ransom Guillem, a fellow parishioner, who had been taken captive during the previous year off the Balearics "and led with his confederates as a captive to Bugia by the enemies of the Cross and the barbaric Saracens."[31]

Among those who contributed money for ransomings, there is Berenguer de Riara of Castellón de Ampurias, who in 1259 gave as a rebate to the Mercedarians of Majorca the rental that they owed him for a vineyard on the island, on condition that the ten morabetins each year be used "for

freeing captives from their chains and from the prisons of the infidel Saracens
. . . from the hands of the pagans." This action, furthermore, was to be done
"for the remission of my soul and those of my relatives and especially for
those to whom I have done any injury." Gerald Adroerius, also from the region of Ampurias, bequeathed for his soul in 1245 wheat from a field outside
Torroella de Montgrí "for the redemption of Christian captives who are held
in chains by the Saracens." [32]

In both instances, the receivers and the givers of money thought it important to stress the character of the captors rather than the poverty of the
captives. Each in its way relates to the rhetoric of the papal bulls, which
themselves give as much emphasis to the "evils" of Islam as the needs of captives. For captives, one may speculate that the expression of enmity toward
Muslims legitimated their demand for Christian alms and made them more
than mere slaves seeking liberty. For donors, these same sentiments seem to
have made the gift worthy of the remission of sin and eligible for the indulgences promised by the papacy.

Royal expressions of ideological fervor, on the other hand, are much
more complicated. We do find sentiments similar to those of captives and
contributors in the privilege that Sancho IV of Castile extended to the Mercedarians in 1289: "[The ransoming of captives from the land of the Moors]
is a great service to God and to me and to Christianity." [33] King James II of
Aragon sought privileges for the order in 1310, using as justification their
"redemption of captives held in stinking captivity in the nations of the barbarians," but one has the sense that the Catalan monarch was pursuing multiple agendas.[34] In a series of letters addressed to the pope and to others
between 1302 and 1310, King James takes pains to depict the Mercedarians
as members of a military or crusading order and, at the same time, to tie the
order closely to his dynasty by making the novel assertion that his grandfather, James the Conqueror, was its actual founder. The correspondence begins in 1302 with a letter to Pope Boniface VIII, in which King James
describes Mercedarians as those who ransom "captives of the orthodox faith
from the custody of the barbarians"; at the same time, he argues that the
order has a rule similar to those of various military orders: the Hospitallers
of St. John, the Templars, the Knights of Calatrava, and the Order of Santiago. In order to establish his right to intervene in Mercedarian affairs, the
king also makes reference to the *guidaticum* that James I had conferred upon
the order in 1251.[35]

The crusading theme is amplified in 1303 by the consuls of the Valencian
municipality of Segorbe, where the order held property. They told Pope
Boniface that in the course of their work as ransomers the brothers "have to
use arms and do other enormities that do not pertain to the clerical office." [36]

James II in 1306 wrote to the new pontiff, Clement V, and again recalled the patronage that his grandfather had extended toward the early Mercedarians.[37] By 1309, when he addresses the Mercedarian chapter, James began to assert that the order received its "initiation" from his ancestors, and this is repeated in his letter to the consuls of Barcelona in 1310.[38] These dual claims—the royal foundation and the military character of the order—are telling because they occur in no previous documents; their novelty suggests that each was meant to serve some specific purpose.

One intention is clearly an attempt to limit papal influence over the order in the course of a series of elections for master during which clerical and lay factions had formed among Mercedarians. King James, suspecting a papal bias in favor of the clerics, consistently favored lay candidates for the mastership and to this end stressed both the military character of the office and his own dynasty's rights of patronage.[39] For similar reasons the king battled for control of the assets within his realms that had belonged to the dissolved Templar order. Ironically, 1317 marked the year that James lost the first battle, with the imposition of a papally appointed clerical master upon the Mercedarians, while gaining victory in the second through his establishment of the new military order of Montesa.

There is also the possibility that the king's purpose extended beyond his desire to maintain a measure of control and influence over the Mercedarian order. His letters of 1309 and 1310, for example, were too late to influence the most recent election, since this had already been decided by Clement V in a letter of February 12, 1308, and his instruction to the Mercedarian chapter of 1309 was intended to uphold the recent papal verdict and maintain the delicate balance within the order's ranks between clerics and laics. Likewise, the letter to Barcelona's magistrates in 1310 had nothing to do with matters of governance, but rather expressed a concern to maintain the order's economic viability, and particularly its ability to seek alms for captives despite the interdict imposed upon the city by the bishop of Barcelona.[40] Together both letters indicate apprehension that the order's ability to function was impaired by a particular crisis. Why this anxiety? A reasonable explanation for this is the joint Catalan-Castilian assault upon Granada in 1309–1310, which in early 1309 had received the designation of a crusade from Pope Clement V. With the objective of conquering Almería, the Catalans sent some two hundred ships against Granada, and their forces began a siege in August 1309. This lasted until early 1310, when James was forced to retreat in chaos.[41]

The first of James's two letters regarding the Mercedarians was written in April 20, 1309, or during the final stages of the king's preparations for the crusade. There he instructs the Mercedarian chapter to meet not at the rural location of Puig, but instead in Valencia under the watchful eye of the royal justiciar so that the latter "insofar as he can take care that the brothers turn aside from undertaking any disorders." Two months earlier James had already instructed his envoys to the papal court to request that the order's revenues be appropriated for use in the Granadan campaign.[42] One might reasonably infer from this that the king anticipated that he needed the Mercedarians and their alms for his upcoming campaign and thus would not tolerate the continuation of any destructive infighting among the brethren. There is little evidence to document a Mercedarian presence at the siege, apart from the citation of a single friar.[43] But the letter of May 4, 1310, to the magistrates of Barcelona is dated just after James's disastrous flight from Almería, and its concern with the order's ability to beg alms for ransoms seems to coincide with a need to redeem his own troops who had been captured during the siege. The negative tenor of his references to Muslims in this letter mirrors that in correspondence to others of the same period.[44] Thus, just as James exploited the notions of crusade to obtain subsidies from his episcopate and a three-year tenth from Clement V, so also the king was willing to evoke images of "stinking captivity" to promote alms for the Mercedarians.

What do these portraits of ransomers and captives tell us about Catalan perceptions of the conflict against Muslims? The verdict is an ambivalent one. A portion of the evidence suggests that medieval Iberians focused upon the caritative nature of the ransoming act and regarded it in the same light as other contemporary works of charity. Such works themselves were the product of complex social, personal, and religious motivations that grew out of the internal dynamics of the particular society. Thus, there is the penchant for calling early Mercedarian establishments hospitals and listing legacies for captives alongside those for other needy members of the community. The promise of indulgences itself was no longer tied exclusively to crusading activities; by the thirteenth century it had broadened to include the entire gamut of good works. Even the Mercedarian custom of parading ransomed captives before audiences of potential donors provides evidence that is equivocal because this tactic came to be mimicked by other types of Barcelonan hospitals.[45] Thus, while many benefactors assisted captives and the Mercedarians for religious motivations, these reasons were not necessarily tied to ideas of crusade.

Then, there is the sense that by the thirteenth century ransoming had become a matter of routine and a practical necessity. Most frequently the order is merely labeled as the *ordo captivorum* and those who were helped as *captivi*. References to their captors or the nature of their captivity are exceptional. Of course, this may merely reflect the cryptic nature of many medieval sources and disguise a myriad of concerns and motivations, but in a sense the ability of Mercedarians to perform their acts of ransoming depended upon an ability to travel as nonmilitant intermediaries to Muslim lands.[46] It seems fairly certain, furthermore, that the Mercedarians came to be regarded by many families and captives merely as one of the several sources of funds to be used in assembling a ransom.[47]

It is undeniable, however, that crusading notions also formed a part of the motivations of Mercedarians and their supporters. This is evident in the Mercedarian constitutions and in the bulls of support that emanated from the papacy. While the sparseness of our information makes generalization dangerous, nonetheless, the fact that both captives and contributors are seen echoing these sentiments is evidence for their existence within lay society. It would be natural enough for a former captive, or his family, to engage in anti-Muslim rancor, but the fact that benefactors did so as well indicates that ransoming did have a connection to the conflict with those "who are against our law." Common sense also suggests that the long succession of papal indulgences would not have appealed to crusading ideas if these had not resonated in some fashion within society.

Royal motivations were more complex than these. One can detect in the evidence a sense of routine: the promotion of a pious act and hostility toward Muslims. During the reigns of James I and Peter the Great, there is little to suggest that royal intentions strayed far beyond these boundaries. The *acta* of James II, and later those of Peter the Ceremonious, however, reveal a political use of the crusade to promote a measure of royal influence over the order and the ability to appropriate its revenues for crown purposes. Indeed, the royal evidence seems to be a mirror of the broader phenomenon. Ransoming, like the wars against Islam, was a mixture of necessity, piety, and opportunism that changed with the needs of the moment.

PART TWO

Cooperation, Conflict,
and Issues of Identity

5

Toleration Denied

ARMENIA BETWEEN EAST AND WEST
IN THE ERA OF THE CRUSADES

JAMES D. RYAN

In the era of the Crusades, the Armenian people were already well acquainted with intolerance and its consequences: they had become well
schooled in the art of war, resisting conquest by Persians, Hellenes, Romans,
Sassanids, Byzantines, and Arabs. Their struggle to preserve national
uniqueness was conjoined, after conversion to Christianity in the fourth century, with defending their freedom to worship; the Armenian Holy Apostolic
Orthodox Church was persecuted in turn by Zoroastrian Sassanids, Muslim
Arabs, and Orthodox Byzantines.[1] In the tenth century Armenians encountered two new societies: Muslim Turks, whose invasion occasioned the Crusades, and Frankish crusaders with their Latin Church of Rome. This paper
focuses in particular on the confrontation between the Roman and Armenian Churches during the Crusade period, exploring the growth of intolerance
in the interaction of these two cultures. Although only an introduction to a
long and complex tale, it should provide insights into the causes of mutual
antagonism that developed during this period.

The bare outline of the story is as follows: the Crusades brought into
contact two cultures sharing a common religious heritage, Franks and Armenians. They made common cause against both Muslims and Greeks, and despite occasional mutual skullduggery, became allies, intermarried, and
united their churches during the first century of this interaction. During the
next hundred years, however, although political and matrimonial connections continued, the union of their churches dissolved. Finally, in the third
century of this period, serious attempts were made to restore the communion
of churches. But this had become an impossible task because during these
centuries both churches had undergone an attitudinal change, a shift from
accommodation to mutual hostility. As will be seen, this was based on nei-

ther ignorance nor simple prejudice, but on increased knowledge of each of the other, and on dawning self-awareness. In short, the process of interaction made each church define itself more deliberately, and each ultimately chose not to tolerate the other.

First, a brief look at the Armenians with whom the crusaders interacted, and at their church. The crusaders barely touched the historic homeland of the Armenians, eastern Anatolia, where they had held intermittent lordship from at least the sixth century B.C.[2] During the Bragratid period (885 A.D. to c. 1045), an Armenian monarchy (under Muslim suzerainty) governed frequently unruly, largely independent *nakharars,* the land-owning nobility.[3] Byzantium annexed western Armenia between 1020 and 1042, but lost it to the Seljuks soon thereafter (1048–64).[4] Following the Battle of Manzikert (1071), Turkic hordes overran virtually all of Anatolia.[5] The Armenians whom crusaders encountered were the few *nakharars* and their retainers who had established themselves in and around Cilicia. Although catholicoi (patriarchs) of the Armenian Church tended to gravitate there, most of the Armenian faithful and clergy continued to dwell in Greater Armenia, under Turkish overlordship.

Armenians were very proud of their church, which they believed to be both Apostolic and autocephalous because founded by Bartholomew and Jude Thaddeus.[6] Armenia as a nation became Christian early in the fourth century, when its king was baptized by St. Gregory the Illuminator, the first catholicos of the new national church.[7] Throughout the medieval period, most subsequent catholicoi were linear descendants of St. Gregory, who sired a line of ecclesiastic aristocrats. Gregory's descendants included Nerses the Great, who refined church government in the fourth century, and Sahak I, who in the next century sponsored creation of the Armenian alphabet and translation into Armenian of the Bible and liturgy.[8]

Their church was not in communion with either the Orthodox Church of Constantinople or the Roman Church when the Crusades began. Because the Armenian Church did not consider the Council of Chalcedon (451) canonical, the Greeks condemned them as Monophysite and heretical.[9] Byzantine intolerance and persecution engendered in most Armenians a strong antipathy toward the Orthodox Church and things Greek.[10] They held a different opinion of the Roman Church, however. According to Armenian traditions, St. Gregory the Illuminator had established a pact with Pope St. Sylvester (314–335), and during succeeding centuries, in which they had no interaction with the papal see, Armenian respect and affection for Rome remained undiminished.

Armenian sentiment toward Rome was reinforced for those in Cilicia by their encounter with the crusaders. Cavalier treatment of Armenian princelings often soured political relations.[11] First contact with the Western church and its practices, however, deepened Armenian respect for the Latin Church, and Westerners showed toleration for non-Greek eastern ecclesiastics, giving them a free hand in religious affairs.[12] Michael the Syrian, Jacobite patriarch of Antioch at the end of the twelfth century, contrasted the Latins' attitude with that of the Orthodox Greeks: "The Franks never raised any difficulty about matters of faith, or tried to reach an agreed statement of belief among Christians ethnically and linguistically separated. They regarded as Christian anybody who venerated the Cross, without further inquiry."[13] Perhaps because of frequent intermarriage with Armenian nobility, the Franks treated the Armenian Church with great respect, and clergy from both confessions sometimes shared facilities with mutual toleration.[14] The twelfth century Armenian poet St. Nerses the Gracious gave voice to Armenians' affection for the Western church when he wrote: "Oh Rome, magnificent and revered mother of cities; See of St. Peter, the rock against which the gates of hell will never prevail. You are like the Garden of Eden."[15]

Throughout the twelfth century the Armenian and Roman Churches drew closer together, and a union of churches was established by century's end. At an 1141 synod convened in Jerusalem by Alberic, cardinal bishop of Ostia and pontifical legate, the Armenian catholicos Gregory III made a personal profession of faith and promised to restore his church to union with Rome.[16] Following the lead of the Maronites of Lebanon, who acknowledged papal primacy about 1182, the Armenian catholicos Gregory IV sent a profession of faith to Pope Lucius III (1181–85) in 1184.[17] Lucius accepted this as an act of submission and sent the catholicos a *pallium* (the woolen symbol of archiepiscopal authority), along with a copy of the *Rituale Romanum,* which was subsequently translated into Armenian.[18] Later, when Prince Leon II of Cilicia approached both Pope Celestine III (1191–98) and Emperor Henry VI, seeking a royal crown, they dispatched legates to Armenia to grant his request.[19] Only then, in 1197, did Rome attempt to exert authority over the Armenian Church by delaying Leon's coronation until the union of the Armenian and Roman Churches was reaffirmed. Ultimately twelve Armenian prelates swore they would bring their practice into closer conformity with Rome's, and the kingdom of Armenia was inaugurated on the Feast of the Three Kings, 1198, as a vassal state of the Empire, in communion with the Roman Church.[20]

Considerable controversy surrounds the submission of Armenia to Rome and the establishment of church union. Neither Catholicos Gregory IV's 1184 letter of submission to Rome nor a text of the papal demands of 1197 has been preserved, and many details are known only through Armenian historians, who began to reinterpret these events as soon as union collapsed in the next century.[21] In one such report, Leon is said to have told his prelates that he would submit merely in word and not in deed.[22] Whatever the circumstances, in subsequent correspondence with Armenia both Innocent III (1198–1216) and Honorious III (1216–27) studiously avoided doctrinal issues. This was not done though ignorance; an 1199 letter from Innocent to Leon makes clear that the papacy was well aware that only part of the Armenian Church had accepted union with Rome.[23] The popes seem to have been in no hurry to put pressure on Armenia and contented themselves with gentle prodding. Only under Gregory IX (1227–41), and probably as a result of friction over dynastic change in Cilicia, did the papacy threaten the traditional position of the Armenian Church by making it subject to the Latin patriarch of Antioch.[24] In the face of vigorous Armenian protestations, however, the pope immediately did a *volte-face* and in 1239 explicitly recognized the rites and customs of the Armenian Church: "By apostolic authority We confirm to you and to your kingdom the reasonable customs which have obtained there from the time of Pope Sylvester and of St. Gregory, Catholicos of the same kingdom, who are said to have been contemporaries, in so far as they do not contravene the rulings of the Holy Fathers or the canons of the church."[25] Resistance from conservative Armenian churchmen continued, however, and although a 1251 Armenian synod, at the urging of Innocent IV (1243–54), affirmed belief in dual procession of the Holy Spirit, only formal union had been achieved in Cilicia, and no steps to effectuate union were being taken in Armenia proper, where the bulk of the faithful resided.[26] It was only natural, therefore, that the Western church ultimately took a new tack in the quest to unify all Christian churches under Rome.

The adoption of a new approach to achieve union with the Armenian Church was part of the larger story of the medieval missionary movement, which blossomed in the thirteenth century.[27] In 1246, Innocent IV had dispatched a Franciscan, Lawrence de Orte, with the special mission of reconciling Eastern Christians with Rome.[28] The next year he sent another friar, Andrew, to work specifically with the Armenian Church.[29] Relations with Armenia were clouded at this point, however, because of the Mongol menace, something that Armenia and Rome viewed quite differently. The popes saw the Mongol khans, who claimed a mandate from heaven to rule the entire world, as an evil to be resisted and believed no pact was possible with them.[30] Armenia's King Hetoum I (1226–69), on the other hand, submitted and in 1247 made the Cilician kingdom a Mongol vassal state. He also persuaded his nephew, Bohemond of Antioch, of the advantages of Mongol alliance.

Armenian relations with the papacy became more strained thereafter. Even before Hülegü's 1260 invasion of Syria, Pope Alexander IV (1254–61) authorized the preaching of an anti-Mongol crusade, urged Latins in the

Holy Land to oppose the Mongols, and threatened to excommunicate leaders, like Bohemond, who lent them support.[31] Nevertheless, Hetoum and Bohemond rode with the Mongols and entered Damascus in victory with them. Church union may now have seemed a liability for Cilicia, and dialogue with Rome was broken off in 1261.[32] When the Latin bishop of Bethlehem summoned Catholicos Constantine I (1221–1267) to Acre, Constantine sent as proxy an antiunionist theologian, Mekhitar of Daschir. In the course of discussions, Mekhitar launched an attack on papal primacy: "Whence does the Church of Rome derive the power to pass judgment on other Apostolic Sees while she herself is not subject to their judgments? We ourselves [the Armenians] have indeed the authority to bring you [the Catholic Church] to trial, following the example of the Apostles, and you have no right to deny our competence."[33] Such views Armenians had previously kept to themselves. The conference ended with no resolution, and union seemed at end as well.

The thirteenth-century papacy is frequently castigated for its unbending, legalistic rigidity in dealing with other churches. It was difficult for leaders of the Roman Church to compromise because they held strong convictions concerning the nature of the church and the unique position of the Roman pontiff in dispensing grace necessary for human salvation. Right or wrong, they deeply believed in their position, and throughout this period buttressed it with legal, philosophical, and theological arguments. In spite of this intolerant mind-set, the papacy exhibited gentle toleration in its interaction with other Christian peoples encountered in the Levant and Asia between the late twelfth and early fourteenth centuries, as their initial interaction with Armenia demonstrates. This acceptance of other churches is in striking contrast to Latin hostility toward the Greek Orthodox Church, which was briefly reconciled to Rome at the Second Council of Lyons.[34] The schism between the Orthodox Church and Rome, which had been in existence for more than two hundred years, was declared over at Lyons after Greek representatives made solemn submission, chanting the phrase *ex patre filioque procedit* three times during the recitation of the Nicene creed.[35] It was another symbol (creed), *Credimus Sanctam Trinitatem,* which had been used in negotiating this reconciliation. Drawn up in the pontificate of Clement IV (1265–68) as terms and conditions of union with no room for compromise on papal primacy, it included paragraphs emphasizing the unique position of Rome.[36] In contrast with the approach taken *vis-à-vis* the Armenian and other Eastern churches, the papacy held the Greeks' feet to the fire of submission before compromise.[37] This different attitude resulted from the long and acrimonious debate with Orthodox churchmen over ritual and belief. By the thirteenth century the Latins had come to believe Greeks perfidious and haughty, in addition to simply wrong. Familiarity breeds contempt, and an unwillingness to be tolerant. But, because the Armenian and other Eastern Christians were not a known quantity, it was easier for Rome to accept their customs. To rework the cliché: The new, the exotic, the unfamiliar had engendered patience and reserve that, in this context, one might call toleration. Interestingly, the same paradigm, applied to the Armenian Church, helps explain why its relationship with Rome altered in the fourteenth century.

Despite the many points of belief on which the Roman and Armenian Churches readily agreed, there were differences that were highlighted by the ways in which each of the two confessions expressed its belief. One example was the matter of the "mixed chalice," that is, the addition of a drop of water to the wine before consecration, standard in the West but not an Armenian tradition. As is generally the case, this ritual expressed deeper meaning. The mixing of water and wine symbolized for the West the two natures of Christ, divine and human, and an unmixed chalice might be interpreted as an affirmation of Monophysite heresy. That notwithstanding, in matters of ritual there were clear limits to Armenian willingness to compromise with Rome. The Armenian people and clergy were very attached to their traditions and practices, which were central to the culture the Armenian Church had helped create, and the majority within that confession resisted any alteration in customary rituals. Cilicia was exceptional because political considerations and cultural interaction facilitated the movement toward a union of churches there. Cheek by jowl with newly formed crusader states, the *nakharars* intermarried with Frankish counterparts and Latinized the government of their kingdom.[38] Increasingly Cilicia became less representative of the bulk of the Armenian people and more open to the compromises necessary for church union. This readiness to compromise on religious matters, whether toleration or expediency, was not endorsed by conservative clergy, the majority in Greater Armenia, who had had little direct contact with Westerners and who viewed changes in ritual practice, even if for the sake of union with another church, with suspicion and hostility.

This situation changed when missionaries of the Latin Church entered Greater Armenia under Mongol protection, as a consequence of rapprochement between the Western church and the Mongols in the last third of the thirteenth century. Hülegü, brother of Qubilai Khan and first Ilkhan (subking) in Persia and Mesopotamia, had sent an embassy west in 1263–64, suggesting military cooperation, and his successors welcomed ambassadors and missionaries into their realm.[39] Western missionaries were allowed into every part of the Mongol empire thereafter and given permission to preach in all subject lands.[40] Franciscans and Dominicans quickly seized this opportunity, and by the third decade of the fourteenth century at least forty convents had been established in the East, on the shores of the Black Sea and beyond, in Qipchaq, Georgia, Greater Armenia, Persia, Mesopotamia, and even China.[41] As the fourteenth century dawned, the papacy built upon this foundation by establishing a Latin hierarchy in Asia, bringing the scattered outposts of the western church under two new archbishoprics: Khan-baliq (Qubilai's capital, modern Beijing, established in 1307), and Sultaniyya (capital city of the Ilkhanate in northern Iran, created in 1318).[42] Although the Franciscans had more houses in Persia, John XXII invested the Dominicans with the archbishopric of Sultaniyya, perhaps to advance a long-range crusade plan involving Christian communities to the east and south of Islam.[43] As it turned out, because most of the new diocese's suffragan sees lay along the main road through eastern Anatolia, Dominican bishops in the new jurisdiction focused their attention there, and assumed an apostolate in Greater Armenia.[44] The Dominicans thereafter joined the Franciscans already at work in Cilicia and Greater Armenia, attempting to reconcile Eastern Christians to Rome.[45] Because of Mongol support, Armenian clergy were powerless to prevent or regulate the activities of Western clerics who entered their territory.

Dominican and Franciscan missionaries did make converts in both Greater Armenia and Cilicia, including some influential church leaders whom they brought into full union with the Roman Church. Among the earliest of these was Catholicos Constantine II, who was secretly received into the Roman rite about 1285, probably by Franciscans resident at Sis. Because relations between Cilicia and Rome were still strained at that point, his reconciliation was considered apostasy, and when it became known, in 1288, Hetoum II deposed and exiled him.[46] More significant were the conversions made in Greater Armenia in the fourteenth century, after the see of Sultaniyya had been established. One of these was John, the *aradjorn* (superior) of the monastery at Qrna. After spending a year (1329) with Dominicans in Maragha, teaching them Armenian while he studied Latin and Western theology, he became personally committed to church union. Following a conference he convened at Qrna, many monks and clerics subscribed to union with Rome, among them his entire monastery, which was thereafter given in perpetuity to the Dominicans. From these beginnings a new order, the Brothers Unitors, emerged, and from about 1340 they worked assiduously to bring the Armenian Church into full union with Rome.[47] Another notable convert was the monk Zachary of Zorzor, archbishop of St. Thaddeus and exarch (governor) of Greater Armenia, whose adoption of Roman Catholicism gave first the Franciscans and later the Dominicans a strong presence at Zorzor.[48] Mendicants, teaching scholastic theology and supervising the translation of a variety of works from Latin into Armenian at both Zorzor and Qrna, convinced many, including two Armenian bishops, to submit without reservation to the Roman Church.[49] Through their teaching at least one Armenian monk, John of Zorzor, qualified as a doctor of theology.[50] So complete was the conversion of Unitors that they rejected Armenian rituals, replacing them with Roman usage. Convinced by scholastic theology that the Roman Church was the true church of Christ, they attacked their own traditions as tainted with Monophysitism, and some went so far as to have themselves rebaptized and reordained in the Roman rite.[51]

These were the exceptions, however, and not the rule in Greater Armenia, where the majority of clergy and faithful remained unmoved by Western missionaries. Both the individual conversions to the Roman Church and the converts' rejection of Armenian traditions made the bulk of Armenian clergy even more hostile to compromise for the sake of union than before.[52] Thus hostility toward the Roman Church blossomed in Greater Armenia because of contact and interaction with Latin clergy, and traditional Armenian respect for the church of Rome gradually disappeared. Not surprisingly, when Western missionaries lost the support of Mongol overlords, who ultimately adopted Islam, the orthodox among the Greater Armenians shut Latin clergy out of their territory and treated the Unitors as schismatics. Once again, familiarity had bred intolerance.

A very different dynamic was at work in Cilicia as the fourteenth century opened. There Armenian clergy, despite their deep attachment to traditional rituals, officially capitulated and embraced the Roman Church and its creed. With the loss of the Latin outposts in Syria (1291) and the conversion of the Ilkhanate to Islam, Armenia was bereft of erstwhile allies.[53] Because only Lusignon Cyprus, Western kings, or the pope could provide military succor, the union of the Armenian Church with Rome seemed a good move once again. These facts certainly helped inspire the 1307 synod at Sis, at which Armenian prelates adopted all the reforms Rome asked, chief among which were recognition of all seven ecumenical councils (including Chalcedon), an expression of belief according to the Roman formula, and adoption of the mixed chalice for the Eucharist.[54] The last had become particularly important as a clear statement of Armenia's rejection of Monophysitism. Although the Armenians had always argued that this symbolic mixing, not part of their tradition, was not essential, and had always stressed their differences with Monophysite Nestorians, they yielded on this and every point to Rome. The union was not acceptable to the Armenian Church as a whole, however, and it was promptly repudiated.[55]

The Cilician capitulation to Roman demands at Sis did not achieve the desired results, because by this point Rome was conscious of the many reservations held by Armenian clergy, even in Cilicia, and began to demand greater proof of Armenian commitment to church union. Ironically, Western suspicion of Armenian adherence to union with Rome was fueled largely by some Unitors, who denounced their confreres for less complete submission to Western ritual and belief. Foremost among these was Nerses of Balienz, the Unitor bishop of Qrna, who made his way to Avignon about 1338.[56] Nerses impressed Benedict XII (1334–42), who named him archbishop of Malazgerd and set him the task of examining the Armenian faith.[57] When King Leon V (1320–42) sent an embassy to Avignon to plead for immediate aid in 1336, Benedict was slow to respond because, as he explained in letters of 1341 to Leon and the Armenian Catholicos, he had been informed that execrable errors had arisen in the two Armenias, and had ordered a *libellus* (pamphlet) drawn up, which Leon's envoys were carrying back so it could be discussed in a synod, which would correct errors and restore orthodoxy.[58] Titled *Fides Armenorum,* the *libellus,* which Nerses had drafted, listed 116 articles accusing the Armenians (except for the Unitors) of a wide variety of errors. These included rejecting both the *filioque* and the Council of Chalcedon, professing Monophysitism, not adopting the mixed chalice, and rebaptizing those who had been baptized under the Greek or Roman rite.[59] This lengthy text elicited quick response from Cilicia, where a 1342 synod refuted the *libellus* article by article and affirmed that the alleged errors were not the common doctrine of the Armenian Church.[60] A large entourage of Armenian nobles and clerics arrived in Avignon later that year to bring these conclusions to the papal court. Although the pope was heartened by Cilicia's commitment to union, and some financial aid was dispatched to assist Lesser Armenia, the papacy henceforth sought continued reassurances of Armenian goodwill and devotion to real church union. When the ambassadors returned to Cilicia in 1346, they were accompanied by two Latin bishops who were charged to examine Armenian books to expunge their errors and to hold a synod for that purpose.[61]

Clearly, the attitude of the papacy toward Armenia underwent a sea change and took on a new, harder edge as the fourteenth century progressed. From the reign of Benedict XII onward, popes began to insist that the Armenians align both their belief and their ritual with that of the Roman Church. Benedict had explicitly linked assistance for Armenia to reforms in religious practice, and demanded that "errors" be corrected before military aid would be sent.[62] The toleration and latitude that characterized earlier relations between Rome and the Armenian Church were gone. Clement VI (1342–52), in a 1351 letter to the Armenian Catholicos, stated the new situation clearly: Armenians not only had to believe as the Latins, they had to adhere closely to the papal mode of practicing their common faith.[63] Trust had disappeared because, over a long interaction, the two parties had alienated each other. Since the Armenians (in the papal view) had said one thing but done another by professing union but refusing to implement it, the test of determining orthodoxy now became full compliance with Latin ritual as the outward sign of agreement with Latin belief and discipline. The papacy was no longer willing to endorse Armenia's unique national style of religious expression, as it had a century earlier. Toleration had become a victim of familiarity, and Armenians were henceforth treated with suspicion formerly reserved for Greeks.[64]

In conclusion, this brief and partial recapitulation of the waxing and waning of relations between Rome and the Armenian Church in the High Middle Ages is little more than the outline of a remarkable story that needs a larger canvas to be traced in proper depth and detail. This survey should, however, provide insight into causes and occasions of intolerance, and call into question conventional "wisdom" that deeper knowledge and broader intercultural experience promote fellowship and toleration. Too often the opposite is true; the worst enemies are those who have learned over long periods of interaction to know and to despise each other. That level of hatred probably did not mature between the Roman and Armenian Churches, but the warm feelings for Rome that Armenians had cherished in the earlier Middle Ages were supplanted by resentment and suspicion of Western aims, and Latin toleration of Armenia's unique institutions vanished. To find an example of more mature intolerance, one must look at the relations between the Armenians and Turks, or, more currently, between Bosnian Muslims and Serbs, but an exploration of those topics would be another paper entirely.

6

Muslim Taxation under Crusader Rule

PAUL L. SIDELKO

The survival of native administration after a foreign conquest is a commonly assumed historical phenomenon. A good deal of scholarship has addressed the extent to which crusader society adapted the customs and administrative policies of Muslim society and how the daily lives of the Muslim and Syrian Christian inhabitants were changed under crusader rule.[1] Depictions of crusader society have ranged from the integrated model put forth by French historians of the nineteenth century to Prawer's conceptualization of an apartheid regime under European colonial rule.[2] Although conclusions and interpretations vary with individual authors, many scholars have argued that there was some degree of continuity of Muslim social organization and administrative practice within the boundaries of the Latin East.[3]

This paper will evaluate the continuity of the Muslim administration in the crusader states with regard to rent and taxation. The evidence related to tax payments by cultivators to their lords is limited; the occurrence of Muslim tax terms in the considerable source material of Latin charters contained in the various cartularies of the military orders and ecclesiastical organizations is even slighter.[4] A few charters indicate that the basic rent paid by cultivators for their parcels of land, usually called *carruca*, was the *carragium*, also known as the *terraticum* or *terragium*.[5] Most authors have seen these terms as either a corruption *(carragium)* or a Latin synonym *(terraticum, terragium)* of the *kharaj*, which continued to be collected from cultivators under crusader lordship.[6] With regard to the term *carragium*, the assumption of a direct connection to the Arabic *kharaj is* especially troublesome. The problem is largely a linguistic one. To begin with, the term *carragium* may instead be formed from the Anglo-French *caruage* or *carruga*, misleadingly similar in appearance, no doubt, to *kharaj*, but deriving its meaning from the Latin *carruca* or chariot, later the wheeled or heavy plough.[7] Of course, this word serves as the basis for the crusader land terms *carruca* and *carrucae*, meaning plough-land. In fact, the *carruca* is sometimes called *caruge* in the charters.[8] It is also possible that the term *carragium* is not synonymous with *terragium,* but rather indicates a carriage service or a toll on carts, most likely charged when bringing the harvest to the lord's curia. This is the definition provided by Latham under the entries for *carragium* (c. 1160) and *carragium* (c. 1170). *Carregium* is also found as a variant spelling under the entry for *carreda* in Du Cange, who provides a similar definition of a fee for carriage. Indeed, this appears to be the sense in which the word is used in a Templar document of 1142 from Arles.[9] In this document, reference is repeatedly made to *carreig,* for example, "lo carreig xii deniers raimondegz." Surely this money payment is not at all related to *kharaj,* but, rather, most probably to a fee for carriage or transportation of the harvest from the fields to the lord or his agent. Such a fee is often found in medieval Europe.[10] A perhaps similar payment is indicated in a document from the Hospitaller cartulary, which transfers the right of two "bêtes de charge." [11]

In particular, the identification of several instances of *kharaj* in the crusader cartularies by Jonathan Riley-Smith warrants detailed reexamination. Of the five documents he identifies, only two are possibly references to *kharaj* in Latin form. It must be kept in mind that variations in spelling make any precise definition impossible, so that any conclusions must remain tentative. One charter, dated 1193, concerns the dispute over tithes at Margat between the Hospital and the church at Valenia. The Hospital agrees to hand over to the church the tithe held "in villages and rents from the same incomes, *caragiis,* agreements." [12] Another Hospitaller charter, dated 1238, contains the following lines: "Besides, when the aforesaid Master and the brothers paid only five bezants to him for the twentieth of the *caragium* of the same village, he demanded the same to be paid to him and they should be held to the account of those who receive for a greater payment owed to him according to the number of the receivers." [13] It may be the case, as suggested above, that, as used here, the term *caragiis* could just as plausibly be a spelling variation of *carruca,* the land measurement commonly found in the charters of the Latin East, and with a number of variant spellings, e.g. *carrega,*[14] *carrugas,*[15] and *caruge,*[16] as well as *carruc[cagio]* and *carrugag[iis]* from two English documents, dated 1199–1200.[17] Significantly, Du Cange has an entry for *charuagium,* which carries the following definition, "terra quae caruca seu aratro colitur" (land cultivated by a *caruca* or *aratrum*[types of plows]). Such a meaning for this word would fit in the context just as nicely as an adaptation of *kharaj.* It is also important to note that the document from 1238 is issued under the name of Pope Gregory IX at the Lateran. It certainly casts some doubt on the authenticity of *caragiis* as a Muslim term if it originates in the chancery of the pope.

In a third example, the French variation *karrage* appears in Raybaud's summary of a Hospitaller document, dated 1139. The caption reads, "Donation faite à l'Hôpital de Hierusalem par Raymond I, prince d'Antioche, . . .de six besans et demy censuels et neuf écus de karrage, qu'il prenoit sur le jardin que Trigaud avoit donné à l'ordre." [18] Without the text itself, the details of this document are too vague to allow for more than speculation. There is no indication as to the size of the garden or what was grown in it. There are no prohibitions against the leveling of *kharaj* on fruit trees, but it should be noted that this is a money payment and not a portion of the harvest. This fact makes this item an anomaly even among the rare, scattered documents under discussion here.

Another document from the cartulary of the Teutonic Knights, dated 1257, is more detailed, but by no means definitive in its description. It describes a settlement between the bishop of Acre and the Knights over a wide range of payments and dues. It contains the following reference: "Et debent solvere dictam quintam decimam de vino suarum vinearum et de charagiis et de oleo suorum villanorum de tanto quantum inde recipiunt et de suomet oleo, de computagio caprarum, de apibus, et de exeniis villanorum suorum" (And they ought to pay the said fifteenth from the wine of the vineyards and from the *charagia* and from the oil of their villains, from the accounting of goats, from bees, and from the gifts of their villains). The exact meaning of this term is debatable, and its placement in the text is perplexing. If it is indeed a reference to *kharaj,* it would seem unnecessary to include it among payments of wine and oil, since a portion of these goods would constitute a payment of *kharaj.* The charter continues to list a variety of goods and animals, including she-goats, bees, geese, eggs, and cheese. The content of this listing allows for the possibility that here the word *charagia* may refer to another such product, namely, the carob nut. The tree was quite common in Syria, and its fruit was valued by the inhabitants. The carob may be considered here because a French variant of the word for it is *carrouge,* which when rendered into Latin may have taken the form displayed in this charter.[19] The final document, from the Order of St. Lazarus, makes no mention of *kharaj,* despite Riley-Smith's assertions to the contrary.[20] Rather than *kharaj,* it refers to cavage, a capitation or head tax, which was a common feature of European lordship.[21] Finally, Ibn Jubayr's statement that the inhabitants of a village outside Acre paid half their harvest as rent to their Frankish lord is often cited in support of the survival of *kharaj.* It should be noted, however, that an examination of the passage in Arabic clearly shows that he does not use the term *kharaj.* Rather, he writes only that *nisf,* or half, of the harvest is collected as tax. A variant manuscript reading gives *thulth,* that is, a third.[22]

The various suggestions provided in this examination indicate that no consistent and definitive explanation can be provided for the exact meaning and usage of the term (or, more likely, terms) contained in these charters. But this is perhaps the point to be made. These scattered and ambiguous references provide little support for concluding that the Muslim *kharaj* survived under crusader rule. Even if these terms do indeed represent adaptations of the word *kharaj*, it is vital to understand that the appearance of an Arabic term for taxation in crusader documents in no way proves that Arabic taxation practices survived. The validity of this point is further proved by the overwhelming continuity of European practices in crusader rural administration.

That the Latin terms *terrage* and its variants appear in charters from the Latin East is not surprising because these terms have a long tradition in Europe. *Terragium* and *terraticum,* in contrast to *carragium,* correspond closely with the kind of rent payment that historians have found in the Latin East, that is, rent paid in the form of a share in the harvest.[23] According to Du Cange, the earliest mention of *terraticum* is in a charter of Emperor Ludwig II in 869. *Terrage* is first mentioned in a charter of Count Otto in 1030. In western France, *terrage* appears between 1030 and 1060, but given the long time before these terms are written into text, they could have appeared before 1000.[24] In this region, the proportional rates vary from one-seventh to one-third of the harvest, but almost two-thirds have a rate of one-fourth.[25] It is possible as well in certain cases that several redevances (dues) are imposed upon the same land, so that when combined with the tithe at one-tenth, the rate of one-fourth is raised to one-third. On lands subject to the tithe, *terrage* was taken from what was left of the crop after the tithe had been deducted. It is worth noting that such a procedure contradicts one of the major Islamic jurists, Abu-Hanifa, who prohibited the exaction of *kharaj* from lands subject to *'ushr.*[26]

In Provence a similar arrangement is found under the name *facherie,* a contract by which the lord concedes land for a fixed term against the payment of a quarter, a third, or a half of the harvest. Four acts from the Cartulaire de St. Thomas de Trinquetaille between 1190 and 1198 contain the term *facherie,* one of which states that the amount charged by the Templars was one-fourth.[27] Similar rates are found in the southwest of France, where rents on vineyards are usually fixed at one-fourth and other crops at one-third.[28] Germany provides an abundance of similar examples, where the introduction of sharecropping or *métayage* is related to the abandonment of direct exploitation. This point will become extremely important when examining the extent of demesne land in the crusader settlements in the Latin East. *Métayage* is a form of cultivation in which the lord provides the land as well as a part or whole of investments such as seeds, tools, plough, and plough team.[29] In contrast, *tenure à champart* or *terrage* requires the tenant to put up all the expenses and equipment and assume all the risks. The lord invests nothing, so he receives a comparatively smaller portion of the harvest, often one-eighth to one-sixteenth. Share cropping is also found throughout Germany, except in the colonized regions of the east, where only fixed rents are found. For vineyards, the rate is typically one-fourth to one-half of the harvest; for cereals, one-half or one-third, depending on the crop, the more precious, such as autumn wheat, requiring a higher proportion from the cultivator.[30] It is worth noting that in the Cistercian rules of 1134 in Germany, *métayage* is expressly forbidden, but the prohibition could not withstand the movement to this form of revenue exaction by the lord. Two centuries later, in the county of Württemberg in 1380, the ratio of land in direct exploitation to that under *métayage* stood at 1:36, from a ratio of 1:4 thirty years earlier.[31] Such examples from Europe indicate that the origin and nature of taxation under the crusaders in the Latin East is more solidly based on a European system than in the survival of Muslim administration and the *kharaj*.

Moreover, if we look more closely at the nature and history of the *kharaj*, the arguments for its survival become even less persuasive. The *kharaj* is a tax levied on the land, paid to the state.[32] This designation, it is important to note, immediately distinguishes the *kharaj* from the Latin form, which was a rent paid to the lord.[33] Cahen has argued that the privatization of tax collecting under the feudal regime of the crusaders negated the distinction between *terrage* as a private rent and *kharaj* as a public tax.[34] Such a distinction might have been lost on the worker forced to make the payment, but the shift has a profound theoretical resonance. It is difficult to make an argument for the survival of an institution when the very foundations upon which it is built have been swept away. Once the public nature of a tax is changed into a private rent, how can it be said to survive in anything but a nominal way? And as has been shown, even this nominal survival should be called into question. Chris Wickham, disputing the existence of feudalism under the Ottomans, considers the relationship between lord and serf based on rent extraction to be the crucial aspect of feudalism, not the judicial-political relationship. Thus, he draws a sharp distinction between tax paid to the state as a feature of Islamic lands, and rent paid to the lord as the defining feature of European feudalism.[35] In reply, Halil Berktay has argued in Marxist terminology that such a distinction can be supported only if it can be shown that these two different modes demonstrate different methods in which surplus production is extracted from the cultivator by the ruler.[36] We have seen many examples of methods of extracting production that vary considerably from the Muslim practice. For example, the terms of *métayage* require the lord to put up the materials with which the land is cultivated in return for a larger share of the harvest. These are not at all the terms by which *kharaj* is appropriated from the cultivator, who is responsible for all materials and work and pays a portion of his income to the state as a tax. With regard to the crusader settlements in the Latin East and the survival of Muslim administration, this theoretical distinction between rent paid to the lord and tax paid to the state needs to retain its importance.

A similar argument may be made with regard to the survival of the Muslim *jizya*. It has been argued by some recent scholars that the crusaders took over the Muslim practice of exacting a head tax, only instead of imposing it on Christians and Jews, it was now collected from Muslims.[37] In this case, the writings of Ibn Jubayr do explicitly refer to the head tax on Muslim inhabitants of crusader lands as *jizya,* but such limited evidence certainly does not warrant the conclusions of LaMonte that it represented one of the chief revenues taken by the kings of Jerusalem.[38] Again, the argument being made for survival of *jizya* is refuted by the fact that the tax as administered by the Muslims was specifically intended for non-Muslims. How can it then be said to survive when its fundamental nature and purpose has been removed? The crusaders did not simply adopt this method of taxation; rather, they introduced their own, indigenous system that shared nominal similarities with that practiced in the lands they conquered. Indeed, as with rent in the form of a share of the harvest, the head tax was a common institution in medieval Europe; its appearances throughout England and the continent are too abundant to list. Duby has identified *chevage* as early as the tenth century and speculates that it was an even more ancient practice. Certainly it was well known in the Roman Empire and early Byzantium. Like the *jizya, chevage* was considered a payment indicative of subjection, but in Europe it was not based on religion. Again an important distinction between the two regimes must be made both in theory and in practice. All Muslim jurists and their legal traditions agree that *jizya* is to be collected only from able-bodied adult males who are not Muslims. It is true that the evidence of Ibn Jubayr indicates that under crusader rule, the head tax was now levied on the Muslims, but contrary to Islamic law, on females as well as males. Moreover, the document from Cyprus in 1210 indicates that the *chevage* was collected from Christian cultivators as well as Muslims.[39] The administration of such taxation more clearly resembles European than Islamic practice.

By paying the head tax, the Muslim and perhaps the Syrian Christian cultivators were exempt from the tithe. Several papal decrees related to the possessions of the Abbey of Our Lady of Josaphat indicate that revenues derived from "rusticos infidelium" (the rural men of the infidels) were to be kept in total by the abbey, that is to say, the tithe would not be taken from these rents.[40] As well, it appears that the proposal of Thoros, king of Armenia, to settle 30,000 Christians in Palestine in the 1160s was scuttled when the Church insisted on collecting the tithe from these new cultivators, although it was not being collected from the Muslims.[41] A papal confirmation concerning the possessions of the Abbey of Our Lady of Josaphat contains the phrase "aliisque decimis bonorum hominum latinorum" (and other tithes of Latin *boni homines),* suggesting that only Latin Christians paid the tithe there as well.[42]

In Europe the tithe represented a major form of revenue for religious orders; the situation was no different in the Latin East.[43] The charters are filled with the disputes between various religious and lay organizations over claims to the tithe on produce and lands.[44] In Islamic law, there is a parallel to the tithe, known as the *zakat,* usually levied at 10 percent of property including food harvests, fruits, grapes, and nuts, cattle and animals, and sometimes gold and silver and other merchandise. This practice in both societies clearly has its origins in Judaic tradition and was adapted and institutionalized by the Christian church and the Islamic theocracy. According to the dictates of Muhammad, *zakat* is incumbent upon all Muslims who meet a minimum level of wealth. Until the time of Abu Bakr in 632–34 A.D., the tax was usually given to the recipients directly from the hand of the benefactor. According to tradition, in addition to the destitute, recipients included parents, relatives, orphans, travelers, beggars, and slaves. The reforms of Abu Bakr made the tax a regular institution, which required payment to the state treasury for distribution. Only Muslims paid *zakat.* Payment of the *jizya* by Christians and Jews exempted them from this payment, which, depending on the wealth of the cultivator, probably provided a lower rate. In practice, the collection of the tax was often difficult and evasion widespread. In some cases, the secular tax on land, known as *ushr,* replaced the *zakat.* On a superficial level, this tax appears quite similar to the European tithe, but significant theoretical and practical differences remain. In Islamic administration the *zakat* as well as *ushr* is collected by the state in the name of the Muslim community. It was often used for military and political purposes, in addition to poor relief. Such features provide a stark contrast to the collection and distribution of the European tithe, where the tenth is claimed and collected in the name of the Church by various religious communities.

Rent as paid in a share of the harvest was not the only feature of European land tenure that was brought to the Latin East. Often, as in Tuscany, these dues were accompanied by gifts to the lord, such as chicken, eggs, and cheese.[45] There are several examples, such as those concerning the Venetians at Tyre, of these gifts in the Latin East as well. Here too it is difficult to accept survival of the Muslim system.[46] It is as hard to follow other conclusions that the Franks did not introduce any features of feudal Europe into the Latin East.[47] One need only look at the Hospitaller settlement at Beit Jibrin to see a clear example of a European form of settlement.[48] Prawer has studied this colonization custom extensively. He has concluded that the number of the first settlers, around 1153, was thirty-two families, between 100 and 150 people. All of them were Franks, and the majority were newcomers from Europe. Their terms of settlement stipulated that they were obliged to pay the annual *terragium* on crops and fruits. Here is an example of cultivators, none of them Muslim or Syrian Christians, who paid a proportion of their harvest to their lord as rent. Here too did the *kharaj* survive?

We may ask the same question of another settlement founded by the canons of the Church of the Holy Sepulchre on lands given to them by Godfrey of Bouillon.[49] Magna Mahumeria (al-Bira) established a custom of settlement that was copied throughout the twelfth century until the territorial gains of Saladin in the 1180s. The terms of settlement are clearly laid out along European lines. The Frankish settlers, about 150 families at the most, were mainly involved in viniculture, although there were a number of craftsmen and artisans as well. As at Beit-Jibrin, land was granted against a share of the harvest, *terraticum,* in this case, ranging from one-third to one-half. Prawer has also identified grants of land that he associates with a variation of the *champart* or *complant* contract, known as *medietaria*.[50] With these contracts in Europe, lands are usually given at a fixed lease, after which the cultivator would return half the land and retain the other against a share of the harvest. At Mahumeria, however, the contract stipulates that the lands are held in perpetuity and heritable against a payment of one-half. If the cultivator wishes to sell the land, then he is obliged to return half the price to the canons of the Holy Sepulchre. In this settlement custom, as in that of Beit-Jibrin, there is not a trace of Muslim survival. The sharecropping arrangements are clearly elements of European origin.

One of the main arguments against the introduction of European forms of land tenure assumes the almost total absence of demesne land in the Latin East.[51] But again, the lack of demesne is not a convincing proof that a European system was not imposed. For security and cultural considerations, the crusader lords were rentiers, residing in the cities and not on their lands. At first glance, one may assume that the absentee lord was merely following the Muslim custom. After all, the Middle East in the Middle Ages was largely an urban society, centered around the great cities of Cairo, Baghdad, and Damascus. Europe at this period, on the contrary, was a predominantly rural society, centered around the great manors in the countryside, where the lord lived directly off the produce of his estates. Thus, it would have been natural for the crusaders in the Latin East to attempt to impose their manorial customs in place of the native Muslim customs, and to introduce the demesne and its accompanying labor services. That this effort did not succeed is seen as proof that the Islamic land tenure system survived. Such a view, however, is misleading from two perspectives. Ronnie Ellenblum has recently published a brief but important article effectively challenging a generation of historical writing on crusader settlement in the Latin East. According to his findings, the assumption that the Franks did not settle in the countryside and only collected a share in crops "is not based on documentary or archaeological sources and is in no way accurate." [52] In his archaeological field study, undertaken between 1985 and 1991, Ellenblum has identified the remains of more than two hundred rural sites settled by the Franks. These usually took one of two forms, both commonly found in Europe: rural *burgi* attached to fortified castles and *maisons fortes,* located in remote areas and organized around the manor for agricultural exploitation, including pathways to the fields and extensive irrigation. Ellenblum uses the large numbers of these settlements to refute the prevailing view that the Franks created a largely, if not exclusively, urban society of rentiers and absentee landlords who lived off the share of the harvest that they extracted in kind from their predominantly Muslim subjects. Through the plotting of these sites, Ellenblum also suggests that Frankish settlement took place, following a stratification dating from the era of Byzantine control, mainly in areas where Syrian Christians were a large minority or majority of the population and that they avoided those areas with a large Muslim population. Although these conclusions warrant further elaboration and research, they suggest that the crusaders were much more involved in rural settlement and administration than has previously been assumed.

Even if Ellenblum's preliminary findings do not withstand future scrutiny, the view that the crusaders continued Muslim practices falters for other reasons. When analyzing the features of crusader lordship, there is solid ground for suggesting that the supposed lack of demesne land and feudal services in the crusader states in the Latin East may in fact derive from contemporary developments in the feudal system of Europe, where there was a movement at this same period away from holding demesne land and towards the elimination of services. In England and France, especially, the elimination of demesne land took place under three specific conditions: 1) shortage of labor; 2) difficulty of cultivating newly acquired or remote territory; and 3) preference of lords to reside in cities for comfort, security, and convenience.[53] These were precisely the conditions that most historians believe to have obtained in the Latin East. Because of the scarcity and reluctance of Muslim workers and the difficulty in encouraging European peasants to settle abroad, labor was in short supply. This short supply made it difficult to exact the labor services necessary to maintain a demesne. More-over, the political and military instability of the crusader states made travel to and residence in the rural areas impractical and dangerous. For these reasons lords preferred to reside in the cities and live off the rents they collected from their lands in the country. Indeed, this situation, which was typical of the Latin East in the twelfth and thirteenth centuries, became increasingly more common in Europe over time.

The lack of demesne land and the shortage of labor also reduced the demand for *corvée,* or labor services required from the peasants by the lord. There is a parallel in colonization activities in eastern Europe. For German colonists in eastern and central Europe, labor services were exceptional, amounting to only a few days per year.[54] In fact, the first German colonists had no work to do for their lord. They paid little money to landowners and for the first ten to twenty years were entirely free from taxes.[55] In much the same way, in the Crusader states labor services were for the most part also very light or non-existent, exacted only in very difficult and labor-intensive tasks, such as olive grove cultivation and sugarcane production. Rather than concluding that the crusaders conformed to the indigenous pattern of rents and services, it is equally plausible that the crusaders responded to the labor shortage and impracticability of living on their lands in a manner similar to that which their counterparts in Europe had begun to follow by the twelfth century and would increasingly follow in the next two centuries.

As this paper has shown, much of the evidence for the survival of Muslim administration under crusader rule is fragmentary and scattered; conclusions must therefore remain tentative. Indeed, given the rudimentary knowledge of rural life in Islamic Syria and Palestine before the Crusades, it is difficult to establish an acceptable standard of comparison. As other scholars have observed, we must also be cautious about reading too much into brief descriptions and making broad generalizations from a singular reference. I would argue, however, that given what we do know about crusader land tenure, a framework for further research may be established. In a compelling article presented at the University of Western Ontario, Riley-Smith discussed his personal views on the future of research on the origins of the First Crusade.[56] He urged further study of the social and political environment of eleventh century France and a return of crusader scholarship to the European mainstream. On the matter of the survival of Muslim taxation, I would second that call, for there too I believe a better understanding of the subject is to be found.

7

Edward of England and Abagha Ilkhan

A REEXAMINATION OF A FAILED ATTEMPT
AT MONGOL-FRANKISH COOPERATION

REUVEN AMITAI

In the spring of 1271, Edward, prince of England, landed in Palestine and
soon sent an embassy to Abagha Ilkhan, Mongol ruler in Iran. It would
appear that in his message, Edward suggested to Abagha that they would
launch a concerted attack against their common enemy, the Mamluk sultan
of Egypt and Syria. Although Abagha's answer was enthusiastic, little was to
come of this *démarche*. The actual force that the Ilkhan sent into north Syria
was not large, and Edward wasted his strength on pointless raids in Palestine. This paper will attempt to reexamine this failure to cooperate in what
was one of the few opportunities, if not the best, to effectively do so in the entire history of Mongol-Latin relations. One question that may be asked is, To
whom do we ascribe the blame for this unfulfilled hope? Was it that Abagha
was unable—or unwilling—to act more decisively, or that Edward did not
respond appropriately to the initial Mongol advances, or was constrained
from doing so? In my conclusions, I will try to bring back my discussion to
the theme of this volume, tolerance and intolerance during the Crusades.

Because the actual events themselves have been chronicled in some detail
in previous scholarship,[1] I will limit myself to a brief rendition.[2] Having witnessed the final stages of Louis IX's debacle in Tunisia (1270), Prince Edward
made his way to the Holy Land via Sicily and Cyprus, and arrived in Acre on
May 9, 1271. Edward's aims were certainly militant, and in spite of what appears to have been a lack of similar feelings among the local Frankish leaders, he began making preparations for an offensive against the Muslims. His
most important step was the dispatch of an embassy to Abagha Ilkhan, ruler
of the Mongols in Iran. While Edward's original letter has not come down to
us, we do have at least the gist of Abagha's reply: "After talking over the matter, we have on our account resolved to send to your aid Cemakar at the head

of a mighty force; thus, when you discuss among yourselves the other plans involving the fore-mentioned Cemakar be sure to make explicit arrangements as to the exact month and day on which you will engage the enemy."[3] Cemakar, of course, can be easily identified with Samaghar, the powerful Mongol commander in Anatolia at this time.[4] I might add that there is no indication of whether Edward answered this letter, or in other words, whether he continued to pursue this policy of a joint campaign by actually attempting to coordinate the movement of troops. I will return to this point below.

While waiting for Abagha's response, Edward indulged in a *chevauchée* (raid) to the east, leading a column against Sieser (al-Shaghur) and St. George-de-Lebeyne (al-Bi'na) in mid-July. Little came of this raid except a few burnt houses and crops and the Frankish troops' many casualties from heat and food poisoning.[5] This was certainly not an auspicious start to the English prince's endeavors.

When exactly Abagha's letter, which was written in early September, reached Edward is unknown, but it seems likely that it arrived before the Mongol attack which it announced. Around mid-October 1271, a Mongol force raided north Syria. It was, however, eventually to withdraw with the approach of the Mamluk army; more will be said about this offensive shortly. Edward's reaction to this news—as well as the performance of his troops—cannot by any stretch of the imagination be called impressive. On November 23, he headed south from Acre at the head of a column composed of his own forces (which had been somewhat reinforced since his previous raid), men of Acre, Cypriots, Templars, Hospitallers, and Teutonic Knights. In the region of Qaqun (Caco, in the Sharon plain), a group of Türkmen were surprised, many of them were supposedly killed and a large number of animals were taken as booty. As for the local Mamluk garrison, one officer was killed and another one—of some importance (Baybars al-Jaliq)—was wounded, while the governor (Bajka al-'Ala'i) was forced to temporarily withdraw from the fortified town.[6] With the approach of reinforcements from the Mamluk unit stationed at 'Ayn Jalut, the Franks fell back towards Acre; some Franks were killed and many horses and mules perished, while a number of captured Türkmen were freed.

This second campaign of Edward, whose goals were certainly very modest, was also not a spectacular achievement.[7] But it was about as close to one as Edward was to have in his war against the Mamluks, and it was also the nearest thing to real Mongol-Frankish military coordination that was ever to be achieved, by Edward or any other Frankish leader.[8] Could a more effective joint campaign have been launched, and if so, who is responsible that it was not?

It is first worth examining in greater detail the actual Mongol campaign

into north Syria. Initial reports of this attack reached Baybars at Damascus
and spoke of Mongols raiding 'Ayn Tab and moving on to 'Amuq al-Harim,
which they reached around 20 October 1271 (mid-Rabi' I 670). From there
the Mongols continued on Harim and al-Ruj (to the west of Aleppo), killing
many people. This information is originally found in the biography of Baybars written by his secretary Ibn 'Abd al-Zahir, and is copied by several later
writers, including Maqrizi, who is perhaps still the best-known Mamluk
writer among historians of the Crusades.[9] Another group of Mamluk historians, mostly hailing from Syria, provide additional important information
of this campaign. The Mongol expeditionary force was indeed led by Samaghar, as promised in the letter by Abagha cited above; these sources explicitly state that the Ilkhan gave the order for this campaign. Samaghar was
accompanied by the pervane, Mu'in al-Din Sulayman, the strongman of
Seljuq Rum. The latter's presence is not surprising, as the sources write that
the force numbered 10,000 horsemen (i.e., a *tümen)*, composed of Mongols
(al-mughul)[10] and Rumis, i.e., the Turkish soldiery of the subservient Seljuq
sultanate. This army reached as far as Mar'ash (today in southeast Turkey),
from whence an advance force of some 1,500 elite Mongol troops *(min
a'yanihim, min akabir al-mughul,* or just *min al-mughul)* was dispatched to
reconnoiter and raid to the south.[11] The report by this group of sources
about the continued advance of this smaller force is similar, but slightly more
detailed than that found in Ibn 'Abd al-Zahir: the raiders reached 'Ayn Tab
and then went on to Qastun, in the region of al-Ruj. Between Antioch and
Harim, they came across a group of Türkmen and inflicted great casualties
upon them. With the approach of a Mamluk army under Baybars, this Mongol force retreated from Syria.[12] By the time, a Mamluk strike force reached
Mar'ash (at an unknown date), the larger Mongol force had also with-
drawn.[13] It may be noted that the Syrian Türkmen appear to be the greatest
victims of this so-called Frankish-Mongol campaign.

Before I examine the possible reasons for a lack of a more substantial
Mongol response to Edward's overtures, the record can be set straight on one
minor point, but one perhaps not without interest. The second report cited
above is often summarized by modern writers, but almost invariably they explicitly state that the entire force numbering 10,000 men invaded Syria.
There is, then, no mention by these twentieth-century historians that only a
smaller, albeit elite, force actually penetrated into Mamluk territory.[14] This
omission, however, is perhaps unjustified, given that two earlier historians,
the early nineteenth-century savant D'Ohsson and in his wake Grousset, give
a good rendition of this report, including the detail in question.[15]

Would we be correct in attributing the failure of the nascent Mongolian-
Frankish cooperation to the small size of the Mongol expeditionary force?

Before I answer that question, it should be clear that whatever the extent of this force, this was apparently a deliberate choice by Abagha, and he was not constrained by his preoccupations in other matters, particularly fighting on other fronts of his extensive kingdom. There is no reason to accept the suggestion made by a number of scholars, starting with Grousset, that Abagha was unable to send a larger force to aid Edward because he was busy on the Chaghatayid front in the east.[16] In fact, the war with Baraq in Khurasan had been successfully concluded by Abagha in the previous year (1270), and his own campaign into Transoxania was over the winter of 1272–73.[17] Perhaps, the basis of this mistaken assertion is the information regarding a letter from Abagha brought to Edward in 1277, in which he apologized for the inadequate assistance earlier offered to the English prince.[18] It would appear, then, that some modern scholars have read into this apology more than was actually there.

On the other hand, in this last-mentioned letter Abagha had felt the need to express some contrition if not explicitly to justify himself. It appears then that in retrospect, at least, he believed that he could have done more to turn the negotiations for the joint campaign into a reality. What kept him from doing so in 1271? As mentioned above, things were quiet on the eastern (Chaghatayid) front. To the north, on the border with the Golden Horde, there was also a hiatus in hostilities. A perusal of the Persian sources emanating from the Ilkhanate does not indicate any major matters, strategic or political, that seem to have weighed heavily on shoulders of the Ilkhan at this time.[19] So we are left with the tentative conclusion that we have before us a strategic decision on Abagha's part to send a force of such-and-such size at this juncture. Unfortunately, but not surprisingly, the deliberations of Abagha and his advisors in this matter (and many others) have not come down to us. We have no choice, therefore, but to speculate on his reasoning in this case.

A couple of preliminary points should first be made. First, it is clear that Abagha had a long-standing desire to effect an alliance with the West against the Mamluks. This is evidenced, *inter alia,* by the many missions that he sent to Europe to drum up support for a joint campaign.[20] Secondly, a corps of 10,000 horsemen, while representing only part of the entire Ilkhanid army, was a not insignificant force by the standard of the time.[21] By way of comparison, the Mongol army that fought at 'Ayn Jalut in 1260 numbered in the neighborhood of 10,000 (or perhaps slightly more),[22] while the Mongol army that gave Baybars so much trouble at Abulustayn in 1277 was composed of only 11,000 Mongol horsemen and 3,000 Georgian troops.[23] With these points in mind, I would suggest that there was a certain logic in Abagha's decision to send at this stage only one corps of 10,000 to the Syrian frontier. There had been some preliminary negotiations with Edward, and these had augured well, but up to now there had been no effective Frankish response to several Ilkhanid calls for help, starting with that of Hülegü in 1262.[24] By accepting Edward's proposal for a joint campaign, the Mongols were in a sense "buying a pig in a poke." How were they to know ahead of time of the extent and nature of the Frankish expedition, assuming that one would be made? It made perfect sense for Abagha to send at this time a medium-size probing force, from which a component of particularly good troops would detach itself and move forward, in order to test both the response of the Mamluks and, no less important, the actions of the Franks. If the latter had evinced some sign of effecting a joint campaign, then the main force would have been poised to enter Syria. Although Abagha himself in retrospect may have regretted his decision, it appears that at the time this was a particularly wise move. Given the character of the actual performance of Edward and his troops, the modern historian would not go amiss in giving Abagha high marks for his thinking.

Edward's second campaign has already been discussed in some detail, and the inescapable conclusion that can be drawn is that even had it been successful, the Franks would have gained little except for some local tactical advantage; it certainly would have had little effect on developments in north Syria. Had the Franks taken Qaqun, they might have attenuated Baybars' communications with Egypt, but reinforcements could still have come from that direction, simply by traveling further to the east. What should Edward have done? Following Professor Riley-Smith, it would appear that in theory the total force that Edward had at his disposal was not an insignificant one.[25] Personally, I would be wary of attempting an exact quantification, but Lockhart has written that he commanded 7,000 troops.[26] It could be suggested then that the options open to Edward were not limited to an attack against a minor, albeit fortified, center to the south, even if his goal was its conquest and occupation. It is interesting to note that Baybars himself, in a letter that he wrote from Syria to the emirs in Egypt just previous to the Mongol attack in north Syria, writes that it had been learned (probably via his intelligence network) that the Franks were preparing ladders and were expected to strike at Safad.[27] Whether the force at Edward's disposal could have launched and persevered in a siege of that fort remains an open question, although it appears that the Mamluk leadership thought them capable of giving it a try.

This option, however, does not exhaust the strategic possibilities open to Edward. One certainly bold, but potentially decisive, move would have been to strike to the north, and to attempt a truly joint campaign with the Mongols, either as one body or in a two-pronged attack against Baybars and the Mamluk forces at his disposal. Such a plan offered a number of advantages: first, Baybars had only part of the entire Mamluk army under his command in north Syria; second, in principle, Edward could have picked up on his way north the troops of the military orders and Syrian towns, especially Tripoli; third, a move to the north, coordinated with the Mongols, would have brought into play at least the main part of the corps at Mar'ash, and perhaps other Mongol detachments in the area.[28] In any event, Edward's army and the 10,000 Mongol horsemen was certainly a force to be reckoned with, and Baybars would have been hard pressed had he met them on the open battlefield.

There are, however, reasons that would have argued against such a strategy. Foremost, it would have necessitated exact coordination with the Mongols. As it is, we have no evidence that Edward responded to Abagha's request for precise details of his movements. In fact, one wonders whether Edward would even have had time to make an effective diplomatic response: after all, Abagha's letter was written in early September, and less than a month and a half later, the Mongol raiders were in north Syria. In addition, and perhaps no less important, an offensive of this type would have required troops possessing large degrees of willpower, stamina, and fighting ability. If the two chevauchées of Edward are anything to go by, there is little evidence that these traits were held in large abundance by the majority of the troops at Edward's disposal. The prince may well have known this and planned accordingly. Whether Edward himself was up to the task is another, difficult question, which can be left for those better qualified to answer.[29]

What then was Edward's objective in attacking Qaqun? Perhaps he thought it would be an easy win with Baybars preoccupied up north, and thus it would improve morale and increase his standing among the various factions in Outremer. It appears that Edward was realistic enough to understand that he was unable to launch a serious offensive, even in conjuncture with the Mongols. I might speculate that it was possible that he was waiting for them to send a larger force that would do the actual job of destroying the Mamluks, and he then would be in position to pick up the pieces. If so, this is reminiscent of at least some of the opinions expressed by Frankish leaders in Acre before the battle of 'Ayn Jalut.[30] However, the poor performance of his troops against a small Mamluk force at Qaqun, his growing disgust with the political reality of Outremer (including the conclusion of a treaty between the kingdom of Jerusalem and Baybars in May 1272), let alone the assassination attempt inspired by Baybars, combined to convince him not to wait around for the possibility of another, larger Mongol offensive that might lead to the desired results. He departed the Holy Land on September 24, 1272, just two months before another Mongol attack upon Syria, this time a large-scale attack on the border fortress of al-Bira, which probably was intended as a prelude to a massive offensive into Syria proper.[31] Had Edward remained, one could speculate on the effects of some type of Mongol-Frankish coordination on Baybars' ultimately successful efforts to frustrate this siege. The possibilities are intriguing: but, of course, all conclusions remain unprovable.

I must, then, express my lack of agreement with Röhricht, who places the weight of blame for the failure of the joint campaign squarely on Abagha's shoulders when he writes: "In reality that which most irritated [Edward] was that Mongols had completely abandoned him."[32] The textual foundation of this statement is unclear, and, as my discussion here indicates, there appears little basis for such supposition. Edward, who had done little to live up to his side of the nascent bargain, had no right to express irritation. On the other hand, while Abagha may have expressed some remorse in his letter of 1277 for not doing everything he could to bring the project to fruition, at least he did something, and I have attempted to show that his actions could have been of some significance if there had been a proper Frankish response. It is for this reason that I also cannot accept the assertions of Boyle and Prawer, that the attempt at a coordinated Frankish-Mongol operation was doomed from the start.[33] To reiterate: the principal responsibility for this failed campaign must be laid at the doorstep of the Franks, both because of Edward's faulty strategic thinking and because of the inability of the Frankish troops to effect a serious campaign.

It has recently been suggested that "it is perhaps expecting rather a lot of [Abagha] to have been ready to mount a major expedition to Syria the following spring [i.e., after the campaign against Baraq in the summer of 1270]. Although it was technically an opportunity missed, Abaqa's failure to take advantage of Edward's presence shows partly the debilitating effects of fighting on several fronts."[34] The point is certainly well taken, but I would now suggest that even 10,000 horsemen was a respectable force, although from a Mongol point of view it would not have hurt matters to have a few more troops in the vicinity. Since the onus of responsibility for this failed operation is now placed more firmly on the shoulders of the Franks, and Edward in particular, it was not perhaps as important as previously thought (including by myself) that the bulk of the Ilkhanid army did not play a role in the events of 1271 in Syria.

How does all of this relate the theme of the present volume: toleration in the time of the Crusades? In the realm of international relations, at least, it seems that in the early 1270s most participants were, in the long run as well as often in the short term, not interested in finding a *modus vivendi* with their traditional adversaries. It is true that the negotiations between Edward and Abagha were an important step in the rapprochement between the Mongols of Iran and the Latin west. Both sides got to know each other a little better, and gradually the haughty rhetoric and the unrealistic demands were eschewed. As we have seen, however, nothing of substance was to come of these relations—and, for that matter, from later attempts at communications. In other spheres, even this small extent of understanding and acceptance did not bear fruit. The Mongol-Mamluk war continued unabated, although, as one commentator has recently written, it did at times only "simmer."[35] Edward was certainly not a proponent of peaceful coexistence with his newly found Mamluk neighbors, although as we have seen, he was unable to realize his aspirations. Perhaps some of the leadership of Outremer would have been happy to maintain the status quo. This perhaps was the best that they could hope for. Their own participation in Edward's raids, let alone agreement—perhaps only passive—to his attempts to reach an accord with the Mongols, did little to further that goal. While Baybars was soon to conclude a treaty for ten years and ten months with the kingdom of Jerusalem, this was only an expedient move so that he could be in a better position to deal with the Mongols. As I have suggested elsewhere, even at this time the long term goal of the Mamluks was the eradication of the crusading entity,[36] and this was just postponed until a more propitious time. In fact, I would argue that this entire episode, which brought no tangible results to the Franks, was in the long run to contribute to their fall. The Mamluks were aware that the Mongol and Frankish raids were the result of some type of agreement.[37] This knowledge might well have strengthened their long-term resolve to preempt the possibility of Mongol-Frankish cooperation by eliminating the Frankish entity. All in all, little toleration was to result from Edward's visit to the Holy Land.

8

Crusading for the Messiah

JEWS AS INSTRUMENTS OF CHRISTIAN
ANTI-ISLAMIC HOLY WAR

ADAM KNOBLER

In 1221, at the siege of Damietta during the Fifth Crusade, a rumor swept through the crusader camp that an army in the East had soundly defeated a large Muslim host and was advancing on the Holy Land to assist the crusaders in recapturing Jerusalem.[1] Nearly four and half centuries later, during the protectorate of Oliver Cromwell, the *London Gazette* reported that an army in the East had just soundly defeated a large Muslim host, and was advancing on the Holy Land to assist Christendom in recapturing Jerusalem.[2] Both armies were borne of rumor and prophecy, and both were fictitious constructs. The former was supposed to be an army of Prester John—the Christian king of the East whose coming was to bring a new day. Prester John was powerful, wealthy, and on the verge of overthrowing those Muslims who had run roughshod over crusading armies of the West for over 120 years.[3] The second army was supposed to be the army of Jeroboam of Aden, whose Biblical namesake had been granted dominion over ten of the twelve tribes of Israel—and whose return was to bring a new day.[4] He, too, was powerful and on the verge of overthrowing the Ottomans, the same polity with which much of the West had been fighting for over two centuries. The difference was that, unlike the first army, the second army was not comprised of eastern Christians but, rather, of Eastern Jews: members of those lost tribes whose "gathering in" had been predicted in both Jewish and Christian apocalyptic texts.

It would be easy to dismiss both the thirteenth century and the seventeenth century rumors of these Eastern armies as fanciful pieces of crusading marginalia. Yet while Prester John existed no more than did monstrous races, much of Western extra-European diplomatic activity in the late thirteenth, fourteenth, fifteenth and early sixteenth centuries was predicated on a belief in his existence and in the existence of his kingdom.[5] Likewise, the army of the Eastern Jews proved to be far more than a single, casual reference of interest only to the most rabid of Protestant chiliasts. For while some millennialists wrote extensively of the role of the Jews in bringing about the eschaton, stories of Jewish armies threatening Muslim power (directly paralleling the Prester John mythologies) appear in Christian circles, well before the Reformation and its Puritan millennial by-products. And it is these reports that provide the focus of this study.

Most discussions of Judaism and Jews within a crusading context have heretofore focused on the pogroms of the First Crusade, the collection of crusading taxes from European Jewry, or the treatment of Jews in the Latin East or in Reconquista Spain.[6] In each of these cases, the Jews under discussion were treated as a people under siege and under attack: social outcasts, persecuted for their faith and their way of life. The Jews under consideration here, as fictitious as they might have been, are of a very different breed, and their treatment at the hands of Christian writers, clerics, and monarchs is of a markedly different tone. Nowhere do we find them condemned as foul, groveling beings. Nor are they held up for ridicule. Rather, they are portrayed as brave, powerful, and well organized. But why should an army of Jews, members of a race subject to great persecution in Europe, be treated with such respect? Were they any more or less credible as allies than the Mongols or the Ethiopians, about whom so much had been written and in whom so much expectation had been placed? And why were such stories given the level of credibility that would make them a subject for continued reportage in official circles in Cromwell's Britain?

The Christian belief in the existence of Jews dwelling in the Indies originated in the same text that refers first to Christians living in the Indies: the *Acts of Thomas,* where the apostle's first convert was a girl who was "a Hebrew by race."[7] Thus, as the West learned that there might well be Christians dwelling in the East from at least apostolic times, so too did they learn of the Jews. And just as Eastern Christians became embedded in Christian geographical mythology, so too did Eastern Jews—most often identified with the so-called "lost" ten tribes of Israel, whose return was prophesied in Isaiah and Jeremiah.[8] The Christian canon continues the story of the exiled Jews, whose return came to be seen as a necessary feature of the eschaton.[9]

Throughout the Middle Ages the fate of the ten tribes came to have great geopolitical significance for both the Jewish and Christian communities. If they were, in fact, dwelling somewhere in Inner Asia, as the ninth century Jewish traveler Eldad ha-Dani claimed and as the twelfth century letter of Prester John described, then somewhere in the East there was a Jewish polity.[10] This conclusion is significant, because earlier Christian commentators and polemicists had long denied the existence of such an entity, ignoring, for example, the Jewish Khazars of the eighth and ninth century—known to Muslim and Jewish authors but described by Christians as a people without a known faith.[11] As far as Christians were concerned, Eldad's claims were quite fanciful. A distant polity of Jews was a source of both hope and wonder for Western Jews, but also, perhaps, a cause of some concern for the Western Christians. Otto of Freising, the Christian chronicler who first used the name "Prester John" and described his Eastern victories, also wrote of many Jews dwelling near the Caspian Sea who were expected to burst forth in the last days.[12] While not expressly calling them Ezekial's Gog and Magog, as Godfrey of Viterbo did,[13] Otto noted that these Eastern Jews were cause for Christian concern: a concern that manifested itself notably at the time of the initial Mongol invasion of eastern Europe in 1240/1241.[14] Matthew Paris in his *Chronica Majora* speculated that the Tartars were those "of the ten tribes who, having forsaken the Mosaic law, followed after the golden calves, and whom Alexander the Macedonian endeavored at first to shut up in the rugged mountains of the Caucasus . . . There arises, however, a doubt whether the Tartars now coming from there really be they, for they do not use the Hebrew tongue, neither do they know the laws of Moses."[15]

This is a rather telling passage. The new force might possibly be Jews or, at least, Judaic. Yet they did not speak Hebrew, nor did they follow *halakha*, Jewish law. In other words, they did not conform to Matthew Paris's notions of what a Jew is supposed to be, which, at a time when Jews were subject to increasingly harsh treatment in England, was not surprising.[16] Furthermore, they were clearly fierce and powerful, traits not generally attributed to Jews by medieval Christian commentators. The passage might have simply been pure polemic on Matthew's part, aimed at instilling fear in his English Christian readership, but the fact that he distances himself from any claims to certainty casts some doubt on such an interpretation.

Matthew's rather distressing account of the ferocity of the Mongols (Jews or not) became a rather passé view in the Latin West by the early 1250s, when diplomacy with Mongol Eurasia began in earnest.[17] Gradually, by the 1280s the Mongols came to be seen as potentially valuable allies.[18]

The Mongol polity came and went, but Western interest in forming some type of profitable crusading relationship with a powerful Eastern polity continued throughout the fourteenth and fifteenth centuries. At the end of the fifteenth century, it was the Portuguese who most vociferously maintained both the search for such potential allies, along with a crusading desire to recapture Jerusalem.[19] Their voyages down the western coast of Africa, deemed crusades by the papacy, were couched in crusading language by royal chroniclers who also denoted the desire of the Portuguese crown to make contact with potential allies, believed to live somewhere in Africa or beyond.[20] Yet, when Vasco da Gama reached India, the Christian community he found there was hardly that of Prester John. Small and without a state of its own, the Thomas Christians were able to advance Portuguese regional goals only on the most limited scale.[21]

But Ethiopia still retained a certain allure—and its Christian king, now granted the title Prester John by Western observers and courts, was still sought after as a potentially important ally.[22] King Manuel I of Portugal, who had his own messianic pretensions as a crusader at the beginning of the sixteenth century, looked at Ethiopia's strategic position at the mouth of the Red Sea as critical in his own, personal designs to recapture the Holy Land.[23] Yet, it gradually became clear that Ethiopia was not especially strong militarily, nor was its Christianity of a brand that was thoroughly palatable to a Roman Church embroiled in its own reassertion of Orthodoxy.[24] In essence, the power of Prester John—the great king of the East—had been greatly reduced as his geographical locus came to be understood and mastered by the West. Familiarity bred contempt.[25] However, the rise of the Ottomans and their conquest of Palestine, Egypt, and North Africa made contact with an ally who had ready access to Muslim lands desirable. And into this void, created by decreasing Portuguese interest in Prester John and his rather weak and unorthodox empire, came David ha-Reuveni.

Claiming to represent a Jewish nation in the East whose troops were massing for an assault on Islam, David ha-Reuveni appeared in the West in 1523 and for the next seven years traveled throughout Europe seeking papal and royal backing for a joint Jewish-Christian military campaign against the Turks.[26] His broad scheme was to convince Pope Clement VII to broker a peace between France and the Empire, which then, in conjunction with the Ethiopians and the Jewish army, would conquer the Holy Land. Scholars have debated the origins and sincerity of Reuveni for many years.[27] Reuveni's actual origin was in many ways no more important than was the origin of the very first "Prester John," who appeared at the papal court in 1122. What is striking is that he was given such serious attention in Christian circles. Reuveni's proposal, with its claims of a massing Jewish army, ran counter to the commonly held belief that no Jews were living under their own dominion. The pope, while admitting that a peace between France and the Empire was unlikely, *did* recommend Reuveni to João III of Portugal. Reuveni spent nearly two years in Portugal. When it was felt that he was attempting to reconvert *conversos* to Judaism, he was expelled, but only after he had been treated with great ceremony as a legitimate Eastern ambassador.

Eventually, Reuveni's claims and, more importantly, his preaching aroused imperial ire, and he was imprisoned, dying in Spain in 1538. But his exploits had lasting consequences. Here was a Jew whose actions and claims to power both intrigued and dismayed the Latin West. His claims about a Jewish army and polity were taken quite seriously, and it was only the fact that he seemed to wish to bring converted Jews back into the fold and empower them that drove him into the hands of the Inquisition. The prophetic strain in his words and in the idea of a Jewish army at the gates of Mecca or Jerusalem was not lost on either his Jewish audiences or the Christians who heard of his claims, or who read of his exploits, through Latin and vernacular accounts. It should not, thus, be surprising that millennialists and millennialism, heightened in both communities in the seventeenth century, should have looked to Reuveni's claims of a Jewish army awaiting the word to strike at the heart of Islam as an important point of reference for their own beliefs.

The mid-seventeenth century was a time of greatly heightened eschatological expectations. Preachers of many radical Protestant stripes in Holland and England, but also Catholic millennialists in France and Portugal, published extensive exegeses on the ten tribes, their imminent return, and, in most cases, their imminent conversion.[28] Jews were, for most millennial thinkers, crucial participants in the eschaton, as 4 Esdras (2 Esdras), Revelation, and, of course, the biblical prophets had foretold. While some saw the Jews being converted and led to the Holy Land by a temporal Christian monarch, other millennialists described how the tribes would return of their own volition and overthrow the Turks, converting once Jerusalem was taken. Correspondence, attributed in 1665 to the English Puritan Nathaniel Homes and the Dutch preacher Peter Serrarius, notes the arrival of news that Mecca itself was under siege "by Israelites, who appear in great numbers, and are said to be sent by the Ten Tribes."[29] Likewise, an anonymous letter "from Aberdeen," also published in 1665, noted the arrival (or so it was claimed) of a ship filled with Hebrew-speaking sailors, who carried news that there were 160,000 Jews gathered in Arabia who had slaughtered Turks in great numbers.[30] Reports from Italy went so far as to say that all caravan traffic to Mecca had halted because of the fighting.[31]

These texts could be dismissed as purely fanciful and without any broader significance to Western attitudes. Yet similar stories find their way into official or semiofficial documents, and of these we must take some notice. In September 1665, for example, the Royalist Sir George Rawdon wrote from Lisburne in Ireland to his patron, Viscount Conway, noting that "We hear many strange stories of the Jews marching to Jerusalem, and are in great expectation of good news from the fleet."[32] Rawdon, a supporter of Charles II, was no millennialist. Likewise, we find that almanacs written in late 1665 for use in 1666 speak of similar rumors.[33] It is, in fact, in late 1665 that Jewish communities in the West first begin to hear tell of the rise of the pseudo-messiah Sabbatai Sevi.[34] Philo-Semites among the Christian millennialists, such as Serrarius, clearly became aware of Sabbateanism and took up Sabbatai's cause with great fervor.[35] But the Sabbatean movement was a pacifist endeavor. It was Christian rather than Jewish sources that most clearly spoke of Jewish armies, and it was such detailed reports on this theme that made their way into the *London Gazette* in early 1666.[36] The official *Gazette* reported in late January 1666 the formation of a military alliance between Jews and Arabs in Arabia under the leadership of one Jeroboam of Aden.[37] Jeroboam was a name that would have invoked a specific biblical memory of one who had been chosen to lead the ten tribes—but who had himself gone astray. The story, as followed by the *Gazette* through February and March, related how this joint Semitic army conquered Mecca and Medina, and was marching toward the Holy Land, having destroyed Muhammed's tomb.[38] By the end of March, the story was finally declared a falsehood, and soon afterward Sabbatai Sevi himself converted to Islam at the Ottoman court.[39] The very fact that such a story existed is noteworthy, particularly its image of a powerful Jewish army being able to accomplish militarily what Christians had not—the destruction of Islam's holiest of cities. These "Jews" clearly fit the pattern of earlier potential allies such as the Mongols and Ethiopians. This strong army of united Jewish tribes, whose coming was prophesied, was from a land (here identified as the Hejaz) unseen by all but a few Western eyes. English Puritan chiliasts linked the Jews to a spiritual purity denied the rest of the corrupt world. Feeling besieged after Cromwell's rise to power, many of the radicals hoped the Jewish army would supply the means necessary for the armies of the apocalypse to defeat the Antichrist and his minions. These ideas, as we know, came quickly to be marginalized, both in English and Continental thought, and less millennially inclined Protestantism came to the fore. No longer did states actively seek out allies for war from among the unexplored reaches of the globe.

As this global conception of Christendom fell out of favor during the Enlightenment, it was replaced with the more humanistic notion of "civilization." If allies or models for Christian behavior were no longer to become the subject for any serious search, there were still those who felt that there might be hidden "civilized" races or polities, whose standards of living, codes of behavior, and general cultural sophistication would not only be of service to the larger civilizing mission but would also serve as a cautionary reminder to the West not to abandon Enlightenment ideals.

Why should this be so? Why Jews? And why such power? Several answers, taken together, might shed some light on this phenomenon. The first concerns what could be called the "power" of geographical distance. Part of what endowed these Jews with their power was the very fact that they lived afar. As the anthropologist Mary Helms has demonstrated, most cultures imbue a special aura or magic or romance to peoples and travelers from unknown lands.[40] By the middle of the sixteenth century, and certainly by the middle of the seventeenth, Western geographical knowledge about the earth and its peoples was ever increasing. New peoples and new lands were being discovered by the West, and old frameworks for understanding the earth were being reevaluated. The Bible, after all, did not mention the American Indians or the continents upon which they lived. Yet, with millennial expectation rising, biblical prophecies could not simply be ignored. The ten tribes were a necessary ingredient for the eschaton. If they were not found among the newly discovered places or peoples (and, indeed, some thought the American Indians to be from the tribes), they were still needed.[41] Thus, to create Jews in the very heart of Dar al-Islam was to place them where Christian eyes and Christian explorers had not yet gone. Once located there, they must be granted a power that would accord with Western concepts of "large tribes": theirs would be a unified military power at a time when military might and national unity was coming to determine political supremacy in Europe. Add to the fact that, like the Mongols and Ethiopians before them, these Jews were seen as convertible, Christian prophecy would thus be fulfilled. It was only when David Reuveni began to reconvert converted Jews, or when Sabbatai Sevi himself converted to Islam, thus acting contrary to prophecy, that Christian support and interest waned. Only in a world where the forces of evil would be overcome by mysterious, unexplainable (but, in the end, convertible) powers of good would the failings of the medieval crusaders be finally and permanently erased in both the Heavenly and the Earthly Jerusalem.

PART THREE

Orthodoxy and Western Christianity
in the Crusader East

9

Images of Tolerance and Intolerance in Cypriot Historical Writings Between the Thirteenth and Sixteenth Centuries

ANNETTA ILIEVA

When I took to writing this paper, my first thoughts, as a historian of Frankish Greece and Cyprus, did not differ much from a well-known dictum: the opposition between the relative tolerance of second- and third-generation Crusaders and the intolerance of newcomers from the West is a theme common to all the Latin states in Outremer (the East).[1] But being plagued by the *imagologie* fashion, I moved away from reality with ease; it seemed much more interesting to look at how the approaches of tolerance and intolerance were *viewed* in an Outremer society where confrontation had long been the order of the day.

Thus, plunging into the realm of mentalities, we have immediately to admit that approval or denial of tolerance goes hand in hand with verbalized expressions of identity. Exclusive identities, both individual and collective, are less likely to tolerate the otherness; a group with an exclusive identity and a supreme position in society can become the exponent of violence and enforce its identity upon the less well placed individuals or even groups. An external frontier can be another frequent catalyst of behavioral extremities. In the age of the Crusades, exclusiveness and frontierness blended in a unique amalgam: Western patterns of behavior were tested and implanted in the ethnically, linguistically, and religiously alien environment of the *partes ultramarinae*. It was not only the Saracens. Despite a somewhat more favorable view towards Jacobites and Armenians, the native Christians of Outremer were regarded as second-class citizens.[2] The paradigm of language—Latin and eventually Old French—and Christian religion were most insistently put to work as agents of denigrating differentiation with regard to the Greeks.

Generally speaking, an intolerant approach was backed by the exclusive Frankish identity and grounded in the psychology of Christianity: pride, covetousness, anger, and envy were deadly sins demanding strong action even against one's own kind.

Viewed from this perspective, Frankish Cyprus certainly invites investigation. The island is a holy place related to the cornerstones of Christianity. Besides, "the dominant fact which has affected Cypriot history from antiquity to the present day [is] its frontier status."[3] With its conquest by a crusading Western king in 1191 and the subsequent colonization from Latin Syria, Cyprus was incorporated within the larger frontier of the Crusading States in *Outremer*. When in 1291 all positions in the Holy Land had been lost, the island became the outpost of Christianity against the miscreant Saracens. The disaster of 1426 tipped the balance in this single stand to the "sultan [of Cairo]."[4] By the end of the century, Venice was the full master of the island but not for long: some two months before their crushing defeat at Lepanto (October 7, 1571), the Ottomans were in total control of Cyprus.

The inner development of Cypriot society under the Lusignans followed those transformations. To quote Jean Richard, the thirteenth century seems above all a time of "juxtaposition of cultures and inhabitants who live a parallel life."[5] By the mid-fourteenth century the ruling Frankish elite was still extremely corporate, but the following one hundred years witnessed its decline and assimilation.[6] The "old order dominated by a French crusader nobility and a Catholic hierarchy gave way to a cosmopolitan Mediterranean society" represented by James II (1464–73), the last effective Lusignan king.[7] The *Venetokratia* in turn incorporated Cyprus in the colonial empire of the *Serenissima*.

Since all authors to be discussed below were in one way or another in the service of the governing regime, the evolution of Cypriot historical writing under the Latins underwent the same general changes. It was fathered as Old French prose writing by Ernoul (after 1197?), then acquired a Greek discourse with Leontios Machairas and George Boustronios (the middle and second half of the fifteenth century), and finally, in the sixteenth century, produced either plain translations from a Greek original, as in Diomede Strambaldi's chronicle, or works deriving material from Greek sources, as in the *Historia* by Florio Bustron (1580). For the time being, I shall leave aside the latter's works as having been written under unique, post-Latin circumstances. At the same time, the authors of the first period ending in 1320–25 will now be treated only briefly, since I have dealt with them from the same perspective and in detail elsewhere.[8]

Some twenty years ago Margaret Ruth Morgan was the first to suggest Ernoul's Cypriot connection, identifying him with Arneis of Jubail. She saw

Ernoul as a layman—a *Poulain* (trainee) squire of Balian II Ibelin, who had been firmly established in Cyprus in the late 1220s and early 1230s. In his now lost Holy Land chronicle (covering the period ca. 1100–97?), he focused on the Hattin disaster and its background. Ernoul himself was not a continuator of William of Tyre, but all other compilers of the "Eracles" tradition drew on his chronicle, mostly indirectly.[9] Shortly before ca. 1280, a Cypriot text *(d_o)* of the second quarter of the same century and quite close to Ernoul's chronicle was used, together with an "Eracles" covering the period for the year 1275, by another Cypriot *poulain* (a Frank born in the East) to produce the most important account of the years 1184–97.[10] The result was a redaction *(d)* now surviving in a single manuscript: MS 828 of the City Library of Lyon reaching to the year 1284. Around 1290 *(d_o)* served as a model to the last, abridged *Outremer* compilation, which stopped at the end of 1277 and is now preserved only in MS Plu. LXI .10 of the Bibl. Med. Laurentiana in Florence *(Fl)*.

The Lyon and Florence "Eracles" make a clear distinction between *Frans* and *Franceis* and are quite sure when exactly to use them. On the other hand, both texts not only abound in Griffons but even consider them worse than the *felons Sarrazins*. It is in the narrative on the Latin conquest of Cyprus that the somewhat earlier *(d)* demonstrates a strong religious element by opposing "les Griffons de Chypre" to the Latin Christians of Roman law. Thus, from the local perspective it was not the French in Cyprus but the Latin Christian Franks, already viewed as a Cypriot race of their own, the "gens de Chypre," who stood against the Griffons/Greeks.

Obviously, Frankish historical writing in Cyprus emerged as initially embedded in the patterns of *Outremer Poulain* tradition established by William of Tyre. What Ernoul introduced was a strengthened dislike of European crusaders, Ibelin intolerance—openly persistent until at least the middle of the thirteenth century, and a strongly expressed Griffon stigma, possibly Cypriot born. Redaction *(d)* preserved Ernoul's preoccupations, but by 1275 the Ibelin connection was more a reflection of the earlier model than a contemporary imperative.

Philip of Novara, who around the middle of the thirteenth century first took to writing nearly contemporary Cypriot history, was to establish a strong, at times denigrating ("griffonized") sentiment against Frederick II that was still topical in the 1320s. His Ibelin partisanship nourished the "gens de Chypre" theme, in which the Griffon convention of the conquest did not matter any more.

About 1320–25, in the so-called "Gestes des Chiprois," the *Poulain* Templar of Tyre preserved the "Eracles" outlook on the earlier crusades, but the Third Crusade (i.e., the conquest) was no longer that important to him; it was the post-1291 settlement that troubled his mind. In historically appropriating Cyprus ("le plus aize païs") as Frankish, he challenged Greek Cypriot awareness with a new, peace-mongering attitude. It was Leontios Machairas who coined the answer in the first chronicle of the Lusignan dynasty in Cyprus.

A number of qualifications are mandatory before any discussion of Machairas's chronicle is launched. First, the textual and chronological relationship among the three manuscripts containing its versions is yet to be determined; what is beyond doubt is that the "personal and group identity" of the compiler of the Venice text (or *V)* bearing Machairas's name "was that of a Greek Orthodox." [11] Second, it is not at all clear how precisely the *Exegesis* relates to the so-called "Chronique d'Amadi" in Italian, having been in the possession of Francesco Amadi (d. 1566, in Venice) and itself a basic source of Bustron's *Historia* for the fourteenth century. It seems, however, that the "Chronique," ending in 1441 but preserving fresh the historical tradition of the first stage, drew on the same sources, French and Greek, as Machairas himself.

Finally, by the time when Machairas took to writing his work, another group with exclusive identity had had its decisive say in the history of Cyprus: the Genoese. A negative differentiation between French and Italians appears as early as Ernoul's epigones: "the French . . . knights—the Italians . . . usurers or pirates or merchants or sailors." [12] The Genoese, however, had served the first Lusignans well and acquired their privileged status in Cyprus as Ibelin supporters in 1232.[13] Venice would have to wait until 1306, although the first administrative representatives of both republics would appear on the island almost simultaneously (the Genoese *podesta* in 1292 and the Venetian *bailo* in 1301).[14] Elsewhere I have suggested that the extreme intolerance of Machairas toward the Genoese in his narrative of the 1360s and the war of 1373–74 could be explained by his immediate proximity to sources presenting the history of Cyprus from the survivors' point of view: first John, prince of Antioch (d. 1375), then his brother James, constable of Jerusalem, and finally the same James but as king of Cyprus and Jerusalem (1382–98), installed with Genoese intervention. While on more than one occasion 'Amadi' and Bustron abbreviate substantial portions of this narrative, with obvious pro-Constable propaganda in Machairas, the enemy claim that the Constable is the only noble man among the defenders; more, the Genoese and "the nobly nurtured men of Cyprus" are two mutually incompatible species.[15] Machairas is also much more eloquent on the psychology of the violence on both sides: with the Genoese it was their anger and their frustration at the short memory of Genoese services to the kingdom.[16] It is worth noting here that the anti-Genoese crescendo is the loudest in the anonymous Oxford version of Machairas's text *(O)*. It gives the floor to the enemy even at the very moment of overmastering the twelve Cypriots left in the castle of Famagusta: "Leave the gates open. Tell us: will you treat us as Christians, or will you be treating us as enemies of God, treating us like dogs, that you do not follow our bidding?" (f. 168v). This speech is, in fact, telling us what should have been—and perhaps was—the real Cypriot view of the Genoese nation. The dramatic tension is intensified when *(O)* bluntly reports that it was the Genoese who in the event maltreated the three royalties (Peter II, his mother, and his uncle, prince of Antioch) locked in all day and night without food, drink, bed, and servants. The motif is repeated in a proverbial phrase on the morrow when the queen mother voices her protest before the Genoese admiral: "Such a thing has never been done either among the Turks or the Saracens; and to put us to sleep like dogs!" [17] But to sum it up, while the opposition of "Constable/Cypriot/God" to "Genoese" is the peculiar feature of *(V)* and especially *(O)*, what is common to Machairas, "Amadi" and Bustron is a fully developed juxtaposition between the non-traitorous Cypriots in general and the traitorous Genoese. [18] Some decades after Machairas, now that the Genoese had been expelled from Famagusta, George Boustronios would go even further: identifying Queen Catherine Cornaro "with the interests of the Cypriots against the foreign party of Catalans and Sicilians with their pro-Neapolitan policy," he would label the latter "Franks" and "traitors." [19]

The time allotted will not allow me now to treat the much discussed tolerance (or, according to others, fanaticism) of Machairas with regard to the Latins in Cyprus and its metamorphoses in "Amadi" and Bustron. Instead, I will conclude by focusing my attention on the group's treatment of the "world of the infidel." Ignorant or not of the catastrophe at Hattin, Machairas is alone in presenting Hugh-Guy of Lusignan as requesting the support of Saladin, "the sultan of Cairo," against a possible threat of another Greek revolt. Since "it is the will of God that peoples should love their neighbors," he declares that Cyprus and the Saracens are neighbors "by the grace of God." [20] The attitude of the sultan is also most telling: "And know neither of you nor those who shall be born of you will suffer any vexation from me; or who shall come after me, *unless it is caused by you.*" Furthermore, the sultan claims readiness for "a firm alliance" if only the king would convert to Islam. To this, of course, Hugh-Guy answers with a wholehearted "no": "I would rather be enslaved to the emperor [of Byzantium?], than deny my faith in my God." And yet he sends "word to the sultan, asking advice from him how he should rule his people [*sic*]". The piece of advice is rather courteous: "Better for you to give abundant gifts and bring to yourself great men, than to give little and lose the rest. And send envoys of prudence and worth."[21]

I believe that this first Saracen "message" of tolerance to the new regime in Cyprus is not accidental in the opening section of the chronicle. Later, Machairas or his source(s) are at great pains to present the long and painful negotiations with Egypt after the sack of Alexandria (October 10, 1365) as having ended with a moral victory for Peter I: he took the initiative, and the final judgment over "that dog," "the thrice-accursed sultan," belonged to him by God's will.[22] Then, within the narrative of Peter II's reign, the mood evolves into its antipode. The sultan's envoys greet fittingly neither the king nor the regent prince of Antioch. With "great haughtiness" they dare to say that "the most high lord the great sultan . . . has pardoned you for your error: *because your father King Peter was the cause of this war, for he beguiled our master and invaded his lands and carried away many captives at Alexandria and in many other places.*"[23]

The metamorphosis is complete within the narrative of Cypriot-Saracen hostilities that started in the early fifteen century and led to the tragedy of July 7, 1426. Moreover, it is for the first time that the text assumes a first-person-plural position and we hear of Cypriots against Saracens; both "novelties" persist further. And Machairas is quick to denounce Cypriot plundering raids upon Syria—"coined" in his view, after the piracy in the region—as "shameless."[24] This would not blind his view to exploits in the name of the "sweet Lord Jesus." In 1425 two Christian prisoners of war, Rekouniatos and Andronikos of Gorhigos, suffered death as martyrs. "And they chose to die in the faith of Christ rather than to live in lies and to turn Moslem; and they reviled the sultan and those who tormented them."[25] This piece of news was unbearable even to a Saracen holyman in Damascus.

The next paragraphs (nos. 661–67) are among those I call "a program" for the whole work. They are charged with the most important messages and come as a dramatic counterbalance to nos. 22–25. Since justice is on the side of the sultan, the king's intention to face him is wicked; besides, the sultan is said to have made a fatal decision: "I sent word to him twice by my ships to send to me to confirm the peace, and he makes no sign; he must be, I think, either very brave or very mad. So I give him my promise that by God's will I will use all my power to see if I can come forward and be done with him; and I will burn up the stinking island of Cyprus, rather than be troubled by them for ever." Yet to Machairas or his source the effect must have seemed inadequate.[26] A long and passionate letter to the king, sent by the same Saracen with his only son, is "quoted" next to hold the audience spell bound. Because of the boy's efforts (he is twice called upon to speak), the sheikh's letter is also read before the council. The answer Janus sends back with the sheikh's son is totally absent in our text, for evidently it is as defiant as the counsel of his "vain men." Thus, the megamessage we should grasp is that King Janus had no responsibility for the catastrophe that followed.

But should we? Back, far back in the opening pages of this long chronicle (if indeed one is to consider it a work by a single compiler), there appeared a king who sought and seemed to have listened to the sultan's counsel. His kingdom survived. Now it was not to be. The sheikh's final reaction is unequivocal: "it must . . . be the will of God that [the king] shall abide under the lordship of my lord the sultan, because of their pride." [27] The sin of sins into which both Saracens and Genoese as enemies have constantly fallen—pride, is now committed by the king and his counselors! Nonetheless Machairas tries his best to prevent the Cypriots in general from losing face. If not the people, then what they have created should make the Saracens feel fear: "they were afraid to go into Lefkosia, seeing that the town was so great." [28] Nicosia escaped burning, but the Saracens "carried off the Christians and the plunder, and went away, and a curse be upon them." [29] Thus the "anathema" phrase frames a section of the narrative that has been most compassionate and most instructive at the same time. I would say it cuts off the logical end of the entire *Exegesis*.

The mosaic of images just reviewed reveals the predicaments of a bicultural society on an island "built upon rock in the midst of the sea and surrounded by the infidels, Turks and Saracens." [30] While inner boundaries were gradually disappearing by the end of the fifteenth century, the establishment of the *Venetokratia* and the growing Ottoman threat turned the clock back. Cyprus under the *Serenissima* was ready to compromise against the Ottoman Empire, but we should not forget that Florio Bustron did not choose to expand his narrative much beyond 1489.

10

The Frankish Encounter with the Greek Orthodox in the Crusader States

THE CASE OF GERARD OF NAZARETH
AND MARY MAGDALENE

ANDREW JOTISCHKY

The growing mutual hostility of the Latin and Greek Orthodox Churches during the course of the twelfth century has for long been a fruitful source of scholarly endeavor. Organically evolving differences in custom—use of leavened or unleavened bread in the Eucharist, the correct day for fasting, etc.—and in the interpretation of theological doctrine—the *filioque* issue, for example—became frozen into fixed cultural reference points. Whether the context was ecclesiastical, diplomatic, or military, contact between Franks and Byzantines steadily gave rise to friction and intolerance.[1] Thus theological or ecclesiological issues can be seen to have been exacerbated by contemporaneous confrontations in other spheres of activity, for example, the relations between Alexius I Komnenos and the crusaders. The problem is partly that the exact relationship between ecclesiastical and secular politics is intangible; partly, also, that the nature of the ecclesiastical politics is itself so elastic. As Jean Darrouzès has remarked, schism between Latin and Greek Churches in the Middle Ages was not a single act, but endemic.[2] Yet the "schism" of 1054 was technically not a formal rupture, but simply a striking instance of animosity between individual representatives of their Churches. One might, indeed, argue that all instances of hostility in which the theological and ecclesiological arguments are rehearsed[3] are separate "moments" that should not stand for a continuum of relations in a similar vein throughout the twelfth century.

An earlier version of this paper was published in *Levant,* 29 (1997): 217–226; published with permission.

100

It is tempting to revolve all points of friction around a geographical axis based on relations between Rome and Constantinople, and determined by, for example, the *filioque* issue or the Roman primacy. Yet we cannot assume that "official" policy handed down from pope or patriarch of Constantinople, and devised in the context of high politics, necessarily reflected the concerns of Latins and Orthodox in their dealings with one another at a local level. In fact, relations in one geographical sphere of intensive contact between the Churches—the crusader states in the twelfth century—embraced a variety of issues of a more pragmatic nature than is suggested by study of the surviving documents of theological controversy. Discord, where it can be seen, sometimes took expression in oblique and unexpected ways; at the same time, where mutual hostility might be expected, we find examples of cooperation and tolerance.[4]

The evidence for polemical dispute between the Frankish ecclesiastical authorities and the local Christian peoples in the kingdom of Jerusalem is meager, perhaps surprisingly so.[5] It is true that Jacques de Vitry, on taking up his appointment as bishop of Acre in 1216, was outraged to find the Greek Orthodox communities in his diocese practicing customs such as the use of leavened bread in the Eucharist, and the Jacobites even practicing circumcision; but Jacques's intolerance is important evidence partly because it is so rare.[6] What strikes one about Jacques's grievances is their indiscriminate nature. They cover matters of local custom, such as the tendency of Eastern clergy to wear beards, or the absence of clerical celibacy, that had nothing to do with pure doctrine, in addition to the well-known theological and doctrinal aberrations over the *filioque,* or the persons of the Trinity. Jacques de Vitry was not alone in such apparently loose thinking about the beliefs of other traditions.[7] Byzantine canonists of the eleventh and twelfth centuries regularly produced *opuscula* listing the errors of Latin doctrines and traditions. Some of these derived from the ninth-century patriarch Photius's letter to the Eastern patriarchs on the five major errors of the Latins.[8] Another genre seems to derive from the letter of the eleventh-century patriarch of Constantinople, Michael Kerularios, to Peter, patriarch of Antioch, in which Michael, incoherent with rage, lists grievances against Latin beliefs in a manner that even his correspondent found disorderly and unhelpful. As Peter complained, Michael had mixed up serious and minor points of difference, with the result that the grave doctrinal errors are not given sufficient emphasis because they are obscured by unimportant differences of local custom.[9] Michael's letter, and indeed that of Photius, continued to be read and copied in Greek Orthodox monasteries in twelfth- and thirteenth-century Palestine, along with works such as the treatise of Michael's contemporary Leo of Ochrida against the Latins, copied in the twelfth century by the Orthodox community at the Holy Sepulchre, and the catalogue of the Greek Orthodox Church written by Nilus Doxopatris for Roger II of Sicily, which was copied at St Sabas in the thirteenth century.[10] The genre inspired by the letter of Michael Kerularios enjoyed wide currency throughout the crusader period and, as one might expect, expanded still further after the establishment of Frankish rule in Constantinople.[11] The characteristic feature of such works is the unhierarchical nature in which doctrinal errors, misinterpretations of Scripture and aberrant cultural practices are grouped together. One might easily conclude that the difference between variations of custom, which derived from localized cultural norms, and larger points of doctrine or theological interpretation was simply not understood by Latin or Byzantine clergy. Intolerance took root in such easily observed examples of "otherness" as whether one made the sign of the cross with one finger instead of three, or whether one's priests married or wore beards, rather than in what people believed about the procession of the Holy Spirit, the nature of the Trinity, or the interpretation of Scripture.

An exception to this general rule may serve to make the point. One of the ambassadors sent by Manuel Komnenos to the Armenians in 1171 to negotiate a possible reunion with the Orthodox Church was the theologian Theorianus.[12] Around the same time Theorianus also wrote a letter in response to queries raised by a group of Orthodox priests serving the church of St. John the Baptist at 'Ain Karim, near Jerusalem. This church was by 1166, and perhaps from earlier in the twelfth century, in the hands of the Latin canons of the *Templum Domini* in Jerusalem,[13] but the Orthodox clergy evidently remained to serve the needs of their parishioners. The letter takes the form of an arbitration in a debate over how the Orthodox were to regard the ecclesiastical customs of their Latin superiors.[14] The issues raised are familiar from Orthodox/Latin polemic. The priests were not concerned with theological issues such as the procession of the Holy Spirit, or with ecclesiology, but with matters such as whether the Eucharist should be celebrated with leavened or unleavened bread, on which days one should fast, and whether priests ought to wear beards. The really troublesome affairs for parish clergy were the visible differences of practice that emphasized the alien nature of Latin Catholicism to the local Orthodox population.[15] Theorianus's treatment of these problems is remarkable for its tolerance and breadth of vision. These matters, he assures the priests, should never be allowed to stand between coreligionists: they are not differences of belief, but of habit. The Orthodox, he insists, ought to love the Latins as brothers.

The realization by some thoughtful observers that there was a distinction to be made between belief and local practice makes it legitimate to wonder just what the relationship between the two was in the context of

Latin/Orthodox relations. Were polemicists who blurred the distinction between belief and practice simply reflecting the loose way in which people normally thought; or were they, by scrutinizing local customs and traditions, deliberately stoking the flames of intolerance? Could the high-minded views of a theologian like Theorianus be helpful to Orthodox communities confronted with having to share churches with Latins?

The career of a little-known Latin bishop of Syria, Gerard of Nazareth, bishop of Latakia in the mid-twelfth century, allows us to explore further this relationship between belief and practice, and sheds new light on the Orthodox/Latin confrontation.

The importance of Gerard of Nazareth was first realized by Benjamin Kedar, who in 1983 published the extant fragments of his work on hermits and monks in the Latin East.[16] Gerard was a Benedictine monk, perhaps in the monastery of Mt. Tabor, and by 1140 had been made bishop of Latakia, in the patriarchate of Antioch. In 1159 he was present at Antioch when Emperor Manuel Komnenos received the submission of Prince Reynald; according to the French translator of William of Tyre, Gerard played a major role in bringing about the reconciliation between emperor and recalcitrant prince. In 1161, Gerard appears as witness to a deed of Baldwin III in Nazareth; this is his final appearance in the sources, and he can be assumed to have died in that year or soon afterwards.[17]

Besides his work on the hermits, Gerard also wrote a treatise called *De una Magdalena contra Graecos,* in which he presented the standard Latin patristic arguments for identifying Mary Magdalene with other Marys mentioned in the Gospels, and particularly with Mary, the sister of Martha, and went on to attack the Greek tradition of identifying the Marys as separate. The surviving portions of this work show little originality or depth of thought.[18] Gerard was familiar with Augustine, Jerome, Ambrose, Gregory the Great, and Bede on the subject: conventional scholarship, if impressive for a bishop in the crusader East. Rather more revealing than what Gerard has to say about Mary Magdalene is the very occurrence of this subject as a topic for polemical writing. Why was the exegetical study of Mary Magdalene such a fraught issue between Latins and Greeks in Outremer, and how did Gerard come to be involved in it in the first place?

A rehearsal of the differing traditions of Mary Magdalene may be helpful. In the Latin patristic tradition from Gregory the Great onward, the woman from Magdala from whom Jesus had cast out demons (Luke 8:2–3) was identified not only with Mary, the disciple of Jesus, who was a witness to his crucifixion and visited the empty tomb in the garden (Matt 27:56, 28:1, Mark 15:40, John 19:25, 20:1), but also with the anonymous woman caught in adultery and brought by the Pharisees before Jesus (John 8:3–12).[19] Bede then made a further connection between otherwise separate figures in the Gospels by identifying Mary Magdalene, now known as the adulteress forgiven by Jesus and healed by him of demonic possession, with Mary, the sister of Martha and Lazarus, with whom Jesus stayed in Bethany on the occasion when he raised Lazarus from the dead, and who then poured a jar of precious ointment over Jesus' feet and wiped them dry with her hair.(Matt 26:6, Mark 14:3, Luke 10:39, John 12:3)[20] The difficulty faced by medieval commentators was that although elements of the Mary and Martha story are told by all the evangelists, they have to be reconstructed with heavy editing to form a coherent narrative. Matthew and Mark tell the story of an unnamed woman anointing Jesus' head with ointment in the house of Simon the Leper in Bethany. Luke's version specifies that the woman was a sinner, and that the incident took place in a Pharisee's house, but he does not say where the house was (Luke 7:37). Luke then tells, as a separate story, the incident of Martha waiting on Jesus when he visited their house in Bethany, while her sister Mary sat listening to his teaching (Luke 10:39). In Luke's second episode, where Mary and Martha are specified, no anointing takes place. In the Gospel of John, Mary and Martha are the sisters of Lazarus, and Mary anoints Jesus' feet with ointment, after he had raised Lazarus from the dead (John 12:3). The "leap of faith" lies in the identification of the sinful woman who anointed Jesus' head with ointment in Luke with the woman caught in adultery and also with Mary of Bethany, the sister of Martha. The link between these figures may have been supplied by the common theme of anointing, by conflating John's version of the Bethany incident with the synoptic Gospels' account of the sinful woman with her alabaster jar of ointment. Because both Matthew and Mark place this latter episode in the house of Simon the Leper in Bethany, such a connection was easy to make.

It has been said with some justification that a list of writers who followed this tradition would effectively be a bibliography of all Western biblical exegetes.[21] The Greek tradition, in contrast, was more precise in its separation of Mary of Bethany, the sister of Lazarus, from Mary Magdalene, the woman from whom Jesus cast out demons and who was a witness to the Crucifixion, and from the unnamed sinner who anointed Jesus with oil. This tradition prevailed among all the Eastern Churches, which therefore recognized three separate Marys rather than the single one recognized in the West.[22]

By the twelfth century the story of Mary Magdalene in the West had become baroque in its elaboration. It was thought that she had been married to John the Evangelist at Cana, but had fallen into a life of sin when he left her alone to become a disciple of Jesus, and was thus caught in adultery and converted to a life of penitence by Jesus. After the Ascension her path becomes harder to follow. The traditional Greek version of Mary (known by Gregory of Tours and, we can assume, current in the West in the sixth century) has her going to Ephesus with John and the Blessed Virgin, and locates her tomb there, but by the mid-eleventh century the standard Western account told of her journey with Martha and Lazarus to Provence, where she became a hermit.[23] By 1037 the abbey of Vézelay, newly adopted into the Cluniac order, was claiming the Magdalene's relics, and this claim was established by a papal bull in 1058 and subsequently by successive twelfth-century popes.[24] Although during the thirteenth century the claim was disputed and the relics awarded to the monastery of St. Maximin, near Marseille,[25] at the time that Gerard of Nazareth was writing, the tradition of the Magdalene being buried at Vézelay was standard in the Latin Church.

This burial tradition did not in itself entail a monopoly on the cult of the Magdalene. Vézelay, like Saint-Lazare at Autun, which claimed the tomb of Lazarus, was a pilgrimage church with strong links to the Holy Land. Bethany was a popular destination among Western pilgrims to the Holy Land. As early as the fourth century, the pilgrim Egeria had described the annual reenactment of the Lord's arrival in Bethany on Palm Sunday.[26] In the sixth century pilgrims were being shown the original tomb of Lazarus,[27] and the seventh-century pilgrim Arculf reported a flourishing monastery with a newly rebuilt church dedicated to Lazarus to the east of the cave-tomb.[28] The crusaders found the seventh-century church still intact in 1099. Under crusader rule the earlier local tradition of beginning the Palm Sunday procession to Jerusalem from Bethany was revived. But by 1114 further pilgrimage evidence suggests that the church of Lazarus had been rededicated to the sisters Mary (that is, Mary Magdalene) and Martha.[29] Between 1114 and 1169–72 another church, dedicated again to Lazarus and housing his original tomb, was built near the old church.[30] During this period the whole site had been transformed. The original owners of the church and village after the Latin conquest, the canons of the Holy Sepulchre, may have established a priory on the site soon after 1099. But in 1138 they exchanged this property for a village in Judaea with King Fulk. The site newly acquired by King Fulk then became the location of a convent of Benedictine nuns.[31] William of Tyre's explanation for the exchange of properties is that Iveta, the sister of Queen Melisende, had entered the Benedictine convent of St. Anne in Jerusalem, but that Melisende, not wanting her sister to live under the obedience of an abbess, was looking for a suitable place to found a new convent of which Iveta could herself be abbess.[32] Bethany, a pilgrimage site close to Jerusalem, was ideal. William describes it as the home of Mary, Martha, and Lazarus, and as "the familiar dwelling of our Lord and Saviour." The descriptions by William and by twelfth-century pilgrims indicate that

Bethany was fortified with a tower (a ruin of which still survives) and richly endowed, and that it could count on generous patronage by virtue of its importance in the Gospel narrative.[33] The addition of a new church dedicated to St. Lazarus built over the pilgrimage site of his tomb is evidence for the nuns' readiness and ability to tap this source of wealth and status. A double church meant that pilgrims' needs could be served without interfering with the running of the nuns' convent.

This digression into the history of the cult and the site at Bethany is necessary for an understanding of why Gerard of Nazareth was interested in Mary Magdalene. His first treatment of the subject took the form of a homily written for the nuns, *Ad ancillas Dei in Bethaniam,* perhaps at their request. Such a homily would have had the purpose of confirming the importance of Bethany in the cult of the Magdalene in order to ensure that a steady flow of pilgrims made the short journey into the hills to the southeast of Jerusalem. In a Western bishop, the interest shown by Gerard might have appeared largely academic. But in the Holy Land exegetical concerns had a concrete basis in everyday reality.[34] Where the narrative of the Gospels could be seen in the landscape itself, exegesis had a tangible application. Gerard was writing not simply about the minutiae of far-off events, but recounting and explaining details of the drama of human salvation in places that could still be seen, and where a Christian community now lived. For that community the kind of exegesis in which Gerard engaged on their behalf was a form of patronage with distinct economic accents. For Western pilgrims visiting Bethany, such exegesis (however it might be translated into more accessible terms) was also welcome. Pilgrims naturally celebrated the composite collection of Gospel narratives while in Bethany. It made sense to cause a number of events to coalesce at a single site. Pilgrims would want to be reassured that their journey to the site was worthwhile, and the more biblical associations that could be gleaned from it, the happier the pilgrim would be. So by the middle of the twelfth century, Mary Magdalene was inseparable from Bethany.

In the period from about 1160 to 1165, however, the pilgrim John of Würzburg found that visiting the site raised questions about the biblical narrative that he had not previously considered. John explains that Mary Magdalene's action of pouring out the precious ointment over Jesus (as told in the Gospel of John) was actually the second time that she had expressed such effusion of love for him. "This same Mary Magdalene, perhaps in the same place or perhaps in another, the House of Simon the Leper, some time before when she was a sinner, was moved to penitence. In the same manner she came to the feet of the Lord when he was reclining at supper."[35] John is wrestling here with the difficulty of reconciling the accounts in Matthew and

Mark, of an anonymous woman anointing Jesus' head with oil in the house of Simon the Leper in Bethany, with the Gospel of John, where Mary, the sister of Martha (Mary Magdalene in Western tradition), is specified as the woman doing the anointing, and the ointment is poured over Jesus' feet. This incongruity had, of course, occurred to people long before, and John of Würzburg knew from Western patristic teaching that there was a solution: that these were indeed two separate anointing incidents, but involving the same woman on both occasions. Although the person was not specified by name in Matthew and Mark, it was in fact Mary Magdalene who had performed this action on two different occasions. This example illustrated how the nature of the woman herself had changed: as John of Würzburg explains, "once she had come as a sinner in bitter penitence, but now she has been forgiven, and comes with overflowing joy." [36]

In Jerusalem, however, John also visited the Jacobite (Syrian Orthodox) church of St. Mary Magdalene and learned something there that shook his confidence in the traditional Western exegesis of the Magdalene at Bethany. The Jacobite monks told him that their church was built on the site of the house of Simon the Leper, where the Magdalene had poured out the ointment over Jesus' head, as related in the gospels of Matthew and Mark. They convinced John that this was so by showing him a relic of the Magdalene's hair, kept in a glass jar.[37] John's confusion at this point can be imagined: what about the church of Mary and Martha in Bethany, supposedly built on the site of the anointing incident? The Jacobites explained that Mary of Bethany was not the same as Mary Magdalene, and that the two anointing incidents had involved different women: the Magdalene in Simon the Leper's house in Jerusalem and Mary, the sister of Martha in Lazarus's house in Bethany. So, although the Jacobite tradition, like the Latin, identified the anonymous sinner of Matthew (26:6) and Mark (14:3) as the Magdalene, the Jacobites, in common with the Greek Orthodox, kept her distinct from Mary of Bethany.[38] John of Würzburg did not know what to believe. The Jacobite claim about the site of their church dedicated to the Magdalene was clearly, in his view, wrong, since the Gospels all located the house of Simon the Leper (or, in Luke, Simon the Pharisee) in Bethany rather than Jerusalem. The advantage of the Western tradition that John had been taught was that it was compact and convenient: it made sense of different narratives by explaining them as aspects of the same individual's changing relationship to Jesus. If Mary, the sister of Martha, and Mary Magdalene, the penitent sinner, were separated into distinct identities, the force of this symbolism was lost. This was troubling to a conscientious pilgrim, who wanted to be sure of what each site was supposed to be commemorating. But to the community of nuns at Bethany, the Eastern and Greek Orthodox interpretation, had it prevailed, would have been disastrous, because it threatened the source of the convent's status and wealth.

Consideration of this problem led John into deeper waters. "The Gospel reading about these things is clear," he mused, "but even to a careful listener it brings doubt upon the other factor, namely whether Simon the Pharisee [as in Luke 7:40] hosted a party in Bethany, and whether he invited the Lord to it." [39] In Matthew, Mark, and Luke, the incident had taken place in Simon's house, whereas in John it happened in the house of Mary and Martha. The Gospels could not contradict each other, but neither could any of them be wrong. Clearly, then, there had been two distinct incidents, and the Gospel accounts each described one of them. But John is still left in doubt about the location, and his doubt had an unbiblical source. Had the first anointing incident, which apparently took place in the house of someone described as either Simon the Leper or Simon the Pharisee, been in Jerusalem, as the Jacobites claimed, or in Bethany? Locating Simon's house in Bethany rather than Jerusalem raised problems of social conventions. It was more appropriate, John of Würzburg thought, for Jesus, when in Bethany, to have been a guest of Mary, Martha, and Lazarus, than of Simon the Leper, because Mary, Martha and Lazarus were lords of the village of Bethany. This conviction came from the Vulgate reading of John 11:1, where Jesus is described as going to the *castellum* of Mary and Martha in Bethany. A *castellum* indicated to Western Christians of the twelfth century proprietorship of a fief, the exercise of delegated office, or, in some wider sense, authority over a community. Contemporary Western conventions of landownership were thus transposed on to the Gospel narrative and used to formulate an interpretation that would have a moral as well as a literal sense. Naturally, this was an interpretation supported by the nuns of Bethany, the successors of Mary and Martha. As landowners of the village by the foundation charter of 1138, and guardians of the holy site, they had inherited the proprietorship once exercised by Mary Magdalene and Martha. Their status and prosperity depended on locating the entire complex of traditions in Bethany, and more specifically in the house of Mary and Martha, which had by a process of "natural inheritance" come to be their own house. The nuns were the heirs of Mary and Martha, not of Simon.

John of Würzburg ends his account of Bethany in confusion. "If anyone wishes to know more about these things, let him come himself, and ask the more intelligent subjects of this land the sequence and truth of this story. As for me, I have not found quite enough to explain it in any of the Scriptures." [40] This candid admission reveals one of the dangers of pilgrimages. Narratives that seemed comprehensible when read far away might not make sense when the geography and the text were put together. Even more worrying, from John's point of view, was that seeing the sites themselves seemed to challenge rather than confirm his received ideas about Mary Magdalene and Bethany. His understanding had been taught; in contrast, the local Orthodox, who had grown up in the sacred topography of the Gospels, had developed other traditions. Ought not they, with this local knowledge, to know better? Pilgrimages could expose Westerners to rival, Orthodox influence, and thus to alternative exegesis of the Scriptures, and ultimately lead them to question the authority of the Western patristic tradition.[41]

John of Würzburg's pilgrimage account and his doubt over the role of Bethany are reminders that the interest of a bishop like Gerard of Nazareth in Mary Magdalene was not merely academic, but had immediate application to the pastoral supervision of his flock. Gerard was not simply promoting the prestige of the nuns of Bethany; he was also safeguarding the Western understanding of the Scriptures from doubts that might be cast upon it by the influence of the indigenous Orthodox people. Moreover the polemical context in which Gerard wrote his treatises on the Magdalene shows how an exegetical problem could become the expression of a larger issue of controversy between the Latin ecclesiastical authorities and the Orthodox under their control. This polemical context must now be examined more closely.

The nuns were established at Bethany probably at about the time that Gerard of Nazareth became bishop of Latakia. Gerard's involvement with the Bethany community seems to have begun with a homily addressed to the nuns for the octave of Easter, *Ad ancillas Dei apud Bethaniam.*[42] Gerard was presumably making use of the well-established cult of Mary and Martha at Bethany to provide material for an Easter sermon, perhaps at the request of the Bethany nuns. Following Western tradition, Gerard took the joint patron of the nuns' church, Mary, to be Mary Magdalene, the penitent sinner whose touching penance at Bethany a few days before Jesus' death and resurrection provided an example of how Christians ought to prepare for Easter.

Of Gerard's five known works, three can be related to the cult of Mary Magdalene localized at Bethany. The *De una Magdalena contra Graecos,* in which he rehearsed the authorities supporting his identification of the Magdalene, was a polemical response to criticism engendered by his initial homily to the nuns of Bethany. That the criticism had a Greek Orthodox source, obvious in any case from the content of the *De una Magdalena,* is further borne out by his final work, entitled *Contra Salam presbyterum.* To recapitulate: first, Gerard wrote and disseminated a homily on Mary and Martha for the nuns of Bethany, in which he presented the thesis that Mary of Bethany was Mary Magdalene; then, in response to criticism from an Orthodox quarter, he wrote the treatise *De una Magdalena,* part of which survives; finally, in response to further criticism, he wrote *Contra Salam*. Neither the initial homily nor the *Contra Salam* survives, except for a single extract from the *Contra Salam* quoted by the sixteenth-century Centuriators of Magdeburg. This passage shows us something of Gerard's method: "Although necessity forces me to read the words of this Sala, it is as though my teeth were being clogged by pitch or something sticky which I can hardly chew or swallow."[43] The precise identity of the man who took such exception to Gerard's works is not revealed by the surviving extracts. This, however, can be surmised from two further short references elsewhere in the Centuriators' work. These passages show us how the quarrel between Gerard and Sala had originated and developed. According to one, "Sala the priest presumed for a long time to dedicate cemeteries, which is the bishop's prerogative: as Gerard of Nazareth writes in his defence against Sala the priest."[44] According to the other, "Sala was a priest, against whom Gerard of Nazareth contended. Gerard objected that he had presumed to dedicate a cemetery, although that pertained to bishops. And also that he [Sala] introduced a Greek bishop against the Latin into the city."[45]

These two issues of grievance against Sala suggest strongly that Gerard's polemical opponent was an Orthodox priest in his diocese of Latakia.[46] Benjamin Kedar suggested, when he first discussed Gerard of Nazareth, that Sala might instead have been a Templar, and that the dispute between them referred to the long-standing grievance of bishops against the privileges and exemptions enjoyed by the order.[47] Following such a hypothesis, Sala may initially have incurred Gerard's anger by contravening the ruling of Pope Eugenius III in 1145 that Templar cemeteries must be blessed by bishops.[48] Doubtless the text of Gerard's *Contra Salam,* had it survived, would resolve the issue of Sala's identity. In its absence, however, we can rely instead on a further reference to the text by a fourteenth-century English Carmelite, John Hornby, who apparently knew Gerard's works. This reference gives the full title as *Girardus episcopus Laodicensis contra Salam philosophum Grecum vel Cretum,* and therefore supports the view that Sala was indeed an Orthodox priest. Hornby incidentally gives some indication of the kind of argument Gerard used against Sala on the question of the identity of the Magdalene. He quotes part of Gerard's discussion of names, where Gerard, with reference to Mary of Bethany being identified as Mary Magdalene, argues that two different "cognomens" or epithets can indicate the same person.[49]

In his initial response to Sala, in the *De una Magdalena contra Graecos,* Gerard had struck a note of tolerance: "There is no greatly pernicious error in this," he said, "and one can believe one or another without grave danger. But it is good, if possible, to hold to what is more truthful, not only in this but in all controversy."[50] The extract quoted above about chewing pitch shows how far from this equanimity Gerard was led in his personal attack on Sala. Of greater interest than the intricacies of the argument is the way in which the controversy shows how an exegetical dispute was engendered by deep-seated grievances of a quite different nature. The root cause of conflict was apparently not the issue of Mary Magdalene at all, but the dedication of cemeteries by a priest without episcopal supervision. That this was already a cause of conflict between them at the time Gerard was writing his works on Mary Magdalene is indicated by the Centuriators' wording: *Sala presbyter iamdudum dedicare coemiteria praesumpsit*. Sala's dispute with Gerard over episcopal authority was a separate issue from the exegetical question of the Magdalene. But once Gerard had entered the arena of exegesis publicly, and in his homily for the nuns of Bethany identified the two Marys as one, Sala evidently saw his chance to strike back at his superior by attacking his interpretation of Scripture. The cause and course of the dispute make perfect sense if we accept Sala as a Greek Orthodox priest of Latakia under the authority of Gerard.

The second extract, in which Sala is accused of introducing a Greek bishop into Latakia, surely confirms his identity as a member of the Orthodox Church. Although Latin Christians can sometimes be shown to have used Orthodox prelates as a sanction against Latin bishops,[51] and although the military orders' relations with the Latin episcopal hierarchy were often frosty, it would be somewhat fantastic to find a Templar espousing an Orthodox view of Mary Magdalene in order to score points off a Latin bishop. The debate over Mary Magdalene reveals a long-running dispute over episcopal authority spilling over into the Latin interpretation of Scripture because this gave an Orthodox priest the opportunity to expose to ridicule his bishop's exegetical method and understanding of Scripture and thus, presumably, to throw doubt on his qualifications for the episcopate.

Gerard of Nazareth himself realized that the immediate issue at stake in the polemical dispute was not the Magdalene but episcopal authority. The bishopric of Latakia lay in the patriarchate of Antioch, which had a larger proportion of Greek Orthodox to Latins than Jerusalem, and where there was probably a more intense level of doctrinal debate.[52] Gerard's superior as patriarch, Aimery of Limoges, was heavily involved in such controversy. Aimery's position may have been threatened by the terms of the reconciliation between Prince Reynald of Antioch and Manuel Komnenos in 1159. In 1165 he was forced out of office by the imposition of a Greek patriarch over Antioch, as part of the terms by which Manuel paid the ransom of his vassal, Prince Bohemond III.[53] There was precedent for this. Odo of Deuil reports, in his account of the Second Crusade, that Emperor John Komnenos had replaced the Latin bishops of Tarsus and Mamistra with Orthodox prelates as a result of his campaign against Raymond of Antioch in 1138.[54]

In the 1170s Patriarch Aimery was a correspondent of Ugo Eteriano, the Pisan theologian in Constantinople who had learned Greek in order to refute Orthodox teaching on the Trinity and on the Roman primacy from Greek patristic sources, and who had been employed by Manuel Komnenos as an advisor on theological matters.[55] Aimery asked Ugo to send him Orthodox theological works, with his annotations, that he could study to use in debate with the Orthodox people in his charge.[56] It is possible (though without evidence this must remain speculation) that the Centuriators' extracts about Sala refer to an actual occurrence: the replacement of Gerard himself as bishop of Latakia by a Greek, as part of the terms of the 1159 settlement in which Prince Reynald acknowledged the suzerainty of the Byzantine emperor. Gerard's only appearance in sources after 1159 locates him in the kingdom of Jerusalem rather than in his diocese,[57] so perhaps he was forced into exile, while his superior, Aimery, managed to cling to office.

The dispute over cemeteries, in any case, has a convincing ring. The dedication of cemeteries raised the vital question of control over churches. By reserving the dedication to bishops, the Latins were of course following standard Western practice. But in the Orthodox Church it was customary for priests to perform dedications and other rites, such as confirmations, that were reserved in the West for bishops. From a Greek Orthodox perspective, the Latin bishop in Latakia was denying the Orthodox clergy control of normal priestly functions within their own parishes. Precisely because of the freedom generally enjoyed by Orthodox clergy to follow their own customs, this insistence on episcopal authority was a provocative reminder of the limits of Orthodox autonomy under crusader rule.

Latin bishops, from their point of view, could not afford to let the Orthodox clergy be seen to flout their authority, for fear that this might spread to their Latin subordinates. To some extent this was already happening. The establishment of cemeteries by military orders was only one example of the weakening of episcopal authority in the patriarchate of Jerusalem. In 1155 a delegation of bishops from Outremer to the papal curia complained bitterly about the loss of tithes as a result of papal privileges to the Hospitallers.[58] Eugenius III had ruled that Templar cemeteries had to be blessed by bishops, but subsequent papal privileges to the military orders had permitted them to establish cemeteries in parishes of which they held the advowson, and thus to queer the pitch for the parochial clergy. Of course, this is not quite the same as Orthodox priests dedicating cemeteries, but it is no less an indication of the threat bishops perceived to their rights. Recalcitrant Orthodox clergy, and autonomous Templars or Hospitallers, could give similar ideas of independent action to Latin clergy. There is some scattered but fascinating evidence that Latin clergy in the eastern Mediterranean could be influenced by their Orthodox counterparts in such ways. For instance, in 1199, Innocent III ordered his vicar in Constantinople to forbid Latin priests (presumably attached to the Italian colonists) to follow the Orthodox custom of performing sacraments, such as confirmation, that should be reserved for bishops alone.[59] In 1204, Innocent was worried that priests in the eastern Mediterranean, both Latin and Greek, were being ordained by Orthodox bishops without proper ceremonial *(absque unctive manuum se faciunt ordinari)* and against canonical sanction.[60] The Latin authorities had to maintain constant vigilance lest their clergy fall under the influence of local ecclesiastical customs that threatened the dignity of the episcopacy.

It is in this wider context of authority in the church that Gerard's interest in Mary Magdalene should be seen. Sala's attack on Gerard's exegesis of Scripture was evidently part of a campaign of resistance against Latin authority. From straightforward flouting of the rights claimed by his Latin superior, Sala carried the campaign into a new field: to an assault on the traditional Latin exegesis of the Scriptures. Here Sala was attacking not only Gerard, but the whole Latin Church's understanding of the Gospel accounts about Mary Magdalene. Gerard raised the stakes, in his *De una Magdalena*, by appealing to the authority of the Latin Fathers. In refuting Gerard, Sala was engaging in a theological debate that transformed a quarrel over local rights into a far-reaching dispute over the nature of authority in the Church. If the Latin bishop could not properly interpret Scripture, by what right did he exercise authority over Orthodox clergy who, with the aid of Greek patristics, could?

Even though they can be reconstructed only by inference, Gerard's works enable us to see the confrontation between Latins and Orthodox in the crusader states at a level that mirrors the more celebrated encounters between representatives of Rome and Constantinople. The problems encountered at Bethany by John of Würzburg show how real the question of the Magdalene's identity could be to contemporaries, and hints at the dangers of exposing Westerners to local influences. In this respect, the emphasis on the Latin patristic tradition in Gerard's work was analogous to insisting on Latin ecclesiastical customs in his diocese.

Sala's refutation of Gerard's thoughts on the Magdalene is a reminder of how varied were the expressions of difference over interpretation and custom between Latins and Greeks. This takes us full circle to the apparently incoherent sets of grievances aired by Latin and Orthodox canonists and clergy against one another. The episode described here may have been a single ripple on the waters, with little long-term effect. Its value for historians lies in the interrelations that it reveals between thought and action, and between belief and practice. Perhaps Peter of Antioch was, after all, wrong to criticize Michael Kerularios's list of anti-Latin grievances for being incoherent and unhierarchical. Perhaps it is precisely this unhierarchic consideration of differences that reveals the truth about relations between the Churches: that Latins and Greeks did not make a conscious and academic separation between theology, exegesis, and custom. All were equally valid as grounds of opposition, or expressions of "otherness." From the Orthodox point of view, the incorrect understanding of Scripture that led Latins into an erroneous tradition about Mary Magdalene undermined the credibility of their understanding of Scripture in general. From this it followed that Latin arguments for the Roman primacy, or the addition of the *filioque,* or the use of unleavened bread in the Eucharist, or the correct days for fasting, or episcopal rights to dedicate cemeteries, or a host of other apparently minor points of difference were also based on a flawed interpretation of Scripture. A theologian and diplomat such as Theorianus might from a distance assure Orthodox parish clergy living under crusader rule that minor points of observance should not obscure the underlying unity of the Church. In the field, however, it was precisely those minor points of observance that rankled, for Orthodox priests no less than for Latin bishops such as Gerard or Jacques de Vitry. An educated priest like Sala realized that one could not separate custom and belief so easily, that one stemmed from the other, and that, no matter what the initial spark that ignited the blaze of controversy, the flame at its heart was always the issue of authority.

PART FOUR

Historical and Intellectual
Perspectives

11

Tolerance and Intolerance in the Medieval Canon Lawyers

JAMES MULDOON

At first glance, a paper dealing with toleration in the writings of the medieval canon lawyers at the time of the crusades would seem to be an easy one to write. One might simply say that there was no conception of toleration in the writings of the canonists and stop. To do that, however, would be to underestimate the complexity of the task involved. There are at least three fundamental issues that would require attention before we could say that the canonists had no conception of "toleration." In the first place, we would have to inquire as to what we and they mean by toleration. In the second place, we would have to consider what and who is to be tolerated. Finally, we would have to examine the tension between theory and practice with regard to toleration.

To consider any or all of these points is, of course, to wrestle with the argument that R.I. Moore presented in *The Formation of a Persecuting Society,* namely, that in the eleventh and twelfth centuries the Christian clerical elite sought to impose its own code of moral uniformity on all members of Christian society.[1] This program, aimed as it was at those defined as social deviants—Jews, heretics, even lepers—was the antithesis of any policy of toleration. It reflected one facet of the great Church reform movement of the eleventh and twelfth centuries that produced the fundamental works of canon law, the *Decretum* (ca. 1140) and the *Decretales* (1234), the law books that provided the legal armature of medieval Christian society.[2] The internal threat, real or imagined, that those defined as social deviants posed to Christendom was paralleled by the external threat of Islam that the crusades were designed to stop. Given these circumstances, it is easy to see why toleration was not at the top of any list of topics that interested the canonists. Even if one rejects Moore's characterization of the eleventh and twelfth cen-

117

turies as the birthplace of a 'persecuting society," one must also accept the fact that the Church reform movement certainly aimed at forming a society shaped according to Christian moral and behavioral standards. Those who did not accept those standards would be, at the very least, marginalized. The problem, of course, is that any society, by definition, has a set of standards by which membership in it is determined. In effect, the question really is, what were the parameters of full membership in the social order in the eleventh and twelfth centuries, and what were the implications of those parameters for those who did not accept some of them?

Given the rather broad nature of the issues involved and the small space of time allotted to considering them here, I wish to consider the issue of toleration in connection with Jewish and Muslim subjects of Christian rulers. This aspect of toleration was, after all, one of the most important consequences of the crusades as crusaders brought more and more Muslims under Christian rule in the Near East, in Spain, and in Portugal.

In order to understand the problem of toleration as it concerned Muslims under Christian rule, it is important to consider two points. In the first place, forced conversion and baptism was forbidden in theology and law. Baptism had to be accepted freely, although what medieval lawyers considered uncoerced conversion would not fit modern definitions of voluntary acceptance. Jews, for example, could be forced to attend sermons designed to enable them to see the truth of Christianity, and they could be enticed by the prospect of various material advantages they could obtain or constraints they could lose if they converted.[3] There do not appear to have been any cases of Muslim subjects of Christian rulers being forced to attend sermons designed to convince them of the truth of Christianity, but the reason for this would seem to have been pragmatic, not theological. There were those who argued that a slave who attended such a sermon and as a consequence accepted baptism would have to be freed. Understandably, Christian masters, such as those in the kingdom of Jerusalem, were not enthusiastic about this consequence, so they generally refused to allow their slaves to hear Christian preachers, even voluntarily.[4]

In the second place, canonists did not argue that nonbelievers had to be exiled from lands that the crusaders had acquired. There were two reasons for this. In the first place, if nonbelievers remained under Christian jurisdiction, they could more easily be led to Christianity.[5] In the second place, crusaders needed the labor that the conquered population could provide. Not unlike the European colonizers of the sixteenth and seventeenth centuries, the crusaders did not intend to labor themselves, and there was no great influx of European peasants to work for them.[6] Thus, both spiritual and economic motives mandated limited toleration of conquered Muslims.

The practical problem was the extent of the toleration allowed the Muslims. This varied according to time, place, and circumstance. It is clear that the papacy and the canonists often found the degree of toleration that a Christian secular ruler authorized his Muslim subjects unacceptable.[7] The Muslims were allowed to believe as they wished, but they were restricted in the external manifestations of their religion. The mullahs were often forbidden to call the people to prayer, for example. On the other hand, some practices that Christians condemned—polygamy, for example—were allowed. The limited toleration of cultural practices, such as polygamy, led, of course, to unique problems when a polygamist decided to convert to Christianity. Could he keep all of his wives? If not, which one could he keep? What if one of his wives converted and wished to marry, could she?[8]

Both those who have seen some limited form of toleration in the eleventh and twelfth centuries and those who do not see any such toleration generally agree that in the thirteenth century the toleration that had existed declined and increasing restrictions were placed on nonbelievers within Christendom. The restrictions that the Fourth Lateran Council imposed on Jews and Muslims can be seen as the turn of the tide of toleration, limited though it was. There were now even more limits on the activities of nonbelievers. Although the Fourth Lateran's restrictions on Jews are perhaps the best known sign of decreasing toleration, James Powell has pointed out that the restrictions on Jews seem equally applicable to Muslims.[9]

If, as I have argued thus far, there was a recognizable, if limited, kind of toleration in the eleventh and twelfth centuries, the question arises as to why toleration of nonbelievers within Christendom seems to have declined during the thirteenth century. Obviously there were a number of factors involved. In the writings of the canonists that culminated in the restraints imposed by the Fourth Lateran Council, there is the repeated theme that Christians will be led astray by non-Christians. It would appear that the Church leadership feared that non-Christian ways of life were somehow seductively attractive to Christians, although the nature of that attraction is not clearly explained.[10] In some cases, special emphasis was placed on the fragility of recent converts' faith, a fragility that required protecting them from associating with their former coreligionists.[11] The ghettoization of Jews and Muslims was a recognition that they would seduce Christians from their faith unless they were clearly identified and marked off from Christians. This stance suggests that hopes for converting Jews and Muslims were fading. It also suggests insecurity on the part of Christendom's leaders that Christianity is indeed attractive to potential converts.

Another way to judge the canonists' attitude toward non-Christians generally is the discussion of marriages between Christians and non-Christians in C. 28 q. 2 of the Gratian's *Decretum*. One problem that runs through the documents here is that of the man who converts to Christianity but whose spouse does not. If the unconverted spouse lives peaceably with the convert, then the marriage is binding. If, however, the unconverted spouse leaves the convert, he can legitimately remarry.[12] This discussion demonstrates that the expansion of Europe would lead to problems about marriage arising from the continued presence of non-Christians under Christian rule. The canonists appear unwilling to offer the possibility of divorce and remarriage as an inducement to convert, their primary goal being simply to protect the religious status of the convert. Presumably, a non-Christian spouse could continue to worship her own gods as long as she did not interfere with her husband's worship.[13]

Other canons forbid Christians to dine with Jews or to employ Jewish physicians (C. 28 q. 2 c. 13), prohibitions certainly applicable to other non-Christians as well. The *Decretales* includes bans on the employment of Jewish nurses for children (5.6.13) and forbids secular rulers from employing non-Christians, specifically Jews and pagans, in public offices.(5.6.16) Here again, the canonists walked a narrow line, forbidding Christians to abuse Jews and, presumably, other nonbelievers (5.6.9) and encouraging efforts to convert them without, at the same time, having too much personal contact with them. The assumption underlying these canons was that there would be nonbelievers dwelling within Christian society and that they should not be persecuted. On the other hand, there is no sense that the nonbeliever had the right to his or her nonbelief. The expectation again would seem to have been that the nonbelievers would be more inclined to become Christians if the advantages, spiritual and material, of doing so were made clear.

By the beginning of the thirteenth century, Christians had a great deal of evidence at their disposal that the Jews and Muslims who dwelled within Christian society were not going to convert *en masse,* which was the way in which medieval Christians understood the process of religious conversion. No Jewish or Muslim Clovis had arisen to lead his people to the baptismal font.[14] Christians had justified the toleration of non-Christians in order to provide them with access to Christian teaching. Rather than using force to bring non-Christian subjects of Christian rulers to the baptismal font, Christians were to teach nonbelievers by their good example and virtuous way of life. While it would be possible to argue that the Christians could have been more patient, waiting longer for the nonbelievers to see the light, it seems to me that they became impatient because they believed that the process of conversion was a rapid one: that is to say, once people were introduced to Christian teaching, they would quickly accept it. The famous conversion stories after all described rapid conversion (that is, baptism) of large numbers of nonbelievers following the lead of their rulers. Constantine and Clovis were the great models of corporate conversion. Reaching back to the New Testament there was also the example of Pentecost, a miraculous event involving the conversion of hundreds of individuals at once. By the thirteenth century, it was even possible for Christians to argue that the failure of Jews and Muslims to convert was due to some fundamental moral flaw that they possessed.

Jews and Muslims did not fit the mold of the ancient Romans or of the early medieval Franks. They were people who possessed a fully articulated theology and institutional structures to maintain their beliefs. Unlike the ancestors of medieval Europeans, they could contend intellectually with Christian teaching and, because they tended to live in autonomous communities, they could reinforce one another's resistance to Christian pressures to convert. Paradoxically, the ghettoization of Jews and Muslims required by the Fourth Lateran Council may well have made it more difficult to convert them to Christianity. If they had been scattered among the Christian population, they might have succumbed more readily to Christian pressures than if they remained in their own communities. It is also worth pointing out that when Jews and Muslims were eventually exiled from European kingdoms, it was the secular rulers, not the Church, that took the lead.

To leave the issue of toleration in the thought of the canonists at this point, however, would be to neglect some mid-thirteenth-century hints of a theoretical basis for toleration in the canonistic tradition. These hints appear in a somewhat peculiar place, Innocent IV's discussion of the right of crusaders to seize the lands of the Muslims. The commentary contains two brief and rudimentary discussions of rights that could contribute to forming a basis for a theory of toleration. What makes these discussions especially interesting is the way in which Innocent at least discusses the application of the same principles to Christian and non-Christian societies equally.

Speaking as a canonist, Innocent IV (1243–54), Sinibaldo dei Fieschi, argued that while the crusaders could legitimately take back the Holy Land and other lands that the Muslims had seized from Christians in unjust wars, they could not legitimately seize other Muslim lands because the Muslims could be presumed to possess them legitimately.[15] He went on to state that all men have the right to *dominium,* that is, the right to property and lordship. As a result, presumably a Muslim or other non-Christian who acquired property in a Christian society could not be deprived of that property simply by virtue of being a non-Christian. That being the case, nonbelievers could not presumably be forcibly deprived of their possessions and forced into exile. Innocent also raised the question of whether infidels could lay a claim to Europe similar to the one that Christians laid to the Holy Land, namely, that the ancient inhabitants of Europe having been infidels and the Christians having deprived them of their legitimate *dominium,* a contemporary infidel ruler could legitimately wage war against Christian Europe in order to reinstate its infidel rulers. Obviously Innocent was not about to accept that argument, but his answer was interesting. He argued that the situations were not identical because ancient infidel societies converted *en masse,* the rulers leading their people to the new faith. Thus, Christians did not conquer Europe as the Holy Land and other areas had been conquered by the Muslims. In the second place, according to Innocent IV, non-Christian rulers were obliged to tolerate the religious practices of their Christian subjects. For example, if a non-Christian subordinate ruler continued to hold land in a region retaken legitimately by Christians, he could continue to govern so long as he did not interfere with the religious practices of his Christian subjects. If he did so, his Christian overlord could deprive him of his lands and jurisdiction. Furthermore, an independent non-Christian ruler must allow Christian missionaries to enter his lands and, presumably, he must leave them in peace. Failure to do so would justify the entry of Christian warriors under papal license to protect the missionaries. Here the right of a people to self-rule is subordinated to the overriding responsibility of the Church to preach its message to all mankind.

The most interesting part of this commentary, however, does not concern the obligation of non-Christians to tolerate Christians, it concerns whether Christians were obliged to tolerate the preachers of other religions who wished to enter Christendom. Specifically, Innocent IV asked whether Christian rulers had to allow entry to such missionaries. In response, he argued that the two cases were not identical, this time because "they are in error and we are on the way of truth." I should add that Innocent did not deny Muslims the right to travel in Christian lands, only the right to preach there.

There is one other point that Innocent IV made relating to religious toleration that is worth examining, although it bears only indirectly on the issue of the toleration of Muslims. The limited toleration allowed Jews and Muslims living within Christian societies was rooted in their links to Christianity by way of the Bible. Islam was, after all, seen as a kind of Christian heresy, though obviously not a heresy in the narrow legal sense of the term because that would have assumed that the Muslims were baptized. Furthermore, the Jews and Muslims were monotheists, as were the Christians, and because of their adherence to the Old Testament ban on graven images, they could not be accused of idolatry. However, those other non-Christians, known collectively as infidels were another matter. According to Innocent IV, idolatry was against the natural law known to all men. Therefore, Christians had the right—indeed, the obligation—to destroy the idols worshiped by the infidel subjects of Christian ruler. Given the importance of rituals attached to idols in various infidel religions, the ban on idols was tantamount to banning the religion entirely. Thus, in practice, it would appear that toleration could not be extended to most, if not all, societies defined as idolatrous. At the very least, when Christians conquered the lands of idol worshippers, they could—and should—destroy the idols.

As I indicated at the beginning, the medieval canon lawyers did not devote a great deal of attention to the issue of religious toleration. At the same time, they were not oblivious of at least some of the issues that toleration involved. In some ways, their writings, brief though they were, were not unlike the debates about religious toleration that roiled Europe during the wars of religion and were also associated with European overseas expansion into the New World. If the twelfth- and thirteenth-century canon lawyers were the creators of a persecuting society, then what were the civil and common lawyers who staffed the early modern European royal bureaucracies? Clearly the problem of religious toleration was far too complicated for simple solutions, then or now. Rather than condemning the canonists out of hand, it is more rewarding to understand why they thought as they did even when we do not agree with them.

12

William of Tyre, the Muslim Enemy, and the Problem of Tolerance

RAINER CHRISTOPH SCHWINGES

To talk of William of Tyre, the Muslim enemy, and the problem of tolerance actually means to thematize the political, juridical, ideological and religious dilemmas of the Holy Land in the era of the Crusades, that is to say, the irresolvable conflict of interests between Christians and Muslims. The renowned chronicler,[1] Prince of the Church, and Chancellor of the Court of Jerusalem, William of Tyre, very consciously placed himself within this conflict, although his attempts to resolve it with the means at his disposal in the second half of the twelfth century were doomed, as we know.[2] He was fully aware of the fact that two powerful religious traditions were struggling against each other for the sole possession of power. William, too, claimed the Holy Land as Christ's legacy to Christianity. Remarkably, however, he did not entirely deny his Muslim opponents' claims to the very same land. Rather, the final Christian victory was in the hand of God.

In William's day and age (he was born in the Holy City in about 1130 and died in 1186), this concession to the enemy of his faith and of his native Jerusalem was an extraordinary political and intellectual achievement. It could be accomplished only by someone able to dismiss the impersonal and rigid concept of the enemy that informed the crusade ideology of the papal church, i.e., the image of an evil and satanic enemy of the faith. This rejection occurred more or less on all fronts of crusading Christianity—for example, in Spain, in the German-Slavic border area, and in the Baltic region. In these areas of colonization and territorialization, the traditional image of the op-

Apart from the notes, the paper is given here nearly unchanged from what was read at the Montréal International Conference of Historical Sciences in 1995. I wish to thank my colleagues, Rifaat Abou-El-Haj, California State University, Long Beach (U.S.A.), and Prof. Fikret Adanir, University of Bochum (Germany), for sympathy and helpful comments.

ponent, and the attitude toward him that had evolved over time, were more influential than the abstract or distant point of view of the ideologues.[3] Nowhere, however, was the religious antagonism more racially undermined than in the Holy Land itself. Here, too, colonization and assimilation supplanted the crusade ideology that had formed the intellectual basis of the Latin Christian domination in the Orient and had guaranteed a continuous flow of pilgrims, warriors, and settlers.

Soon after the conquest of Jerusalem in 1099, the Christian Frankish lords integrated themselves into the Syro-Palestinian political system and found a *modus vivendi* with their Islamic neighbors. Treaties were made and kept, as a rule; battles were fought with and against one another, and the fronts between Christians and Muslims were not always clear-cut. Westerners got accustomed to oriental ways of life. Accordingly, the image of the enemy changed little by little. This is not the least reason for the ambiguous and distrustful relationship between the Christians recently arrived from Europe, who found these changes difficult to understand, and the longer-established Oriental Franks.[4]

William of Tyre was not only a witness to this development but also its most resolute propagator. He was an eminent scholar, part of both the Occidental and Oriental cultures. Educated first at the obviously important school of the church of the Holy Sepulchre, he then studied the liberal arts—theology and Roman law, above all—in Paris, Orléans, and Bologna, and he was able to interpret Eastern writings, whether of Christian or non-Christian provenance. Besides French and Latin, he spoke or read Greek and perhaps Arabic, too. Thus, the intellectual Eastern traditions and the scholastic rationality of the Western schools converged in William of Tyre in a most fruitful symbiosis, making him the most important intellectual of the Oriental Franks in the twelfth century.[5] William of Tyre, one of the *orientales latini* (as he often proudly designated his countrymen and thus implicitly himself), developed a specifically Oriental attitude that went far beyond mere political and economic pragmatism. Any conflicts with the Islamic neighbors were considered separately from the universal sphere of the Western ideologues; William, facing his and the Muslim's *patria,* territorialized or, rather, *orientalized* them.[6]

At this point a methodological remark may be useful: Jerusalem's politician and chronicler did not express his views on the relationships between Christians and Muslims in an integrated way. He did not draw up any guidelines on how to conduct affairs with the opponent. William's views emerge only if one collects the numerous isolated remarks made throughout his *Chronicon.* However, there is a methodological risk inherent in this procedure, since we are dealing with an artificial aggregate that might exaggerate or even falsify William's true position. Fortunately, however, it is possible to verify his statements exactly by examining in the same aggregative manner the Old French translation of William's original, the so-called *Estoire de Eracles* written in Northern France during the first half of the thirteenth century. If one compares these two texts, William's position emerges very clearly from the counterimages and contradictions. His Old French translator often clearly refused to adhere to the original, altering the author's views, reinterpreting, weakening, falsifying, suppressing, or simply misunderstanding them—in conformity with the Western Crusaders' mental image of an enemy. William's position, and thereby the difference between the oriental and Occidental positions, emerges all the more vividly.[7]

I should like to present William's position here under three different but nonetheless related aspects: first, under the aspect of religion, of his interpretation of Islam; second, under a sociocultural aspect of his attitude towards Muslim people, especially towards individual enemies; and, third, under the aspect of law, the juridical aspect of the mutual relationships. And finally, I will make some remarks on the problem of tolerance with regard to William's position.

Islam

William's attitude to Islam corresponds with what was normally expected of a medieval Christian archbishop. He viewed Islam as a "doctrina pestilens" and "superstitio," the Prophet Mohammed as a "subversor" and "primogenitus Sathanae."[8] However, one notices that there are no semantic fields exclusively reserved for Islam, but that the language in which William expresses his ideas is indeterminate, in so far as the same words are also used for those Christians who were guilty of any moral or political transgressions of William's precepts. His linguistic indeterminacy might reveal an undercurrent of indifference beneath his unambiguous rejection of the alien doctrine. The different positions, regarding Islam, of the Greek Orthodox Church, of the Eastern churches, and of the Latin Church, cannot be discussed here. Let it suffice to say that William of Tyre, living on Oriental soil, adopted the Oriental interpretation of Islam. The Byzantines and the Latins generally considered Islam as paganism or occasionally—and only among the educated—as a Christian heresy. In the Oriental opinion, however, Islam appeared as an autonomous world religion, superior to paganism, and related to Christianity in its monotheism and, especially, in having the same God. Islam even participated in the Divine Plan of Salvation, albeit on a level of inferior religious perfection.[9]

William accepted this tradition. In his monumental work, comprising nearly 1100 pages in Robert Huygens's new edition, he strictly avoided the term *paganus*. In the Latin usage, and especially in his sources, *paganus* is a polemical term for the followers of an organized heathen cult that denies God. William preferred the term *infidelis*, which describes, in analogy to the infidelity of Judaism, merely a different attitude to God that diverges from that of the Christians.[10] He was convinced of a fundamental *consensus* between Islam and Christianity, of a *magis consentire*, even, with respect to the Shia.[11] William knew that he was in agreement with the Muslims with regard to their respective worship of the one and only God of Abraham, Isaac, and Jacob. Although he rejected dogmatic Islam as such, he appreciated it as a religious system that might also, even though only within its own limits, teach its followers to fear God and to live piously. Thus, the scholarly Oriental Frank left the Western tradition, actually adopting the Oriental one, a tradition that had originated soon after the expansion of Islam in the seventh century and that always emphasized the resemblances between the two religions rather than the differences, as was the case in the Western idea of the Crusades. The archbishop of Tyre was consistent in that he tolerated mosques in the city of Tyre.[12]

Muslim People

Social and cultural behavior benefited considerably from William's interpretation of Islam. As he did not regard the Muslims as pagans but as believers, although of a different kind, he was freer to view his enemies as human beings in their own right. Although the Muslims were and remained the enemies of his land and faith, he was nevertheless aware of their personal characteristics. In the early days of the Crusades, the authors of his sources would go no farther than to consider their foes as valiant men.[13] William, however, was far more interested in their human virtues and vices, in their abilities and achievements, even if they were used to the detriment of his native Jerusalem. It is significant that in the twenty-three volumes of his *Chronicon* almost all the assessments that emphasize the non-Christian character of the Muslims occur in the first fifteen books, i.e., in those based on and influenced by the major Western chroniclers of the Crusades (for example, Albert of Aachen or Fulcher of Chartres). In the volumes from the sixteenth onward, which are not based on any identifiable model, this aspect fades out and finally disappears entirely. Even a general term such as *infidelis* has been removed from the terminology used to describe personalities; the personal epithet has taken its place (an epithet, admittedly, reserved for princes and noblemen, who were his peers and members of his political class, even though they adhered to a different faith).

Saladin's uncle, Shirkuh, for example, who conquered Egypt, much to the Franks' chagrin, was appreciated by William for his self-confidence, his eloquence and urbanity. As for Saladin himself, William praised his intelligence and political perspicacity, while yet sharply criticizing, in traditional terms of warfare, his tyranny and arrogance—presumably a sign that William was perfectly aware of how dangerous Saladin was to the continued Christian rule over Oriental soil. Of the long-standing ally of the Franks, the Atabeg Unur of Damascus, he spoke with such deep respect that he even bestowed on him the formal social epithet of *dominus,* a term William used quite selectively even for Christian noblemen.[14]

One of the most impressive portraits is that of Nur-ad-Din, emir of Aleppo and Damascus. William credited him with foresight and circumspection, with wisdom and restraint in his judgment, and with prudence. He considered Nur-ad-Din to be a just, godfearing, religious, and hence happy, blessed man *(justus, timens Deum, religiosus, felix)*. These traits, complemented by intelligence, imaginativeness and vigor, qualified him as both an excellent leader of the Muslims and a dangerous opponent of the Christians. William was very much aware of this discrepancy. However, he did not present the two sides separately; rather, he integrated these qualities in a rounded portrait. Thus, in what amounts to an obituary, William noted on the death of the prince: " Nur-ad-Din (is dead), the greatest persecutor of the Christian name and faith, yet a just, shrewd and provident man, and religious according to his people's tradition." [15] It seems to me that William of Tyre has thus acknowledged the Muslim leader as a religious person. One is reminded of St. Peter's speech in the house of the Roman centurion Cornelius in Caesarea, who is said in the Acts to be a *vir religiosus, timens Deum* (Acts, 10:2) and *justus* (Acts, 10:22): "But in every nation he that fears him, and works righteousness, is accepted with him" (Acts, 10:35)[16]. This idea has not exactly had a great influence on the Christian's external relationships. It is all the more remarkable to find one of its advocates on the scene during the Crusades.

Law

William is consistent, in that his views also inform his juridical opinion. To him, the mutual relationships of Christians and Muslims were subject to one and the same juridical and world order. Contrary to the predominant ideas of the Latin church, which granted infidels only inferior rights, if any, William made no distinction whatsoever. He recognized the Muslims as an equal and sovereign people. For William did not hesitate to grant his hostile neighbors the right to their native land, their freedom, property and family, and least so, when the territorial or municipal sovereignty of the Muslim community was attacked and injured by a Christian army, an army which, in its turn, operated in the Holy Land with a claim to defend the *hereditas Christi,* the legacy of Christ. In William's view, moreover, the Muslims were entitled not only to defend themselves against Christian *injuriae,* injuries or injustices, but even actively to take revenge for injuries suffered leading a *bellum justum,* a just war. This right was absolute, that is to say, it was valid even when the Christians also claimed the same right. As a matter of course and logically consistent with this, the Muslims' rights were complemented with the *lex pactorum,* the law of contract, as a formal basis for the equality of Muslims and Christians according to the medieval *jus gentium.* Simply out of political necessity, William was deeply convinced that contracts must be observed without restriction, even with infidels. To the learned jurist, this obligation was founded not only in Roman Church Law *(pacta sunt servanda),* but even more so in the righteousness of God. Thus, a breach of contract by the Christians was ample legitimation for *the justa causa* of war, even on the soil of the Holy Land.[17]

From the great number of relevant observations, I would like to select an early example (bk. 13, chap. 18). This will also show that William's concept of a common juridical order in Palestine did not develop during the years spent writing the *Chronicon.* Rather, it was available from the start for a general assessment of events in the Orient. In 1126 a great battle took place between the Franks, led by King Baldwin II, and the Damascene, led by their Atabeg Tughtigin. William's comment was as follows: "In their zeal, incited by their King, the Franks attempted to take revenge for the injuries done to God as well as to themselves. But Tughtigin, too, encouraged and inflamed his men, asserting that they were leading a *just war* for their wives and children, and for freedom, which is even more important, and that they were defending the soil of their fathers against robbers."[18] By this example, William of Tyre placed right against right, thus gaining insight into the subjectivity of law—an insight that was totally alien to traditional Christian martial law, since there could be no *justa causa ex utraque parte,* no just cause of war on either side.[19] Because of this insight, the chronicler will have to be granted an eminent position in the history of medieval *jus gentium,* or international law.[20]

As I have already observed, the recognition of the opponent's claim to wage a just war in the same place put William in a difficult position. It resulted in a conflict of interests impossible to resolve with humane, legal means. Both the Christians and the Muslims made claims to the Holy Land by adducing historic rights. One party referred to the legacy of Christ, the other to that of their fathers. There, indeed, the decision of whether to favor

Christian or medieval international law lay in the hand of God. William must have been convinced that God did not seem to wish to resolve the conflict solely at the Muslims' expense. In his account of the battle of 1126, mentioned earlier, in which each party believed itself to be in the right, he even has next to God the apostle Paul intercede on behalf of the Muslims to save them from complete defeat. This battle was waged at the heavily symbolic place where Saul, the fierce persecutor of Christians, became Paul, the *doctor gentium,* the teacher of the peoples, or of the infidels.[21]

It becomes quite clear that William of Tyre considered the enmities on the soil of his fatherland as largely separate from the Western ideological context, attempting instead to present them as locally and regionally limited conflicts for domination. Both the Muslims and the Christians attacked and defended each other's territories and rights of ruling. What was at stake on either side was their respective security. Armed pilgrims had become armed settlers who had found a new home in the Orient. The concerns of this new homeland—such as freedom, family, and heritable property—acquired priority. These rights came to be considered as valuable objects of legal protection, for the defense of which no crusading spirit was necessary. An attack against property was a sufficiently just cause for war. William granted his Muslim neighbors the same material grounds for legitimate war, regardless of whether they happened to be allies or enemies. After all, both Muslims and Christians were bound to each other by living in the same area. William felt himself an Oriental, though a Latin Oriental, but he was, nevertheless, very much concerned not to suppress the other, Islamic, Orient. On the contrary, he wished to be part of it; he wished to participate in the culture, politics, and history of the country in which he was born. Thus, he wrote not only the history of the Latins but also that of the Muslims, from Mohammed up to his own times at about 1184, a testimony to his considerable integrative power. Unfortunately, this book, the so-called *Historia de gestis orientalium principum* or *Historia de orientalibus principibus et eorum actibus,* has been lost.[22] However, the very fact that such a work ever existed is, I believe, of extraordinary significance and, in addition, of great rarity. It was a work that for once broke through the Christian official "ideology of silence" which normally considered the deeds of unbelievers in the light of Christian history (which is salvation history) of no written value and their history, therefore, unworthy of any proper representation.[23]

Under all these circumstances, a war waged for purely religious reasons hardly fitted into William's concept of an enemy, much to the displeasure of the Old French translator. In no way did this translator do justice to his original, either with respect to his assessment of Islam and Muslim individuals, or concerning the common juridical system, or with regard to "orientalizing" the conflicts. As an exponent of Western ideology, the translator at one point makes what might be interpreted as an almost angry statement, changing the meaning of the original, when he writes that Christians fought *firstly* for the Faith, *then* for their lives, for their wives and for their children.[24]

The archbishop of Tyre, however, thought of religious war with bitterness and resignation, regardless of who waged it. In such wars, he wrote, humane laws were suspended, hatred and enmity were inflamed to the utmost, and, for lack of other reasons, the mere difference in religious traditions would perpetuate strife.[25] William noted these ideas in about 1175, at a time in which Saladin, sultan of both Egypt and Damascus and the leader in the Holy War (the jihad), was increasingly threatening Christian Jerusalem. The chances of a compromise between the two fronts were exceedingly slight under these circumstances. It is quite tragic that, under the spiritual and intellectual guidance of the archbishop of Tyre, the willingness of the Oriental Franks (at least of an old indigenous part of them) to negotiate was at its height, perhaps at exactly the time when the so-called Muslim *counter-crusade* had acquired its final contours.[26]

The Problem of Tolerance

Some years ago I described William's overall attitudes to Muslims—here summarized under the aspects of Islam, Muslim people, and law—as tolerance or, better and more correct, as *informal tolerance* combined with *dogmatic intolerance.*[27] Some idealists, who fought for arguments of pragmatism or *Realpolitik,* had problems with this description. Nobody, however, forced William to write what he did. No Muslim would likely ever have seen a line of his monumental work, which was composed in the first place for the king, his dynasty, and the Christian public of the court of Jerusalem. Thus, William could have written, had he wanted to, without regard to Muslims or any political or diplomatic affairs.

William's tolerance is not to be seen as opposed to pragmatism or *Realpolitik.* Medieval tolerance has always been a pragmatic tolerance; one tolerated more or less what could not be changed generally or could not be changed at the moment.[28] The problem is that William of course never used the Latin words *tolerantia* or *tolerare* in the modern sense of a conscious holding of other beliefs, doctrines, opinions, or thoughts. William used them only in the sense of enduring or suffering from hunger and thirst.[29] However, when he meant *tolerance,* he, as a well educated man of the "Renaissance of the twelfth century," expressed himself by using known synonyms from classical Latin—for example, *humanitas, moderatus, discretus, clementia, pacientia, pacificus*—and all these were notions that stood for *tolerance* in classical Roman as well as in early Christian thought.[30] So let me close in the words of the distinguished editor of William's *Chronicon,* Robert Huygens: "There can also be no doubt that his tolerance was more than the sum, however important, of political common sense and the lawyer's respect of agreements."[31]

Notes

Selected Bibliography

Index

Notes

Introduction

1. Given the vast bibliography on the history of the crusades and the development of toleration, I can mention only a few of the important recent general histories, such as Hans E. Mayer, *Geschichte der Kruezzüge* (Stuttgart: Kohlhammer, 1963, 1971, 1988; English translation, second edition. (Oxford: Oxford Univ. Press, 1988); Jonathan Riley-Smith, *The Crusades: A Short history* (New Haven: Yale Univ. Press, 1987), and most recently, Jean Richard, *Histoire des Croisades* (Paris: Fayard, 1996). All address these issues. Of special value are: Rainer C. Schwinges, *Kreuzzugsideologie und Toleranz: Studien zu Wilhelm von Tyrus,* Monographien zur Geschichte des Mittelalters, no. 15 (Stuttgart: Hiersemann, 1977) and *Muslims under Latin Rule,* ed. James M. Powell (Princeton: Princeton Univ. Press, 1990). For a brief discussion, see James M. Powell, "Rereading the Crusades," *International History Review,* 17 (1995), 663–69.

2. For a recent adaptation of this view in a postmodernist context, see Karen Armstrong, *Holy War: The Crusades and Their Impact on Today's World* (London: Macmillan, 1988).

3. Wallace K. Ferguson, *The Renaissance in Historical Thought* (Boston: Houghton Mifflin, 1948) is a classic discussion of this development.

4. James Brodman, *Ransoming Captives in Medieval Spain* (Philadelphia: Univ. of Pennsylvania Press, 1986).

5. Bernard Hamilton, *The Latin Church in the Crusader States: The Secular Church* (Aldershot: Ashgate, 1980)

6. Donald Queller and Thomas Madden, *The Fourth Crusade: The Conquest of Constantinople* 2d ed. (Philadelphia: Univ. of Pennsylvania Press, 1997), make a valuable contribution to this discussion.

1. Gender Bias and Religious Intolerance in Accounts of the "Massacres" of the First Crusade

1. John France, *Victory in the East: A Military History of the First Crusade* (Cambridge: Cambridge Univ. Press, 1994), 355; Randall Rogers, in *Latin Siege Warfare in the Twelfth Century* (Oxford: Clarendon Press, 1992), 191–92, makes much the same point about sieges in Spain.

2. See France, *Victory in the East,* 122–42, and Steven Runciman, *A History of the Crusades* (Cambridge: Cambridge Univ. Press, 1951), 1: 376.

3. Fulcher of Chartres, *Fulcheri Carnotensis Historia Hierosolymitana,* ed. Heinrich Hagenmeyer (Heidelberg: Carl Winter, 1913), 767–68; Fulcher of Chartres, *A History of the Expe-*

dition to Jerusalem, 1095–1127, trans. Frances Rita Ryan (Knoxville: Univ. of Tennessee Press, 1969), 280.

4. According to Raymond, "multa milia Sarracenorum ibi interfecit, multaque milia ad Antiochiam reducti venundati sunt. Et illos qui dum obpugnarentur timore mortis se ei reddiderant, liberos ire permisit"; Raymond d'Aguilers, *Liber,* ed. John Hugh and Laurita L. Hill (Paris: Geuthner, 1969), 91.

5. Albara was "capta et caede civium prorsus depopulata" (Hagenmeyer, *Fulcheri Carnotensis Historia Hierosolymitana,* 266).

6. In the Latin, "et occidit omnes Saracenos et Saracenas, maiores et minores, quos ibi repperit"; Anonymous, *Gesta Francorum et Aliorum Hierosolimitanorum* (New York: T. Nelson, 1962), 74–75. The phrase "maiores et minores" may perhaps be more accurately translated as "noble and lesser," as Peter Tudebode's translators do; Petrus Tudebodus, *Historia de Hierosolymitano Itinere,* trans. John H. and Laurita L. Hill (Philadelphia: American Philosophical Society, 1974), 94.

7. In an article analyzing the campaigns in this area, Thomas Asbridge says that Bohemond was "probably" at Albara, basing this on the testimony of Fulcher; see Asbridge, "The Principality of Antioch and the Jabal as-Summaq,", in *The First Crusade: Origins and Impact,* ed. Jonathan Phillips (Manchester: Manchester Univ. Press, 1997), 142–52, esp. 146. But as I show here, Fulcher is not a reliable source because he was in Edessa at the time, and neither Raymond nor (more importantly) the Anonymous makes any mention of his presence; because it was St. Gilles who installed his own man as bishop in Albara, bestowing half the town upon him—acts that one would have expected Bohemond to contest had he actually been there—it would seem likely that Fulcher was misinformed.

8. The axiom is perhaps best illustrated by the work of Matthew of Edessa, who claims that the siege of Nicaea ended with the Franks storming the city and massacring all the "infidels" within; see "The Chronicle of Matthew of Edessa," trans. Ara Edmond Dostourian, (Ph.D. diss. Rutgers University, 1972), 296. In fact, the defenders of Nicaea peacefully surrendered to the forces of emperor Alexius, and few crusaders were even allowed to enter the city; see the *Gesta Francorum,* 17–18; Raymond d'Aguilers, *Liber,* 44; *Fulcheri Carnotensis Historia Hierosolymitana,*188–89.

9. Runciman, *History of the Crusades,* 1: 257.

10. John Beeler, *Warfare in Feudal Europe, 730–1200* (Ithaca: Cornell Univ. Press, 1971), 210–12; Rogers, *Latin Siege Warfare,* 130–31, 135, 142.

11. Matthew Strickland, *War and Chivalry: The Conduct and Perception of War in England and Normandy, 1066–1217* (Cambridge; Cambridge Univ. Press, 1996), 222–24; [Beeler, Warfare in Feudal Europe, 44; Rogers, *Latin Siege Warfare,* 8–9, 101–102, 111–12, 116, 119, 248; John Gillingham, "1066 and the Introduction of Chivalry into England", in *Law and Government in Medieval England and Normandy: Essays in Honour of Sir James Holt,* ed. George Garnett and John Hudson (Cambridge: Cambridge Univ. Press, 1984), 49–50, n. 72; Bernard S. Bachrach, "Enforcement of the Forma Fidelitatis: The Techniques Used by Fulk Nerra, Count of the Angevins (987–1040)," in *Speculum* 59 (1984): 796–819, esp. 817; Ordericus Vitalis, *Historia Ecclesiastica,* ed. Marjorie Chibnall (Oxford: Clarendon Press, 1969–80), 6: 79, 443, 547.

12. *Gesta Francorum,* 79.

13. For a brief discussion of this event and the relevant sources, see France, *Victory in the East,* 314. It should be noted, however, that Raymond d'Aguilers makes it quite clear that the atrocities committed against prisoners took place only after the meager amount and unequal distribution of the booty became generally known (*Liber,* 98).

14. In Latin, "ne gregarii milites repente introirent, et pecunias civium violenter diriperent" (Ordericus Vitalis, *Historia Ecclesiastica*, 2: 214).

15. J.F. Verbruggen, *The Art of Warfare in Western Europe during the Middle Ages: From the Eighth Century to 1340*, trans. Sumner Willard and S.C.M. Southern (New York: North Holland, 1977), 299; Philippe Contamine, *War in the Middle Ages*, trans. Michael Jones (Oxford: Blackwell, 1984), 266. In Northern Europe, however, the practice of killing the men and selling the noncombatants into slavery was still quite common. Matthew Strickland, "Slaughter, Slavery or Ransom: The Impact of the Conquest on Conduct in Warfare," in *England in the Eleventh Century*, ed. Carola Hicks (Stamford, England: Paul Watkins, 1992), 47–48; Strickland, *War and Chivalry*, 304 ff.

16. Strickland, *War and Chivalry*, 30, 288. Fulcher himself was witness to the execution of prisoners in the West. Hagenmeyer, *Fulcheri Carnotensis Historia Hierosolymitana*, 120–21.

17. Penny Cole, *The Preaching of the Crusades to the Holy Land, 1095–1270* (Cambridge, Mass.: Medieval Academy of America, 1991), 16–17, 26–27.

18. France, *Victory in the East*, 355.

19. Penny Cole, " 'O God, the Heathen Have Come into Your Inheritance': The Theme of Religious Pollution in Crusade Documents, 1095–1188," in *Crusaders and Muslims in Twelfth-Century Syria*, ed. Maya Shatzmiller (Leiden: Brill, 1993), 84–111.

20. Cole, "Theme of Religious Pollution," 85, 91.

21. The Latin reads "in modum pristinae dignitatis reformaretur" (Hagenmeyer, *Fulcheri Carnotensis Historia Hierosolymitana*, 305–6); I use the translation of Ryan, (*Expedition to Jerusalem*, 123). For Fulcher's attitude to Islam in general, see also Ryan, 36–37.

22. The Latin is "Dies hec inquam tocius paganitatis exinanicio" (Raymond d'Aguilers, *Liber*, 151); the quotation from Revelation is on page 150.

23. Cole, "Theme of Religious Pollution," 111.

24. As Cole notes, "Theme of Religious Pollution," 92–93.

25. *Gesta Francorum*, xiii–iv.

26. *Gesta Francorum*, 91; the building was in fact the mosque of Omar (*Gesta Francorum*, 91 n. 2).

27. Raymond does not mention the corpses being removed by the inhabitants at all, and Fulcher turns the burial detail into Christians in search of concealed bezants (Hagenmeyer, *Fulcheri Carnotensis Historia Hierosolymitana*, 301–2). Peter Tudebode seems to have been influenced more by the *Gesta Francorum* than by Fulcher and Raymond on these issues, for although he makes extensive use of the pollution/purification metaphor (Cole, "Theme of Religious Pollution," 93–4), he does mention the prisoners and burial party (Petrus Tudebodus, Recueil des Historiens des Croisades Historiens Occidentaux, 3: 109–10); (hereafter cited as *RHC Occ*). However, until the vexed question of Tudebode's relationship with the *Gesta* is conclusively answered, it would be premature to speculate as to why he followed the *Gesta* rather than Raymond or Fulcher.

28. France, *Victory in the East*, 355; S. D. Goitein, "Contemporary Letters on the Capture of Jerusalem by the Crusaders," *Journal of Jewish Studies* 3 (1952): 162–77, and "Geniza Sources for the Crusader Period: A Survey," in *Outremer: Studies in the History of the Crusading Kingdom of Jerusalem* Presented to Joshua Prawer, ed. B. Z. Kedar et al. (Jerusalem: Izhak Ben-Zvi Institute, 1982), 306–22. Goitein also draws attention to the fact that the Jewish community in Jerusalem had been declining in numbers well before the First Crusade ("Geniza Sources", 307–8) and that the Jews of Ascalon remarked that unlike Muslim invaders, the crusaders did not rape women and boys when they took the city ("Geniza Sources," 312). More-

over, the documented cases of ransoms—which would have been extremely difficult to arrange and pay for—hint at much larger numbers of prisoners surviving as slaves; see Ibn al-Athir, in *Arab Historians of the Crusades,* trans. Francesco Gabrieli (London: Routledge, 1984), 11.

29. Albert of Aix, *Historia Hierosolymitana,* in *RHC Occ.* 4: 483–84; France, *Victory in the East,* 356.

30. Joshua Prawer, *The Crusaders' Kingdom: European Colonialism in the Middle Ages* (New York: Praeger, 1972), 15.

31. Stephen Runciman, "The First Crusade: Antioch to Ascalon", in *A History of the Crusades,* ed. Kenneth M. Setton, 6 vols. (Madison: Univ. of Wisconsin Press, 1969–89), 1: 337; Runciman, *History of the Crusades,* 1: 297.

32. Runciman, *History of the Crusades,* 1: 289; cf. *Gesta Francorum,* 92.

33. Terry Jones and Alan Ereira, *The Crusades* (New York: Facts on File, 1995), 74–75.

34. Jonathan Riley-Smith, *The First Crusaders, 1095–1131* (Cambridge: Cambridge Univ. Press, 1997), 44 ff.

35. Riley-Smith, *First Crusaders,* 45–46, 50.

36. Riley-Smith, *First Crusaders,* 47.

37. Hagenmeyer, *Fulcheri Carnotensis Historia Hierosolynitana,* 143–53; see also pp. 163–66, where Fulcher calls the antipope Wibert "stupid" and relates how his supporters attacked the crusaders from Northern France. Evidently, Fulcher's later association with Baldwin, whose brother Godfrey was a supporter of Henry IV (see Riley-Smith, *First Crusaders,* 96), does not seem to have curtailed his enthusiasm for reform.

38. Raymond d'Aguilers, *Liber,* 51, 108; Hagenmeyer, *Fulcheri Carnotensis Historia Hierosolynitana,* 117–18, 196–97, 222–23, 424, 621–24; *Gesta Francorum,* 58; Matthew of Edessa, *Chronicle,* x, 306–9, 324–25, 331, 347, 370–72

39. Raymond explicitly states that his work was undertaken to allay criticism of the crusade (*Liber,* 35); for Fulcher, see Hagenmeyer, *Fulcheri Carnotensis Historia Hierosolynitana,* 115–16, and Ryan, *Expedition to Jerusalem,* 21, 24–25.

40. However, by the time of the First Crusade, the idea that the pope could also personally lead these armies into battle was falling out of favor with the reforming canonists; see I. S. Robinson, *Authority and Resistance in the Investiture Controversy: The Polemical Literature of the Late Eleventh Century* (Manchester: Manchester Univ. Press, 1978), 99–100.

41. See Robinson, *Authority and Resistance,* 44, 96–103, 177–79.

42. The Latin reads "et quos sibi tunc obvios invenerunt gladiis ilico peremerunt" (Hagenmeyer, *Fulcheri Carnotensis Historia Hierosolynitana,* 402). Note that the "ilico," which could be translated as "there" or "immediately," may indicate that Fulcher is up to this point referring only to events on the wall.

43. Ryan, *Expedition to Jerusalem,* 154. The Latin continues: "quod cum Saraceni gentem nostram sic efferatam et urbem iam ab eis captam viderent, ubi diutius vivere putauerunt, illuc perpropere fugerunt. sed nec hic nec illic delitescere potuerint, quin morte promerita trucidarentur. pauci quidem de masculino sexu vitae reservati sunt. feminis quampluribus pepercerunt, ut molas manuales volviturae semper ancillarentur. quas cum cepissent, alii aliis tam pulchras quam turpes invicem vendebant et emebant, masculos quoque" (Hagenmeyer *Fulcheri Carnotensis Historia Hierosolynitana,* 402–3).

44. Ibn al-Qalanisi, *The Damascus Chronicle of the Crusades,* trans. H. A. R. Gibb (London: Luzac & Co., 1967), 49.

45. See, for example, *Gesta Francorum,* 47, 79, 91; Hagenmeyer, *Fulcheri Carnotensis Historia Hierosolynitana,* 234–35, 402–3; Ralph of Caen, *Gesta Tancredi,* in *RHC Occ.* 3: 655. That these authors are usually referring only to the men of the city is shown by the fact that they

often distinguish between the "cives" or "Saraceni" and their "mulieres" and "infantes": e.g., "Boamundus igitur fecit per interpretem loqui Saracenis maioribus, ut ipsi cum suis mulieribus et infantibus . . ." (Bohemond therefore spoke to the Saracens through an interpreter, so that they together with their wives and children . . .) *(Gesta Francorum, 79)*; and "Cives autem . . . rem prout erat arbitrati sunt. Relictis ergo domibus cum uxoribus et liberis temptabant effugere," ("The citizens, however, . . . considered the matter accordingly. They, therefore left their houses with their wives and children and tried to flee.") in William of Tyre, *Chronicon,* ed. R. B. C. Huygens, Corpus Christianorum Continuatio Medievalis, 63 (Turnhout: Brepols, 1986), 301.

46. Ralph of Caen, *Gesta Tancredi, 655.* Other examples are provided by Matthew of Edessa: "Then the Franks turned against Saruj and slaughtered the entire population of the town with the sword. They pillaged the whole town and carried off a countless number of young boys, girls and women to the city of Edessa"; and "Tripoli was set on fire and the inhabitants of the whole city were put to the sword, causing the streets to be inundated with blood. The Frankish forces seized an innumerable amount of gold and silver, and carried off a countless number of captives to their own country" *(Chronicle,* 320–21 and 367).

47. Runciman, *History of the Crusades,* 1: 234–35. More popularly oriented works that copy Runciman almost verbatim continue to be published; see, for example, Jones and Ereira, *The Crusades,* 60, and Ronald C. Finucane, *Soldiers of the Faith: Crusaders and Muslims at War* (London: J. M. Dent and Sons, 1983), 176.

48. The Latin text: "Cassianum, ipsius civitatis tyrannum, cum multis suorum militibus interfecimus, eorumque uxores et filios ac familias cum auro et argento et omnibus eorum possessionibus retinuimus" (Hagenmeyer, *Fulcheri Carnotensis Historia Hierosolymitana,* 262). I have followed the translation given by Ryan, (*Expedition to Jerusalem,* 109). A comparison of this letter with Fulcher's earlier description of events at Antioch shows even more clearly the dangers of confusing the crusaders' conduct towards the adult male "Turcos" and the rest of the population; Fulcher had written that "plebs vero nostra cuncta, quae in vicis aut domibus invenerunt, immoderate adripuerunt. at milites probitatis militiam tenuerunt, Turcos persequendo et occidendo" ("But all our people that they found in villages and houses they killed without mercy. But the knights kept to knightly honor, pursuing and killing the Turks.") (Hagenmeyer, *Fulcheri Carnotensis Historia Hierosolymitana,* 234–35).

49. I must admit that it is often difficult to establish with certainty why any particular author was exaggerating in any particular passage; but the examples I have provided seem to me to prove as clearly as possible that all of the factors that I have identified played some part in Ralph of Caen's description of the fall of Antioch (*Gesta Tancredi, 655*).

50. It should be noted that torture and extortion were parts of the common currency of war in both the West and the East; see Ibn al-Qalanisi, *Damascus Chronicle,* 78, and Strickland, *War and Chivalry,* 197–98.

51. *Gesta Francorum,* 58; Hagenmeyer, *Fulcheri Carnotensis Historia Hierosolymitana,* 243; Raymond d'Aguilers, *Liber,* 66: France, *Victory in the East,* 267–68.

52. Runciman states that at Antioch "The treasures and the arms found there were scattered or wantonly destroyed" (*History of the Crusades,* 1:235. Indeed, it is very difficult to imagine men like Tancred wantonly destroying wealth!

2. Prisoners of War during the Fatimid-Ayyubid Wars with the Crusaders

1. Maqrizi, *Itti'az al-Hunafa',* ed. M. H. M. Ahmad (Cairo: Lajnat Ihya' al-Turath al Islami, 1973), 3: 26, 54, 230, 234, 262.

2. Ibn al-Qalanisi, *Dhayl Ta'rikh Dimashq,* (ed.) H. F. Amedroz (Leiden: Brill, 1908), 140, 192, 197.

3. Maqrizi, *Itti'az,* 3: 32. For a full ramification of these events, see Steven Runciman, *A History of the Crusades,* (Cambridge: Cambridge Univ. Press, 1965), 2: 77–78.

4. Ibn al-Qalanisi, *Dhayl,* 149, 151; Maqrizi, *Itti'az,* 3: 37.

5. Ibn al-Qalanisi, *Dhayl,* 168; Runciman, *History of the Crusades,* 2: 95–96.

6. Abu Shama, *'Uyun al-Rawdatayn min Akhbar al-Dawlatayn,* (ed.) A. al-Bayumi (Damascus: Wizarat al-Thaqafah, 1992), 2: 201.

7. On other occasions in early Islam, however, orders given by military commanders to execute prisoners of war were not always obeyed. For a refusal to carry out such an order during a raid against Banu Jadhima in 8/630, see Ella Landau-Tasseron, "Features of the Pre-Conquest Muslim Armies in the Time of Muhammad," in *The Byzantine and Early Islamic Near East: States, Resources and Armies,* ed. Averil Cameron (Princeton: Princeton Univ. Press, 1995), 320–21. For the events of Badr, see Muhammad Hamidullah, *Muslim Conduct of State* (Hyderabad: Government Central Press, 1942), 129. The Muslim law is examined by E. Gräf in his "Religiöse und Rechtliche Vorstellungen über Kriegsgefangene in Islam und Christentum," *Die Welt des Islams,* n.s., 8 (1962–63): 89–139. Gräf provides extensive extracts and translations from Islamic legal literature. My work differs from his in the choice of sources, chronicles rather than legal writings.

8. Malcolm C. Lyons and D. E. P. Jackson, *Saladin: The Politics of the Holy War* (Cambridge: Cambridge Univ. Press, 1982), 131–32. 'Imad al-Din's motives were complex not necessarily humanistic. See Nasser Rabbat, "My Life with Saladin: The Memoirs of 'Imad al-Din al-Katib al-Isfahani," *Edebiyat* 7(1997): 282–83.

9. Al-Bundari, *Sana al-Barq al-Shami,* ed. R. Sesen (Beirut: Dar al Kitab al-Jadid, 1971), 1: 255 (this work is an abridgment of 'Imad al-Din's *Al-Barq al-Shami);* Abu Shama, *'Uyun,* 1: 38.

10. Al-Bundari, *Sana,* 307; Abu Shama, *'Uyun,* 1: 50–51; Maqrizi, *Kitab al-Suluk li-Ma'rifat Duwal al-Muluk,* ed. M. M. Ziyada, 2d. ed. (N.p., n.d.), 1: 1, 89, 90–91.

11. 'Imad al-Din, cited by Abu Shama, *'Uyun,* 2: 190, 191; Ibn Shaddad, *Al-Nawadir al-Sultaniyya wa-'l-Mahasin al-Yusufiyya,* ed. J. al-Din al-Shayyal (Cairo: al Mu'assasah al Misreyah al Amanah lil-Talif wa-al Anba, 1964), 177, 178, 179, 183, 184, 193.

12. The Mamluk historian al-Yanini explains that the massive slaughter committed by the Mamluks following the conquest of Acre in 1291 was a retaliation for the execution of the garrison of Acre by the crusaders one hundred years earlier. Clearly, this explanation is an apologetic one, an attempt to justify the cold-blooded killings of a defeated enemy who sued for amnesty. For these events, see D. P. Little, "The Fall of 'Akka in 690/1291," in *Studies in Islamic History and Civilization in Honour of Professor David Ayalon,* ed. M. Sharon (Jerusalem: Cana, 1986), 176–77.

13. Lyons and Jackson, *Saladin,* 185–87; G. Leiser, "The Crusader Raid in the Red Sea in 578/1182–3," *Journal of the American Research Center in Egypt* 14 (1977): 92, 94, 96.

14. 'Imad al-Din al-Isfahani, *Al-Fath al-Qussi fi 'l-Fath al-Qudusi,* ed. C. de Landberg (Leiden: Brill, 1888), 28–29. Ibn al-Athir provides a different explanation, saying that the killing of prisoners was aimed at enfeebling the military orders, see Alan Forey, "The Military Orders and the Ransoming of Captives from Islam (Twelfth to early Fourteenth Centuries)," *Studia Monastica* 33 (1991), reprinted in his *Military Orders and the Crusades* (Aldershot: Variorum, 1994), 259; Lyons and Jackson, *Saladin,* 265–66. However, the version of 'Imad al-Din, who was both an eyewitness of the events and a member of Saladin's inner circle, should be preferred. In fact these two explanations are not necessarily mutually exclusive; the military orders were ferocious

and heated enemies of the Muslims. But the concept that the Franks defiled the land was a sweeping one that did not distinguish between the military orders and other segments of the Latin society in the East.

15. Emmanuel Sivan, *L'Islam et la Croisade: Idéologie et propagande dans les réactions Musulmanes aux croisades* (Paris: Librairie d'Amerique et d'Orient, 1968), 62–63.

16. For the battle of Jacob's Ford, see Lyons and Jackson, *Saladin*, 142; Benjamin Z. Kedar, *Crusade and Mission* (Princeton: Princeton Univ. Press, 1984), 76. For execution of apostates, see Yaakov Lev, "The Suppression of Crime, the Supervision of Markets, and Urban Society in the Egyptian Capital during the Tenth and Eleventh Centuries," *Mediterranean Historical Review* 3 (1988); 83.

17. Abu Shama, *'Uyun*, 2: 30–31.

18. For instance, he forbade his young sons, or their servants, to kill prisoners, fearing that this would have adverse influence on their moral development. See 'Imad al-Din, *Al-Fath*, 326, and Ibn Shaddad, *Al-Nawadir*, 156 (slightly different). cf.: Lyons and Jackson, *Saladin*, 325 (who follow Ibn Shaddad).

19. For other highly publicized acts of generosity toward prisoners, see 'Imad al-Din, *Al-Fath*, 325–26; also Lyons and Jackson, *Saladin*, 325. 'Imad al-Din tells a story of a release of an elderly prisoner by Saladin. This person and other pilgrims were captured on a naval raid. But the release of the Lady of Burzey on the request of her sister, Sibylla, the wife of Bohemond, was politically motivated. See Ibn Wasil, *Mufarrij al-Kurub fi Akhbar Bani Ayyub*, ed. J. al-Din al-Shayyal (Cairo: al Matba'ah al-Amiriyah, 1957), 2: 297; Lyons and Jackson, *Saladin*, 289.

20. Al-Bundari, *Sana*, 328–29; Runciman, *History of the Crusades*, 2: 420; Lyons and Jackson, *Saladin*, 140.

21. For two such cases see William of Tyre, *History of Deeds Done Beyond the Sea*, translated into English and annotated by E. A. Babcock and A. C. Krey (New York: Columbia Univ. Press, 1943), 2: 252–53; and George T. Beech, "A Norman Adventurer in the East: Richard of Salerno, 1097–1112," *Anglo-Norman Studies* 15 (1992): 25–40, esp. 33–34.

22. Maqrizi, *Itti'az*, 3: 46.

23. Maqrizi, *Itti'az*, 3: 206, 224, 230, 231. For division of spoils, see Ibn al-Tuwayr, *Nuzhat al-Muqlatayn fi Akhbar al-Dawlatayn*, ed. A. F. Sayyid (Wiesbaden: Steiner, 1992), 98.

24. Maqrizi, *Itti'az*, 3: 102.

25. Maqrizi, *Itti'az*, 1: 76, 77–81 passim. For the rebellion of Abu Yazid, see Heinz Halm, *The Empire of the Mahdi: The Rise of the Fatimids*, trans. by M. Bonner (Leiden: Brill, 1996), 298–322. For the other events, see Kindi, *Governors and Judges of Egypt*, ed. R. Guest (Leiden: Brill, 1912), 276; al-Antaki, *Kitab al-Ta'rikh*, ed. L. Shaykhu (Beirut: Matba' at al-Aba al-Yasu'iyin, 1909), 76.

26. The most famous Muslim prisoner held by the Byzantines was Harun ibn Yahya (fl. Ca. 912). There is an extensive research literature dealing with him. See, for example, the studies of A. A. Vasiliev, G. Ostrogorsky, Henri Grégoire, and M. Izeddin republished by F. Sezgin, ed., in *Islamic Geography* 136 (1994). For more recent scholarship, see Marius Canard, "Les relations politiques et sociales entre Byzance et les Arabes," *Dumbarton Oaks Papers* 18 (1964): 45–46. Occasionally, Muslim prisoners were pressed into military service; see Canard, "Les relations," 43, and "Deux episodes des relations diplomatiques Arabo-Byzantines au Xe siècle," *Byzance et les musulmans du Proche Orient* (Aldershot: Variorum, 1973), 56, n. 3.

27. Romilly J. H. Jenkins, "The Emperor Alexander and the Saracen Prisoners," reprinted in his *Studies on Byzantine History of the Ninth and Tenth Centuries* (Aldershot: Variorum, 1970); Joel L. Kraemer, *Humanism in the Renaissance of Islam* (Leiden: Brill, 1986), 76.

28. Maqrizi, *Kitab al-Mawa'iz wa-'l-I'tibar bi-Dhikr al-Khitat wa-'l-Athar* (Bulaq, 1324 H.), 3: 5–7, 305; 4: 56 (hereafter cited as *Khitat*).

29. Ibn al-Tuwayr, *Nuzhat,* 94; Maqrizi, *Khitat,* 3: 314. For *munakhat,* see Ibn al-Tuwayr, *Nuzhat,* 138, 141–42; Maqrizi, *Khitat,* 2: 311. For workshops in the complex of the Fatimid palaces, see Maqrizi, *Khitat,* 2: 278; 3: 305.

30. Ibn Zubayr, *Kitab al-Dhakha'ir wa-'l-Tuhaf,* ed. M. Hamid Allah (Kuwait: n.p., 1959), 150; Maqrizi, *Itti'az,* 2: 40.

31. Ibn Jubayr, *Rihla,* ed. W. Wright, 2d ed., rev. M. J. De Goeje (Leiden: Brill, 1907), 52; translation by R. J. C. Broadhurst, *The Travels of Ibn Jubayr* (London: Cape, 1952), 43.

32. Neil D. MacKenzie, *Ayyubid Cairo: A Topographical Study* (Cairo: American University of Cairo Press, 1992), 61, and the sources quoted by him.

33. 'Imad al-Din, *Al-Fath,* 118; Maqrizi, *Suluk,* 1: 2: 305; Lyons and Jackson, *Saladin,* 346.

34. See L. Fernandes, "On Conducting the Affairs of the State: A Guideline of the Fourteenth Century", *Annales Islamologiques* 24 (1988): 81–91, esp. 84; Nasser O. Rabbat, *The Citadel of Cairo* (Leiden: Brill, 1995), 241, n. 30.

35. Ellen G. Friedman, *Spanish Captives in North Africa in the Early Modern Age* (Madison: Univ. of Wisconsin Press, 1968), 67–75.

36. For the *zanj* and their rebellion, see Alexandre Popovic, *La Révolte des esclaves en iraq au IIIe/IXe siècles,* (Paris: Geuthner, 1976). For Tunisia, see M. Talbi, "Law and Economy in Ifriqiya (Tunisia) in the Third Islamic Century: Agriculture and the Role of Slaves in the Country's Economy," in *The Islamic Middle East, 700–1900: Studies in Economic and Social History,* ed. Abraham L. Udovitch (Princeton: Princeton Univ. Press, 1981), 209–49. For al-Ahsa', see Nasir-i Khusraw, *Book of Travels (Safarname),* trans. W. M. Thackston, Jr. (Albany, N.Y.: Bibliotheca Persica, 1986), 87. He says that 30,000 Abyssinians and Zanzibari slaves were employed in the agriculture of the al-Ahsa' oasis. This figure seems to be highly exaggerated. The *zanj* slaves were acquired through the slave trade. In Tunisia most of the slaves were prisoners of war and raids conducted in the Mediterranean. In other cases in medieval Islam, the employment of servile force-work in irrigation projects and agriculture was far less extensive than in ninth-century Iraq and Tunisia. For the consequences of the employment of slaves and other servile people *(mawali)* by the Umayyads on their agricultural estates in Arabia, see M. J. Kister, "The Battle of the Harra: Some Socio-Economic Aspects," in *Studies in Memory of Gaston Wiet,* ed. M. Rosen-Ayalon (Jerusalem: Institute of Asian and African Studies, Hebrew University of Jerusalem, 1977), 33–51, esp. 44. For the employment of prisoners of raids and slaves on large agricultural estates in the Ottoman period, see Halil Inalcik, "Servile Labor in the Ottoman Empire," in *Mutual Effects of Islamic and Judeo-Christian Worlds,* ed. Abraham Ascher et al. (New York, 1980), 30–35.

37. Qadi al-Nu'man, *Risalat Ifttitah al-Da'wa,* ed. W. al-Qadi (Beirut: Dar al-Thaqafah, 1970), 207, 215–16; Maqrizi, *Itti'az,* 1: 63, 66.

38. For the fate of the Fatimid family in the Ayyubid period, see Maqrizi, *Khitat,* 2: 394, 395–96.

39. For example, the Fatimid ruler, al-Mansur, released and conferred honors on the womenfolk of his archenemy, the rebel Abu Yazid, whom he captured in Qayrawan. See Maqrizi, *Itti'az,* 1: 83.

40. For example, when the Abbasid caliph al-Mu'tasim put down a peasant uprising in Egypt, he massacred the men and took children and women into captivity. See al-Antaki, *Kitab,* 57. For the massacre committed by the crusaders after the conquest of Jerusalem, see John France, *Victory in the East: A Military History of the First Crusade,* (Cambridge: Cambridge Univ. Press, 1994), 356. However, in 1101, during the conquest of Caesarea by the crusaders,

women were spared because, as Fulcher of Chartres put it, "they could always be used to turn the hand mills"; quoted by Yvonne Friedman in "The Ransom of Captives in the Latin Kingdom of Jerusalem," in *Autour de la première croisade,* ed. Michel Balard (Paris: Sorbonne, 1996), 181.

41. For examples of bedouin warfare from the bedouin insurrection of 1024–1025 in Palestine, see Musabbihi, *Akhbar Misr,* ed. A. F. Sayyid and Th. Bianquis (Cairo: al-Ma'had al-'Ilmi al-Faransi lil-Athar al-Sharqiyah, 1978), 35, 51, 83. For a wider treatment of the fate of civilian populations in this period, see E. Bareket, "Personal Adversities of Jews during the Period of the Fatimid Wars in Eleventh Century Palestine," in *War and Society in the Eastern Mediterranean, 7th-15th Centuries,* ed. Yaakov Lev (Leiden: Brill, 1997), 153–63.

42. Such events took place in the Byzantine raid on Damietta in 853, during the conquest of Aleppo in 962, and following the offensive along the Muslim-Byzantine border in Syria in 968. See Ibn al-'Adim, *Zubdat al-Halab min Ta'rikh Halab,* ed. S. al-Dahhan, 3 vols. (Damascus: al-Ma'had al-Faransi bi-Dimashq, 1951–1968), 1: 140, 159.

43. For these aspects, see Eric McGeer, *Sowing the Dragon's Teeth: Byzantine Warfare in the Tenth Century* (Washington, D.C.: Dumbarton Oaks Papers, 1995), 365–68; Peter Charanis, "The Transfer of Population as a Policy in the Byzantine Empire," *Comparative Studies in Society and History* 3 (1961): 140–54.

44. M. A. Friedman, *Jewish Polygyny in the Middle Ages: New Documents from the Cairo Geniza* (Jerusalem: University of Tel Aviv, 1986), 4, 95–105, 269, 347 [in Hebrew]. The most interesting document published by Friedman in his book concerns the ransom of a Jewish woman, a survivor of the massacre perpetuated by the Mamluks in Acre in 1291. She was ransomed by Avraham ben Shlomo, who held a position at the court, and the document in question contains the draft of the marriage agreement between them. For women preferring to commit suicide rather than to fall into enemy hands, see Yvonne Friedman, "Women in Captivity and Their Ransom during the Crusader Period," in *Cross Cultural Convergences in the Crusader Period; Essays Presented to Aryeh Grabois,* ed. Michael Goodich et al. (New York: Peter Lang, 1995), 75–118.

45. S. D. Goitein, *Palestinian Jewry in Early Islamic and Crusader Times* (Jerusalem: Yad Izhak Ben Zvi Institute, 1980), 306–12 [in Hebrew]. Rather surprisingly, the Jews who dealt with the ransom of captives following the conquest of Jerusalem by the crusaders in 1099 note that women were not abused in captivity. See Solomon D. Goitein, "Geniza Sources for the Crusader Period: A Survey," in *Outremer: Studies in the History of the Crusading Kingdom of Jerusalem, Presented to Joshua Prawer,* eds. Benjamin Z. Kedar et al. (Jerusalem: Yad Izhak Ben-Zvi, 1982), 312.

46. English translation by Arthur J. Arberry, *The Koran Interpreted;* 2 vols. (London: Allen & Unwin, 1955), 1: 205; 2: 220.

47. Hamidullah, *Muslim Conduct of State,* 128.

48. Patricia Crone, *Roman, Provincial and Islamic Law* (Cambridge: Cambridge Univ. Press, 1987), 58; Fred M. Donner, *The Early Islamic Conquests* (Princeton: Princeton Univ. Press, 1981), 89.

49. Michael G. Morony, *Iraq after the Muslim Conquest* (Princeton: Princeton Univ. Press, 1984), 194–95, 224–25, 226–28.

50. These regiments consisted of infantry *(hamra')* and cavalry *(asawira).* See, Morony, *Iraq after the Muslim Conquest,* index.

51. *Encyclopedia of Islam,* 2d ed., s.v. "Fida'" and "Lamas-Su."

52. al-Tabari, *The History of al-Tabari,* trans. Joel L. Kraemer (Albany: State University of New York Press, 1989), 34, 38–44, 138–41. Both accounts are summarized by late medieval historians; see Ibn al-'Adim, *Bughyat al-Talab fi Ta'rikh Halab,* ed. S. Zakkar (Damascus,

1988), 2: 758–60; Al-Nuwayri, *Nihayat al-Arab fi Funun al-Adab,* (Cairo: al-Mu'assasah al-Misrihah, 1984), 22: 269–70, 287–88.

53. Maqrizi, *Khitat,* 3: 311–12. Maqrizi's information on *fida'* is derived from Mas'udi's *Kitab al-Tanbya wa-'l-Ashraf,* (Beirut: Maktabah Khayyat, 1965), 189–99. For the exchange of prisoners of war between the Hamdanid rulers and the Byzantines, see Marius Canard, *Histoire de la dynastie des Hamdanides de Jazira et la Syrie* (Paris: Presses Universitaires de France, 1935), 1: 757–60, 823–29. Mas'udi's information and other sources are discussed by A. Elad in "The Coastal Cities of Palestine during the Early Middle Ages," *The Jerusalem Cathedra* (Jerusalem: Ben Zvi Institute, 1982), 2: 160. For the exchanges of prisoners between Byzantium and the Egyptian rulers of the ninth and tenth centuries, see Ibn al-Muqaffa', *History of the Patriarchs of the Egyptian Church,* trans. A. S. Atiya and Y. 'Abd al-Masih (Cairo, 1948), 2: 75–76 [Arabic], 110–11 [English]; Ibn Sa'id, *Kitab al-Mughrib fi Hula al-Maghrib,* ed. K. L. Tallqvist (Leiden: Brill, 1899), 18, 19, 22, 23. For a French translation of Muhammad ibn Tughj's letter to Byzantium, see Marius Canard, "Une lettre de Muhammad ibn Tugj al-Ihsid émir d'Egpte à l'empereur Romain Lécapèn," reprinted in his *Byzance et les musulmans.*

54. Al-Qadi al-Nu'man, *Kitab al-Majalis wa-'l-Musayyarat,* ed. H. al-Faqi et al. (Tunis, 1978), 175, 180. For this war see S. M. Stern, "An Embassy of the Byzantine Emperor to the Fatimid Caliph al-Mu'izz," *Byzantion* 20 (1950): 209–58; Halm, *Empire of the Mahdi,* 392–99.

55. For these aspects of al-Mu'izz's policy, see Yaakov Lev, "The Fatimid Navy, Byzantium and the Mediterranean Sea, 909–1036 C.E./297–427 A.H.," *Byzantion* 54 (1984): 235–36.

56. Dhahabi, "Ta'rikh al-Islam," MS London, British Library, Or. 48, fol. 16a-b; Ibn Taghribirdi, *Al-Nujum al-Zahira fi Muluk Misr wa-'l-Qahira* (Cairo: n.p., 1932–1950, 4: 151–52; Franz Dölger, *Regesten der Kaiserurkunden des Oströmischen Reiches von 565–1435,* three parts in one volume (reprint, Hildesheim: Gerstenberg, 1967), 1: 98–99, n. 769.

57. Al-Antaki, *Kitab,* 270–71.

58. Ibn Zubayr, *Kitab,* 74–75; Maqrizi, *Itti'az,* 2: 194.

59. Maqrizi, *Itti'az,* 2: 230–31, 234, and *Kitab al-Muqaffa al-Kabir,* ed. M. Yalaoui (Beirut: Dar al-Garb al-Islam, 1991), 3: 383–89, 425–26.

60. Maqrizi, *Itti'az,* 3: 83.

61. Maqrizi, *Itti'az,* 3: 233, 234. On earlier occasions the Byzantines had intervened with the Fatimids on behalf of the crusaders. In 1102 the army of the crusader kingdom of Jerusalem was defeated by the Fatimids at the battle of Ramla. The Byzantines offered the Fatimids high payment for the release of Frankish prisoners. See Ralph-Johannes Lilie, *Byzantium and the Crusader States,* trans. J. C. Morris and Jean E. Ridings (Oxford: Clarendon Press, 1993), 71.

62. Abu Shama, *'Uyun,* 2: 249; Lyons and Jackson, *Saladin,* 328–333.

63. Al-Bundari, *Sana,* 258–59.

64. Al-Bundari, *Sana,* 257; cf. Forey, "Military Orders," 265.

65. Maqrizi, *Suluk,* 95, 158; Charles M. Brand, "The Byzantines and Saladin, 1185–1192: Opponents of the Third Crusade," *Speculum* 37 (1962); 170; Lilie, *Byzantium and the Crusader States,* 225, 234.

66. An example is the truce signed, following Nur al-Din's death in 1174, between the Zenkids and the Franks and Saladin's criticism of it, see Abu Shama, *'Uyun,* 1: 406.

67. Abu Shama, *'Uyun,* 2: 16; Lyons and Jackson, *Saladin,* 151.

68. Abu Shama, *'Uyun,* 2: 148, 150, 154, 155.

69. For Mamluk attempts to release Muslim prisoners, see J. Wansborough, "A Mamluk Ambassador to Venice in 913/1507," *Bulletin. School of Oriental and African Studies* 26 (1963): 514–15. For Ottomans, see N. Vatin, "Note sur l'attitude des sultans ottomans et de

leurs sujets face à la captivité des leurs en terre chrétienne" and "Deux documents sur la libéra-
tion de musulmans captifs chez les Francs (1573)," both in *Wiener Zeitschrift für die Kunde des
Morgenlandes:* vol. 82 (1992), 375–95, and vol. 83 (1993), 223–32, respectively. Friedman's
conclusion that in seventeenth century North Africa "there was no large scale Muslim ransoming effort" (105) is a result of a study of Spanish archival material, not of Arabic sources, and
must be treated cautiously.

70. Jacob Mann, *The Jews in Egypt and in Palestine under the Fatimid Caliphs* (reprint,
Oxford: Oxford Univ. Press, 1969), 1: 87–94; Solomon D. Goitein, *A Mediterranean Society*
(Berkeley: Univ. of California Press, 1967–1971), 1: 327–30, 2: 137–38.

71. Goitein, *Mediterranean Society,* 2: 137.

72. Mann, *Jews in Egypt and in Palestine,* 1: 88–92. For dating of these documents, see E.
Bareket, *The Jewish Leadership in Fustat in the First Half of the Eleventh Century* (Tel Aviv:
University of Tel Aviv, 1995), 71 [in Hebrew].

73. M. Ben-Sasson, *The Emergence of the Local Jewish Community in the Muslim World:
Qayrawan, 800–1057* (Jerusalem: Y. L. Magness, 1996), 181–83, [in Hebrew].

74. Mann, *Jews in Egypt and in Palestine,* 1: 89; Bareket, *Jewish Leadership in Fustat,* 61.

75. Goitein, "Geniza Sources," 309–10, 313–14, 315–16.

76. This topic is a subject of Giulio Cipollone's monumental work *Cristianità-Islam: Cattività e liberazione in nome di Dio: Il tempo di Innocenzo III dopo "il 1187"* (Rome: Università
gregoriana, 1992). I would like to thank Professor Cipollone for sending me a copy of his book.

77. G. Le Strange, *Palestine under the Moslems* (London: Alexander Watts, 1890), 23.

78. For such cases, see Demetrios J. Constantelos, *Byzantine Philanthropy and Social Wel-
fare* (New Brunswick, N.J.: Rutgers Univ. Press, 1968), 25, 71, 99–100, 110, 268, 280, and
Poverty, Society and Philanthropy in the Late Mediaeval Greek World (New Brunswick, N.J.:
Rutgers Univ. Press, 1992), 113–14; Canard, "Deux Episodes," 59, and "Les Relations," 38;
Jenkins, "Leo Choerosphactes and the Saracen Vizier" and "The Mission of St. Demetrianus of
Cyprus to Bagdad," both in his *Studies on Byzantine History.*

79. James W. Brodman, *Ransoming of Captives in Crusader Spain* (Philadelphia: Univ. of
Pennsylvania Press, 1986); Friedman, *Spanish Captives in North Africa.*

80. For prices and salaries in the High Middle Ages, see Eliahu Ashtor, *A Social and Economic History of the Near East in the Middle Ages* (Berkeley: Univ. of California Press, 1976),
200–201; Goitein, *Mediterranean Society,* 1: 89–90, 95–96.

81. Maqrizi, *Kitab al-Muqaffa,* 6: 246.

82. Usama ibn Munqidh, *Kitab al-I'tibar,* tran. P. K. Hitti as *An Arab-Syrian Gentleman
and Warrior in the Period of the Crusaders* (New York: Columbia University Press, 1929), 110.

83. Safadi, *Kitab al-Wafi bi-'l-Wafayat,* ed. A. F. Sayyid (Wiesbaden: Steiner, 1962), 18:
345, 379–80.

84. Jean-Michel Mouton, *Damas et sa principauté sous les saljoukides et les bourides,
468–549/1076–1154 (Cairo: Institut français d'archéologie orientale, 1994), 87–88.

3. From Intolerance to Tolerance: The Humanitarian Way, 1187–1216

1. Giulio Cipollone, *Cristianità-Islam: Cattività e liberazione in nome di Dio. Il tempo di
Innocenzo III dopo "il 1187,"* Miscellanea Historiae Pontificiae, 60 (Rome: Università gregoriana, 1992; repr. 1996); 2: 449–50.

2. *Relations internationales* 63 (1990), La frontière 1: 225–312; *Relations internationales*

64 (1990), La frontière 2: 341–49; James M. Powell, "The Papacy and the Muslim Frontier," in *Muslims under Latin Rule (1100–1300)* (Princeton: Princeton Univ. Press, 1990), 175–204.

3. See surahs: 2: 62, 120–21, 148, 256; 4: 94, 162; 5: 48, 69; 76: 4–8; 9: 6, 30–33; 22: 67; 60: 8–9.

4. Cipollone, *Cristianità-Islam,* 47 ff.

5. Cipollone, *Cristianità-Islam,* 51–53.

6. A. Fattal, *Le statut légal des non-musulmans en pays d'Islam* (Beirut: Imprimerie catholique, 1958), 77–81.

7. Baha ad-Din ibn Saddad, "Anecdotes et beaux traits de la vie du Sultan Youssof (Salah ed-Din)," in *Recueil des historiens des Croisades. Historiens Orientaux* [hereafter cited as *RHC Or.*], 3: 21.

8. 'Imad ad-Din al-Isfahani, *Conquête de la Syrie et de la Palestine par Saladin,* trans. H. Massé, Documents relatifs à l'histoire des Croisades, 10 (Paris: Geuthner, 1972). This is the privileged source for our study.

9. Cipollone, *Cristianità-Islam,* 122–23.

10. Cipollone, *Cristianità-Islam,* 135 ff.

11. *Recueil des historiens des Croisades. Hist. Occidentaux* [hereafter cited as *RHC Occ.*], 3: 15, 57, 123, 170, 174, 176, 196.

12. George B. Flahiff, "Deus non vult: A Critic of the Third Crusade," *Medieval Studies* 9 (1947): 162–88; Palmer A. Throop, "Criticism of Papal Crusade Policy in Old French and Provençal," *Speculum* 21 (1946): 1–23; Elizabeth Siberry, *Criticism of Crusading (1095–1274)* (Oxford: Oxford Univ. Press, 1985). Among Muslims open to tolerance, one can mention Abd al-Qadir al Jilani, who died in 1166.

13. Flahiff, "Deus non vult," 162–88.

14. Francesco Gabrieli, "Ibn Hawqal and the Arabs of Sicily," *Rivista degli Studi Orientali* 36 (1961): 247–48.

15. Extreme religious violence applied by the High Priests during the capital condemnation of Jesus Christ remains a historic event of an absolute exemplary nature.

16. Giulio Cipollone, "Innocenzo III e i Saraceni: Atteggiamenti differenziati (1198–99)," *Acta Historica et Archaeologica Mediaevalia* 9 (1988): 167–88.

17. For bibliographic references and historic sources, see Cipollone, *Cristianità-Islam,* 393–447.

18. It is the first time in the history that the UN, UNESCO, and the EEC came together on the same theme for the International Year: Tolerance.

19. Cipollone, *Cristianità-Islam,* 133.

20. Cipollone, *Cristianità-Islam,* 453.

21. Baha'ad-Din, *Anecdotes,* in *RHC Or,* 3: 347–48.

4. The Rhetoric of Ransoming: A Contribution to the
Debate over Crusading in Medieval Iberia

1. Reilly cites the "fundamentalist empire of the Murabits," and quotes a Muwahhid source that brags: "The infidel without would taste the wrath of an aroused and victorious Islam." On the other hand, with respect to Pedro of Aragon's siege of Huesca in 1096, he barely acknowledges the presence of French troops and fails to mention any papal participation. See Bernard Reilly, *The Medieval Spains* (Cambridge: Cambridge Univ. Press, 1993), 97, 106, 130. Similarly, crusading ideology is studiously ignored in his explication of Alfonso I of Aragon's

campaigns of 1118–24, although he acknowledges that Gelasius II has raised the effort to the level of a "crusade." See Bernard Reilly, *The Conquest of Christian and Muslim Spain* (Cambridge, Mass.: Blackwell, 1992), 160–62.

2. James Powers summarizes municipal warfare in this fashion: "The lands to be won, the spoils to be divided, the hopes and opportunities of the battlefield, all these became infused in the municipal tradition . . . The towns and their armies contributed to the restless, avaricious mind-set, which gloried and bedeviled Castile in the Early Modern Era"; see *A Society Organized for War: The Iberian Municipal Militias in the Central Middle Ages, 1000–1284* (Berkeley and Los Angeles: Univ. of California Press, 1988), 213.

3. Robert I. Burns, *Islam Under the Crusaders: Colonial Survival in the Thirteenth-Century Kingdom of Valencia* (Princeton: Princeton Univ. Press, 1973), xiii.

4. Angus MacKay, *Spain in the Middle Ages: From Frontier to Empire, 1000–1500* (New York: St. Martin's, 1977), 30, 59, 79, 101–3.

5. Derek W. Lomax, *The Reconquest of Spain* (London: Longman, 1978), 40, 59, 60, 62.

6. Thomas N. Bisson, *The Medieval Crown of Aragon: A Short History* (New York: Oxford Univ. Press, 1986), 14–15, 64, 66, 70.

7. For *alfaqueques* and *exeas,* see my "Municipal Ransoming Law on the Medieval Spanish Frontier," *Speculum* 60 (1985): 318–30; and Maria Teresa Ferrer i Mallol, "La redempcio de captius a la Corona Catalano-Aragonesa (segle XIV)," *Anuario de estudios medievales* 15 (1985): 262–66. The position of ransomer was a source of profit, making it a concession that could be sold off by the monarch. For example, Bernat Marcús of Barcelona received in 1178 the office of *mostolaf* from King Alfonse II, which gave him exclusive right to exchange Muslim and Christian captives, a license for which he was willing to pay the king 500 sous; Stephen P. Bensch, "From Prizes of War to Domestic Merchandise: The Changing Face of Slavery in Catalonia and Aragon, 1000–1300," *Viator* 25 (1994): 73, 87.

8. Such, for example, is the view of Charles-Emmanual Dufourcq in *L'Espagne catalane et le Maghrib aux XIIIe et XIVe siècles* (Paris: Presses Universitaires de France, 1966), 71–76; and more recently of Olivia Remie Constable, *Trade and Traders in Muslim Spain: The Commercial Realignment of the Iberian Peninsula, 900–1500* (New York: Cambridge Univ. Press, 1994), 203–8, 234–35.

9. For a discussion, see my *Ransoming Captives in Crusader Spain: The Order of Merced on the Christian-Islamic Frontier* (Philadelphia: Univ. of Pennsylvania Press, 1986), 10–12.

10. See my "Military Redemptionism and the Castilian Reconquest, 1180–1250," *Military Affairs* 44 (1980), 24–27; Regina Sáinz de la Maza Lasoli, *La Orden de Santiago en la Corona de Aragón* (Saragossa: Institución "Fernando el Catolico," 1980), 123–28.

11. See Cipollone's *Cristianità-Islam: Cattività e liberazione in nome de Dio. Il tempo di Innocenzo III dopo "il 1187"* (Rome: Università gregoriana, 1992), 402–4, 449–53.

12. See my "The Trinitarian and Mercedarian Orders: A Study of Religious Redemptionism in the Thirteenth Century," (Ph.D. diss.; University of Virginia, 1974), 212–40. For the Trinitarians in Valencia, see Robert I. Burns, S.J., *The Crusader Kingdom of Valencia: Reconstruction on a Thirteenth-Century Frontier* (Cambridge, Mass.: Harvard Univ. Press, 1967), 1: 238–41.

13. The rivalry between the Mercedarians and Trinitarians came to a head in 1358 when Pope Innocent VI, citing the casualties suffered by both orders in the Black Death, attempted to merge the two ransoming orders under the control of the Trinitarian master. The consolidation was blocked by King Peter the Ceremonious on the ground that the Mercedarians had strong ancestral ties to his dynasty. Regina Sáinz de la Maza Lasoli, "Los Mercedarios en la Corona de Aragón," *Miscellania de textos medievals* 4 (1988): 259–60, n. 4.

14. For a general survey of the development of the Mercedarian Order, see Brodman, *Ransoming Captives,* 15–40.

15. Arxiu de Catedral de Barcelona, DC(d) 1246, cap. 14 (October 29, 1231); Arxiu de la Corona d'Aragó, Monacales, vol. 2676, 390rv (Aug. 6, 1232) (hereafter cited as ACA); Archivo Histórico Nacional, Clero, carp. 76, 11 (January 3, 1234) (hereafter cited as AHN).

16. Brodman, *Ransoming Captives,* 128.

17. ACA, Monacales, vol. 2676, 530rv and vol. 2662, 61–62; Manuel Mariano Ribera, *Centuria primera del real y militar orden de Nuestra Señora de la Merced redempción de cautivos cristianos* (Barcelona: Pablo Campins, 1726), 172–73.

18. ACA, Monacales, A Rollo 1, ORM, 20; vol. 2676, 216rv.

19. *Bullarium coelestis ac regalis ordinis B. Mariae Virginis de Mercede Redemptionis Captivorum,* ed. José Linás y Aznor (Barcelona: Rafael Figuero, 1696), 6–7.

20. For a study of *pro anima* bequests, see my "What is a Soul Worth? *Pro anima* Bequests in the Municipal Legislation of Reconquest Spain," *Medievalia et Humanistica: Studies in Medieval and Renaissance Culture,* ed. Paul Maurice Clogan, n.s., 20 (1994), 15–23.

21. Among the studies of poverty and assistance in the Middle Ages are Brian Tierney, *Medieval Poor Law: A Sketch of Canonical Theory and Its Application in England* (Berkeley and Los Angeles: Univ. of California Press, 1959); Michel Mollat, *The Poor in the Middle Ages: An Essay in Social History,* trans. Arthur Goldhammer (New Haven: Yale Univ. Press, 1986); Lester K. Little, *Religious Poverty and the Profit Economy in Medieval Europe* (Ithaca: Cornell Univ. Press, 1978); and Bronislaw Geremek, *Poverty: A History,* trans. Agnieszka Kolakowska (Cambridge, Mass.: Blackwell, 1994).

22. *Bullarium ordinis de mercede,* 6–7; ACA, Monacales, vol. 2676, 56rv.

23. For the collection of alms and the use of captives, see Brodman, *Ransoming Captives,* 96–101.

24. ACA, Monacales, vol. 2676, 136rv, 188rv.

25. For the meaning and use of the word, see Irfan Shahfd and C.E. Bosworth, "Saracen," *Encyclopedia of Islam* 9:27–28.

26. For examples, see AHN, Clero, carp. 121, no. 7; ACA, Canc. Reg., no. 109, 318rv; ACA, Cartas Reales, 1335; *Bullarium ordinis de mercede,* 5–6, 11–13. It is also the term for Muslim preferred by King James I in his autobiography and documentation: for examples, see his "Crònica o Llibre dels Feits," in *Les quatre grans cròniques,* ed. Ferran Soldevila (Barcelona: Selecta, 1971), 86 (p. 48), 185 (p. 83), etc.; and Robert I. Burns, S.J., *Foundations of Crusader Valencia: Revolt and Recovery, 1257–1263,* vol. 2 of the *Diplomatarium of the Crusader Kingdom of Valencia: The Registered Charters of Its Conqueror Jaume I, 1257–1276* (Princeton: Princeton Univ. Press, 1991), 16 n. 12; 26 n. 26; 46 n. 53, etc. The term "Moor" appears, but seemingly not as often as it does in Castilian sources, but, like "Saracen," it is no more than a generic term for Muslim. See E. Lévi-Provençal, "Moors," *Encyclopedia of Islam,* 7: 235–36. In Castilian documents, interestingly, even King James I uses the term "Moor"; see Burns, *Foundations of Crusader Valencia,* 12, n. 8. The Castilian chronicler Rodrigo Ximénez de Rada employs "Moor," "Arab," "Saracen," and "Almohad" interchangeably; see his *Historia de rebus Hispanie sive Historia Gothica,* ed. Juan Fernández Valverde (Turnholt: Brepols, 1987), 7.14, 8.10, 9.16.

27. For a discussion of the origin of indulgences and their application to crusaders, see James A. Brundage, *Medieval Canon Law and the Crusaders* (Madison: Univ. of Wisconsin Press, 1969), 145–55. For an overview of the indulgences granted to Mercedarian benefactors, see Brodman, *Ransoming Captives,* 100.

28. *Bullarium ordinis de mercede,* 5–6, 6–7, 11–13, 22–23; AHN, Clero, carp. 1379, n. 8.

29. Brodman, *Ransoming Captives,* 127–28.

30. Typical is the receipt issued to two Mercedarians by Pere de Bosc of Barcelona in 1361 for the 130 duplas that the order paid him for a Muslim slave who was exchanged for Jaume Martí of Tarragona, "who was captive in the place of Tunis in the regions of Barbary"; ACA, Monacales, vol. 2704, n. 3.

31. ACA, Monacales, vol. 2676, 138rv (Jan. 15, 1270); vol. 2704, 1r (Nov. 23, 1321); vol. 2676, 5r-6r.

32. AHN, Clero, carp. 121, n. 7; ACA, Monacales, vol. 2676, 188rv.

33. ACA, Monacales, vol. 2703, perg. 1.

34. ACA, Canc. Reg. 144, 234rv.

35. ACA, Cartas reales, 1335.

36. ACA, Monacales, vol. 2679, 65v.

37. ACA, Canc. Reg. 335, 321r.

38. ACA, Canc. Reg. 143, 213v-214r; 144, 234rv.

39. For an extended discussion of this dispute, see Brodman, *Ransoming Captives,* 70–76.

40. *Bullarium ordinis de mercede,* pp. 35–37. On the interdict, see Sebastián Puig y Puig, *Episcopologio de la sede barcinonense* (Barcelona: Biblioteca Balmes, 1929), 234.

41. For a discussion of Almería, see Norman Housley, *The Avignon Papacy and the Crusades, 1305–1378* (New York: Oxford Univ. Press, 1986), 52, 55; Ferran Soldevila, *Història de Catalunya* (Barcelona: Editorial Alpha, 1962), 1:410–12.

42. Vicente Salavert y Roca, *Cerdeña y la expansión mediterránea de la Corona de Aragón, 1297–1314* (Madrid: Consejo Superior de investigaçiones Cientificas, 1956), 2: 403–4, no. 323.

43. This was Bernat de Figuerolis, who was compensated in May 1309 for the loss of his brown horse during preparations for the Granadan campaign (ACA, Canc. Reg. 345, 189).

44. For example, in correspondence with various Catalan prelates concerning their payment of a crusade subsidy, the king refers to the "eradication of the said king of Granada and of his people and the sect of the abominable and damned Mohammed." See *Documenta selecta mutuas civitatis Arago-Cathalaunicae et ecclesiae relationes illustrantia,* ed. Johannes Vincke (Barcelona: Biblioteca Balmes, 1936), 95–97, no. 151 (Nov. 9, 1309).

45. For example, Barcelona's largest hospital, Sant Macià, regularly exhibited abandoned children on Sundays and feasts as part of its effort to collect alms; Josep Maria Roca, *L'hospital migeval de Sant Macià* (Barcelona: Vidua de Lluis Tasso, 1926), 6.

46. For example, James II sent a letter to the king of Granada on May 15, 1300 stating: "The brothers of the Order of Santa Eulalia of Barcelona intend to enter your kingdom to ransom Christian captives who are there. We ask that when the brothers enter for the redemption they and their possessions not be arrested but that they travel safe and secure" (ACA, Canc. Reg. 117, 87rv).

47. In addition to the instances cited above, there is a list from Vic of subsidies given to sixty-two captives or their families (Brodman, *Ransoming Captives,* 106–7).

5. Toleration Denied: Armenia Between East and West in the Era of the Crusades

1. The traditional date for Armenia's adoption of Christianity is 301. Armenian historians proudly claim Armenia as the first nation to officially adopt Christianity, well in advance of Rome. See Leon Arpee, *History of Armenian Christianity, From the Beginning to Our Own Times* (New York: Armenian Missionary Association, 1946), 15–20; and Malachia Ormanian, *The Church of Armenia,* 2d ed. (London: Mowbray, 1955), 8–10.

2. M. Chahin, *The Kingdom of Armenia* (New York: Dorset Press, 1991), 201. Armenian

overlords built upon and continued the culture of Urartu, which had existed there since c. 1275 B.C.

3. Chahin, *Kingdom of Armenia,* 264–73.

4. See George Ostrogorsky, *History of the Byzantine State,* trans. J. Hussey, rev. ed. (New Brunswick: Rutgers Univ. Press, 1969), 314–15 and 333.

5. Complementary brief accounts of these events are given in Chahin, *Kingdom of Armenia,* 267–69; and *A History of the Seljuks: Ibrahim Kafesoglu's Interpretation and the Resulting Controversy,* ed. and trans. Gary Lieser (Carbondale: Southern Illinois Univ. Press, 1988), 47–50.

6. Armenian chronology places Jude Thaddeus, their first patriarch, in Armenia 43–66 A.D., and Bartholomew from 60 until his martyrdom at Albanus (Albac, Armenia) in 68. Ormanian, *Church of Armenia,* 3–; Aziz S. Atiya, *History of Eastern Christianity* (Notre Dame: Univ. of Notre Dame Press, 1968), 315.

7. Armenia's conversion is a complicated tale, replete with passion and intrigue. During war with Persia, Armenia's Trdat II (217–252) was poisoned by a kinsman and his infant son, Trdat III, spirited off to Rome. He returned to rule Armenia in 287 and persecuted Christians, while his father's murderer's son, St. Gregory the Illuminator, raised a devout Christian in exile, returned to proselytize Armenia. After Gregory converted the king through a miraculous cure, he became the first catholicos. See Agathange, *Histoire du régne de Tiridate et de la prédication de Saint Grégoire l'Illuminateur,* in *Collection des historiens anciens et modernes d'Arménie,* 2 vols., ed. V. Langlois (Paris: Didot, 1880), 1: 105–200; Atiya, *History of Eastern Christianity,* 318–21; and Chahin, *Kingdom of Armenia,* 252–56.

8. See Atiya, *History of Eastern Christianity,* 324–28 and the sources cited therein.

9. Ten Armenian bishops were listed in attendance at Chalcedon, but the Armenian Church maintains it played no role there. A half-century later an Armenian synod at Dwin formally rejected Chalcedon's formula on the dual nature of Christ as Nestorianism, and successive catholicoi reaffirmed this position. See Ormanian, *Church of Armenia,* 11–28; Adrian Fortescue, *The Lesser Eastern Churches* (London: Catholic Truth Society, 1913), 411; Henri François Tournebize, *Histoire politique et religieuse de l'Arménie* (Paris: Picard, 1910), 87; and Atiya, *History of Eastern Christianity,* 327–28. Eastern emperors, who intermittently ruled western Armenia, attempted to correct the Armenian Church's "errors." Heraclitus (610–41), for example, persuaded Catholicos Ezra (629) to accept union with the Orthodox Church, but the Armenian Synod of Manzikert (651) repudiated Chalcedon anew, condemning Ezra's submission. Arab conquests freed Armenia from Byzantium's pressure until the era of the Crusades.

10. In both their homeland and the Byzantine empire, Armenians retained a strong sense of identity and rejected assimilation into the Orthodox community. "The Armenian never became a Byzantine like others [incorporated within the Empire]. He kept his language, customs and his national religion [and] remained in the Byzantine empire an unassimilated foreign element." J. Laurent, "Les origines médiévales de la question arménnienne," *Revue des études Arméniennes* 1 (1920): 47, quoted in Chahin, *Kingdom of Armenia,* 271–72.

11. The best example of Frankish maltreatment of an Armenian lord is Baldwin of Bologne's seizure of Edessa and the demise of its Armenian ruler, Thoros, in 1098. See Steven Runciman, *A History of the Crusades,* 3 vols., (Cambridge: Cambridge Univ. Press, 1951–54; reprint, New York: Cambridge Univ. Press, 1965), 1: 204–6. Along the coast and in northern Syria, "with minor exceptions, all the Armenian possessions outside Cilicia passed into Latin hands," Sirarpie Der Nersessian, "The Kingdom of Cilician Armenia," in Kenneth M. Setton, ed., *A History of the Crusades,* 6 vols. (Philadelphia: Univ. of Pennsylvania Press, 1962–89), 2: 630–59, esp. 636.

12. Although the Roman Church was established in all areas conquered, only Orthodox bishops were displaced by Latin clergy. In other territories Latins founded new dioceses. Bernard Hamilton, "The Armenian Church and the Papacy at the Time of the Crusades," *Eastern Churches Review, A Journal of Eastern Christendom,* 10 (1978): 61–87, esp. 63.

13. *Chronique de Michel le Syrien, patriarche jacobite d'Antioche (1166–99),* ed. and trans. Jean Baptiste Chabot, 4 vols. (Paris: Leroux, 1899–1924), 3: 222 (Bk. 14, chap. 1); Michael the Syrian's comment is translated from the French in Hamilton, "Armenian Church and the Papacy," 64.

14. For example, the Armenian bishop of Antioch during this period was head of the monastery of the Jeuséens in the Black Mountain, where there were also Latin monasteries. (Hamilton "Armenian Church and the Papacy," 64).

15. Saint Nersés Schnorhali (the Gracious), *Elégie sur la prise d'Edesse,* Recueil des historiens des Croisades. Historiens Armenians (hereafter cited as *RHC Arm.*), 1: 228, the lines are translated in Hamilton, "Armenian Church and the Papacy," 61. Nerses later became Catholicos Nerses IV (1166–73).

16. Alberic had invited both the catholicos and the Jacobite patriarch, who also promised to promote church union. See Jean Richard, *La papauté et les missions d'Orient au moyen âge (XIIIᵉ-XVᵉ siècles)* (Rome: École française de Rome, 1977), 10, who cites Michael the Syrian, *Chronique* 3: 255–56; and William of Tyre, *Historia rerum in partibus transmarinis gestarum,* in *RHC Occ.,* 1, bk. 15, chap. 8.

17. After the Fourth Lateran Council (1215), as a consequence of their patriarch's submission, the Maronites became the first uniate church in the Latin East. See William of Tyre, *RHC Occ.,* 1: bk. 22, chap. 8. Kamal S. Salibi, "The Maronite Church and its Union with Rome," *Oriens christianus* 42 (1958); 92–104, esp. 94, believes the Maronite patriarch may also have made initial submission at the 1141 Jerusalem synod.

18. Pontificia commissio ad redigendum codicem iuris canonici Orientalis, *Fontes* [hereafter *Fontes*], ser. 3, vol. 1, Acta Romanorum Pontificum a S. Clemente ad Coelestinum III (Vatican City: Typis Polyglottis Vaticanis, 1943), no. 395, 811–13. The letter of the catholicos has not been preserved. The translation was done by St. Nerses of Lampron, archbishop of Tarsus.

19. According to a colophon by Nerses of Lampron at the end of his translation of the letters of Lucius III and Clement III, Leon II, who had assumed control of Cilicia in 1189, expected a crown at the hands of Barbarossa. See Garegin I. Hovsepian, *Colophons of Manuscripts* [in Armenian] (Antilias: n.p., 1951), col. 538, cited in Der Nersessian, "Kingdom of Cilician Armenia," 646, n. 19. After Barbarossa's untimely death (1190), Leon pressed the issue in embassies to both pope and emperor. Henry VI, preparing to go on crusade, sent his chancellor, Conrad, bishop of Hildesheim, with the papal legate Conrad, archbishop of Mainz, to crown both Aimery of Cyprus and Leon of Armenia, (Der Nersessian, "Kingdom of Cilician Armenia," 643–47).

20. These probably included, in addition to Catholicos Gregory VI; John, archbishop of Sis; St. Nerses of Lampron, bishop of Tarsus; and Joseph, Armenian archbishop of Antioch. See Hamilton "Armenian Church and the Papacy," 71, and Der Nersessian, "Kingdom of Cilician Armenia," 647.

21. Vartan the Great, for example, writing in the next century, recast the 1184 submission as an appeal against persecution begun by Alexius Angelus (1185–95). *Extrait de l'Histoire Universelle de Vartan le Grand, RHC Arm;* 1: 438. See Hamilton's analysis, "Armenian Church and the Papacy," 69 n. 40 there.

22. Guiragos of Kantzag (Kirakos of Kantzag), *RHC Arm.,* 1: 422–24. Details surrounding the coronation were also reported by Sempad (*RHC Arm.,* 1: 634–35).

23. After Leon II and Catholicos Gregory IV wrote to Innocent in 1199, professing devotion to Rome and requesting help against Muslims, the pope's response, *In Ecclesiam suam*, asking the king to further union in the entire Armenian Church, demonstrated that he knew only a part had submitted to Rome. *Fontes,* Ser. 3, vol. 2, *Acta Innocentii PP III (1198–1216),* ed. P. Theodosius Haluscynskyj (Vatican: Typis Polyglottis Vaticanis, 1944), no. 12, 201–2.

24. *Per diutinam experientiam,* making Albert, the Latin patriarch of Antioch, a papal legate, and *Venerabilis frater noster,* to Constantine I, catholicos of Armenia, making him subject to the patriarch *(Fontes,* ser. 3, vol. 3, *Acta Honorii III [1216–1241] et Gregorii IX [1227–1241],* ed. Aloysius I. Tautu [Vatican City: Typis Polyglottis Vaticanis, 1950], nos. 240–41, pp. 319–20). Patriarch Albert made this suggestion during political turmoil in Cilicia, probably at the behest of Bohemond V of Antioch, who sought to undermine Hetoum I's position by challenging the validity of his marriage; see Hamilton, "Armenian Church and the Papacy," 78–79.

25. In *Sacrosancta Romana Ecclesia,* addressed in separate copies on March 1, 1239, to Isabella and Hetoum I, queen and king of Armenia, Gregory confirmed the validity of their marriage and confirmed all customary privileges *(Fontes,* ser. 3, vol. 3, nos. 253–54, pp. 332–33, the passage is translated by Hamilton in "Armenian Church and the Papacy," 79–80). Gregory sent a new *pallium* to the catholicos *(Fontes,* ser. 3, vol. 3, no. 258, 335–36), recognized the autonomy of the Armenian Church, and extended its privileges. No one was to preach in Armenia without special license from the pope, catholicos, or an Armenian ordinary *(Fontes,* ser. 3: vol. 3; no. 255, 333), and Armenian churches in Jerusalem and elsewhere were subjected directly to the catholicos *(Fontes,* ser. 3: vol. 3; no. 256, 334).

26. Concerning this synod see Tournebize, *Histoire politique et religieuse de l'Arménie,* 290–91. Atiya errs in terming this the successful conclusion of negotiations for union, after which "catholicos after catholicos declared the profession of faith in accordance with the Roman creed" *(History of Eastern Christianity,* 333).

27. For an overview of medieval mission activity, see Kenneth S. Latourette, *The Thousand Years of Uncertainty,* vol. 2 of *A History of the Expansion of Christianity,* (New York: Harper, 1938–45). When interest in preaching to infidels and schismatics revived as the thirteenth century opened, mendicant orders took the lead. Papal involvement can be dated from Pope Gregory IX's mission bull *Cum hora undecima,* originally issued in 1235 *(Fontes,* ser. 3: vol. 3: no. 210, 286–87). James Muldoon, in *Popes, Lawyers and Infidels* (Philadelphia: Univ. of Pennsylvania Press, 1979), 36–38, analyzes the bull in the context of canon law.

28. *Quia corporali praesentia* sent Lawrence as plenipotentiary to the Greeks, Armenians, and others in the East. *Fontes,* 3: 4: t. 1, *Acta Innocentii PP IV (1243–54),* ed. Meletius M. Wojnar (Rome: Typis Vaticanis, 1962), no. 31, 73–74.

29. See *Biblioteca Bio-Bibliografica della Terra Santa e dell'Oriente Francescano,* ed. Girolamo Golubovich, 5 vols. (Florence: Collegio di San Bonaventura, 1906), 1: 216 (hereafter cited as *BTS*). Hamilton "Armenian Church," 80, sees this as papal acknowledgment that many Armenian clergy and people rejected union with Rome and remained in schism ("Armenian Church and the Papacy," 80).

30. Several ambassadors dispatched to the Mongols by Innocent IV returned in 1248 with letters demanding unconditional submission to the khan. One ambassador, Friar Ascelinus, brought emissaries from a Mongol general, Baiju, whom he had encountered in Armenia, to the papal court at Lyons. Another, Friar John of Plano Carpini, returned with a letter from Khan Güyük. For Ascelinus, see Gregory G. Guzman, "Simon of Saint-Quentin and the Dominican Mission to the Mongol Baiju: A Reappraisal," *Speculum* 46 (1971): 232–49; and Jean Richard, *Simon de Saint-Quentin: Histoire des Tartares* (Paris: Geuthner, 1965). Plano Carpini's *History*

of the Mongols is translated in *Mission to Asia,* ed. Christopher Dawson (originally published in 1955 as *The Mongol Mission;* reissued, Toronto: University of Toronto Press, 1980), 3–76, along with the khan's letter demanding submission (85–86). Innocent's November 22, 1248, reply to the Mongols urged them to stop their slaughter, but expressed no desire for further dialogue; *Les Registres d'Innocent IV,* ed. E. Berger, 4 vols. (Paris: Thorin, 1884–1921), 2: no. 4682. The papacy was slow to renew even missionary contact. Igor de Rachewiltz, in *Papal Envoys to the Great Khans* (Stanford: Stanford University Press, 1971), 118, concludes that Innocent shut the door to further contact at this time.

31. Steven Runciman, "The Crusader States, 1243–1291," in Setton, ed., *A History of the Crusades,* 2: 557–98, esp. 571–72. The anti-Mongol crusade was authorized by the bull *Cum in hora,* July 15, 1258; August Potthast, *Registra pontificum romanorum,* 2 vols. (Berlin: Decker, 1874–75), 1: no. 17347. Hülegü, who later became the first Ilkhan, began his campaign in Persia in 1256, reduced the Assassins' strongholds in 1256–57, and captured Baghdad in 1258. Bohemond was excommunicated for his Mongol alliance by Urban IV on May 26, 1263.

32. Hamilton explains the ephemeral church union as primarily a political manifestation: "In these circumstances, when the Papacy was hostile to the Mongols and the Cilicians were dependent on [them], it is not surprising that the Armenian union with Rome should have broken down. The Armenian Church was even less willing than the Cilician King to offend the Mongols, since Greater Armenia formed part of the Mongol Empire" ("Armenian Church and the Papacy," 81).

33. *Relation de la Conférence tenue entre le docteur Mekhitar de Daschir envoyé de Catholicos Constantine Ier et le légat du pape à Saint-Jean d'Acre, RHC Arm.,* 1: 697; translated by Hamilton in "Armenian Church and the Papacy," 82. The bishop of Bethlehem was Thomas de Lentini.

34. For diplomacy leading up to the council and the problem of religious union at it, see Deno Geanakoplos, "Bonaventure, the Two Mendicant Orders and the Greeks at the Council of Lyons (1274)," in *The Orthodox Church and the West* (Oxford: Blackwell, 1976), 183–211, and *Emperor Michael Palaeologus and the West* (Cambridge, Mass.: Harvard Univ. Press, 1959); Burkhard Roberg, *Die Union zwische nder griechischen und der lateinischen Kirche auf dem II. Konzil von Lyon* (Bonn: Röhrscheid, 1964); and Donald M. Nicol, "The Greeks and the Union of Churches: Preliminaries to the 2nd Council of Lyons," in *Medieval Studies Presented to Aubrey Gwynn* (Dublin: Lochlainn, 1961), 463–80.

35. The council met from May 7 to July 17, 1274. The Greeks arrived on June 24 and made submission at the fourth general session (July 6) (Geanakoplos, *Orthodox Church and the West, 201).*

36. *Nicol,* judges this creed to have been "terms and conditions of union" *("Greeks and the Union of Churches," 458–59).* Heinrich Denzinger, in *Enchiridion Symbolorum; definitionum et declarationum de rebus fidei et morum,* 31st ed., ed. C. Rahner (Rome: Herder, 1958), notes that the creed (no. 461, 214–17) was patterned on an early formula *("Statuta ecclesiae antiqua")* of interrogations and answers for the consecration of a bishop.

37. The Franciscans who negotiated the submission of Emperor Michael (among them, Jerome of Ascoli, later Nicholas IV) had particular difficulty because they had to win acceptance of the Clementine creed. Michael and his son subscribed, and induced many Greek clergy to do so, ultimately provoking extensive schism within the Orthodox Church (Nicol, "Greeks and Union," 463–70; Geanakoplos, *Emperor Michael Palaeologus,* passim).

38. After Leon II (prince of Cilicia from 1187, king of Lesser Armenia 1198–1219) came to power, the Armenian court was rapidly transformed on the pattern of Frankish courts. As Armenia's ancient feudal system gradually modified in imitation of the Western model, barons

became more closely tied to the king and lost independence, which *nakharars* had formerly enjoyed. Indicative of this change was their adoption of the Assizes of Antioch, translated by Sempad, constable during Hetoum I's reign. Ironically, these assizes have survived only in the Armenian version. Der Nersessian, "Kingdom of Cilician Armenia," 650–51, and Leonce Alishan, *Assises d'Antioche reproduites en français et publiées au sixième centenaire de la mort de Sempad le Connétable* (Venice: Imprimerie Arménienne, 1876).

39. Rachewiltz, *Papal Envoys,* 150–57; Kenneth M. Setton, *The Papacy and the Levant (1204–1571),* 4 vols. (Philadelphia: American Philosophical Society, 1976–84), 1: 115–17; and René Grousset, *The Empire of the Steppes,* trans. N. Walford (New Brunswick, N.J.: Rutgers Univ. Press, 1970), 353–71.

40. Other Mongol rulers also welcomed missionaries in the latter thirteenth century. About 1266, Qubilai used the Polos to request that "men of learning, thoroughly acquainted with the Christian religion" be sent to his court; *The Travels of Marco Polo,* ed. M. Komroff, rev. from Marsden's translation (New York: Modern Library, 1926), 8. Missionaries customarily received a *yarligh* of privileges, which conferred a license to preach and protection from local opposition to their activities, even in the khanate of the Golden Horde (Qipchaq), where a *yarligh* was granted to Franciscans at least as early as the reign of Möngke Temür (1267–80), and later confirmed by Özbeg (1313–41), who had converted to Islam; M. Bihl and A. C. Moule, *Tria nova documenta de missionibus F M Tartariae Aquilonaris,* in *Archivum franciscanum historicum* 17 (1924); 55–71.

41. *De locis Fratrum Minorum et Predicatorum in Tartaria* (British Museum codex *Nero A. IX,* fol. 100 v°, reproduced in *BTS,* 2: 72), compiled about 1330, lists missionary establishments in Tartar lands. For the Franciscans thirty-five are indicated; five in *Cathay* (China), eighteen in *Tartaria Aquilonari* (Qipchaq and the northern Caucasus), and 12 in *Tartaria orientali* (Persia, Azerbaijan, and Greater Armenia). For the Dominicans five are indicated: two in *Tartaria Aquilonari* and three in *Tartaria orientali.*

42. For Clement V's appointment of John of Montecorvino, OFM, as first archbishop of Khan-baliq, see Arthur C. Moule, *Christians in China Before the Year 1500* (New York: Macmillan, 1926), 182–89; and Richard, *La papauté,* 144 ff. For John XXII's appointment of Franco of Perugia *(de Perusio),* O.P., as first archbishop of Sultaniyya, see R. Loenertz, *La Société des Frères Pérégrinants* (Rome: Ad S. Sabinae, 1937), 137–41; and Richard, *La papauté,* 169 ff.

43. The bull *Redemptor noster* (April 1, 1318; *BTS,* 3: 200–4) placed the Ilkhanate, Chaghatai Khanate, India, and Ethiopia in the care of the archbishop of Sultaniyya, apparently responding to an idea raised by William Adam, O.P., whose *De modo Saracenos extirpandi,* written after missionary travels in Persia and across the Indian Ocean, reported the existence of numerous Christian peoples. The pope may have hoped to raise fighting forces there to assist in a future crusade (See Richard, *La papauté,* 70).

44. Of the six suffragan sees established for Sultaniyya by *Redemptor noster,* four (Sivas, Tabriz, Dehkhvaregan [Azar Shahr], and Maragha) were along the chief route between the Cilician port of Ayas and Sultaniyya, and were in or adjacent to Greater Armenia. (Richard, *La papauté,* 175–76).

45. Many Franciscans had entered Armenia in the final decades of the thirteenth century. An OFM convent, enjoying Mongol support, was founded at *Sebastea* (Sivas) c. 1279. The Franciscans were reinforced in 1289 when a large party of spirituals, who had departed for the east with Montecorvino, remained in Cilicia when he went on to China. By 1292 there was a *custodia* in Cilicia, comprising at least three convents, and another at Tabriz. *BTS,* 1: 339 and 355; 2: 516–18.

46. Continuator of Samuel of Ani, *RHC Arm.,* 1: 462–63, cited by Hamilton, "Armenian Church and the Papacy," 84.

47. For the Order of the Friars Unitors of Armenia, see Loenertz, *Société des Frères Pérégrinants,* 141–50. His survey relies heavily upon the work of M. A. Van den Oudenrijn, whose many contributions to this history he cites (141 n. 18). The Unitors' rule was based on that of the Dominicans.

48. Loenertz, *Société des Frères Pérégrinants,* 190. An October 15, 1321, letter to Zachary from Pope John XXII, inviting him to adopt the rite of the Roman Church in celebrating the Eucharist and in extreme unction, suggests that his reconciliation to Rome occurred shortly after that time; *Fontes,* ser. 3: vol. 7: t. 2, *Acta Ioannis XXII (1317–1334),* ed. Aloysius I. Tautu (Vatican City: Typis Vaticanis, 1952), no. 47, p. 99. See Richard, *La papauté,* 203–4.

49. The two bishops were Nerses Balientz (of *Orni,* later titular bishop of Manzikert) and Simeon Bech of Theotopolis (Erzerum); Richard, *La papauté,* 210; and Loenertz, *Société des Frères Pérégrinants,* 188.

50. Richard, *La papauté,* 204–5. Many commentators have identified Zorzor with the monastery of St. Thaddeus, southwest of Maku (now in Iran, some 40 kilometers from the Armenian border), but there is still debate over Zorzor's exact location (see 205, n. 141).

51. Nerses, bishop of Qrna, for example, incurred the wrath of Catholicos James II, when (c. 1335) he traveled to Sis to express doubts about the validity of his own consecration because his baptism and ordination had been according to the traditional Armenian rite (Richard, *La papauté,* 210–11).

52. Hamilton, "Armenian Church and the Papacy," 86. But he errs in blaming church union in Cilicia for having "creat[ed] a prejudice against the Holy See among those segments of the Armenian Church which had not been subject to Frankish influence." Rather, antipapal prejudice and rejection of church union, things not voiced in earlier phases of the relationship between Rome and the Armenian Church, followed exposure to Western missionary influence.

53. Despite political struggles, Hetoum II (1289–1305) had renewed allegiance to the Mongol Ilkhanate under Ghazan (1295–1304), a convert to Islam, and assisted in three unsuccessful invasions of Syria (the last in 1303). Mamluk pressure began anew in 1304, and Cilicia thereafter resumed ruinous tribute to Egypt (Der Nersessian, "Kingdom of Cilician Armenia," 656–58).

54. Sis had become the new seat of the catholicate after Hromgla, its residence since c. 1150, was lost to Mamluks in 1292. This placed the catholicos firmly under the control of the king of Cilicia. Other changes endorsed at the synod include suppression of additions to *Trisagion* and several minor reforms (Hamilton, "Armenian Church and the Papacy," 85–86; Tournebize, *Histoire politique et religieuse de l'Arménie,* 309–10).

55. Atiya notes that although "fifteen patriarchs reigned over Sis from Gregory VII to Gregory IX (1294–1441)," the union was never popular with Greater Armenians (*History of Eastern Christianity,* 334). Those opposed elected their own patriarchs, who reigned at Aghthamar. This dual arrangement constituted a schism which lasted until the collapse of the Cilician dynasty.

56. It was Nerses who had confronted Catholicos James II with his doubts about the efficacy of Armenian baptism and holy orders in 1335; see n. 51, above.

57. On October 10, 1338, Nerses was conditionally reconsecrated and received a *pallium; see Fontes,* ser. 3: vol. 8: *Acta Benedicti XII (1334–1342),* ed. Aloysius I. Tautu (Vatican City: Typis Vaticanis, 1952), no. 60, 232–34. Other Unitor Armenians at Avignon at the same time include Martin, archbishop of Edessa, who died about 1342; and John David, a monk from Zorzor, whom the pope named Martin's successor in 1343 (Richard, *La papauté,* 211).

58. *Quamvis delicti filii*, to Leon, and *Dundum ad audientiam*, to the newly appointed catholicos Mechitar Kernertsi (1342–55), both dated August 1, 1341 (*Fontes,* ser. 3: vol. 8: 114–19).

59. Richard, *La papauté,* 212. *Fontes,* ser. 3: vol. 8: 119–55, transcribes the *Libellus.* These letters and the brief *Fides Armenorum* have been preserved in *Reg. Vat. 62,* a unique collection of 191 letters assembled from fourteenth-century popes (primarily Clement V, John XXII, Benedict XII, and Clement VI) dealing with the "business of the Tartars, the lands of *outremer,* infidels and heretics," which James Muldoon discusses at length in "The Avignon Papacy and the Frontiers of Christendom: The Evidence of Vatican Register 62," *Archivum Historiae Pontificiae* 17 (1979): 125–95.

60. The synod was presided over by Catholicos Mechitar and attended by the archbishops of Sis, Tarsus, Anazarb, Kayseri, Konya, and Sivas, along with numerous bishops, abbots, archpriests, priests, and teachers. It used as its working document a refutation drafted by the Franciscan Daniel of Tabriz, who had been one of Leon V's ambassadors in 1336 (see Richard, *La papauté,* 213, and sources cited therein).

61. The two legates were the bishops of Gaete and Coron (Richard, *La papauté,* 214).

62. In *Quamvis delicti filii* Benedict had declared himself less worried because Cilicia's military situation was deteriorating than because "execrable errors are held by many people in Greater and Lesser Armenia and taught *(dogmatizantur)* there against the Catholic faith" (*Fontes,* ser. 3j vol. 8: 114).

63. *Super quibusdam capitulis,* September 29, 1351, from Clement VI "to brother Consolatori, said to be Catholicos of Armenia," covered both major doctrinal issues, such as the nature of Christ, and quite minor areas of disagreement, including use of the Latin calendar for saints' feasts. *Fontes,* ser. 3: vol. 9: *Acta Clementis PP VI (1342–1352),* ed. Aloysius I. Tautu (Rome: Typis Vaticanis, 1960), no. 192, pp. 301–18. As Muldoon, observes, "Clement IV stressed the need for the Armenians to adhere closely to the papal mode of practicing the Christian faith" ("Avignon Papacy," 154).

64. An early sign of this shift was papal use of the creedal statement *Credimus Sanctam Trinitatem,* originally designed to test Greek adherence to Roman doctrine (see nn. 36 and 37, above), in a 1319 letter from John XXII to Armenia's King Oshin (1307–20). *Fontes,* ser. 3, vol. 7: t. 2, no. 20, 34–41.

6. Muslim Taxation under Crusader Rule

1. A perceptive summary of crusader historiography with regard to this question is provided by Raymond C. Smail, in *Crusading Warfare* (Cambridge: Cambridge Univ. Press, 1956).

2. The French model is presented in E. G. Rey, *Essai sur la domination française en Syrie durant le moyen âge* (Paris: Thunot, 1866); E. G. Rey, *Les Colonies franques* (Paris: Picard, 1883); L. Madelin, "La Syrie franque," *Revue des deux mondes* 38 (1917); 314–58; L. Madelin, *L'expansion française de la Syrie au Rhin* (Paris: Plon, 1918); and René Grousset, *Histoire des croisades et du royaume franc de Jerusalem,* 3 vols. (Paris: Plon, 1934–36). The contrasting view is taken up by Joshua Prawer, *Crusaders' Kingdom* (New York: Praeger, 1972); for the use of the term *apartheid,* see p. 524.

3. See, for example, Claude Cahen, "Notes sur l'histoire des Croisades et de l'Orient latin, II: Le régime rural syrien au temps de la domination franque," *Bulletin de la Faculté des Lettres de l'Université de Strasbourg* 29 (1951): 286–310; and Jonathan Riley-Smith, "The Survival in Latin Palestine of Muslim Administration," in *Eastern Mediterranean Lands during the Period of the Crusades,* ed. Philip Holt (Warminster: Aris and Phillips, 1977), 9–22. George Ostro-

gorsky has taken a similar view with regard to the establishment of the Latin empire of Constantinople in 1204; "[the crusaders] found that they were completely familiar with existing conditions, which they could take over without much alteration"; see "Agrarian Conditions in the Byzantine Empire in the Middle Ages," in *Cambridge Economic History of Europe*, 2d. ed. (Cambridge: Cambridge Univ. Press, 1966), 1: 227. For the opposite view, see Benjamin Z. Kedar, "The Crusader Tax of 1183: Innovation or Adaptation?" *English Historical Review* 89 (1974): 339–45, who concludes: "Consequently the decree of 1183 fits well into the dominant institutional pattern of the crusading Kingdom of Jerusalem: adherence to European practices, minimal adaptation to local conditions." This view is also held, in part, by Prawer: "They [the Crusaders] could look back to Spain, North-Western or Southern France, to find a pattern for settlement. . . . So we might expect that the Crusaders brought with them from Europe some knowledge and experience. Especially religious orders, those persistent keepers of tradition, might have brought with them the knowledge of colonization"; see "Colonization Activities in the Latin Kingdom of Jerusalem," *Revue belge de philologie et d'histoire* 29 (1951): 1068.

4. The major collections of documents relating to the crusaders' settlement in the Latin East consulted for this paper are the following: *Le Cartulaire du Chapitre du Saint Sépulcre de Jérusalem*, ed. G. Bresc-Bautier (Paris: Librarie Orientaliste, 1984) (hereafter cited as *Sépulcre*); *Chartes de Terre Sainte provenant de Notre-Dame de Josaphat*, ed. F. Delaborde (Paris: Thorin, 1880) (hereafter: *Josaphat*); *Cartulaire général de l'Ordre des Hospitallers de Saint-Jean de Jérusalem (1100–1310)*, ed. J. Delaville Le Roulx, 4 vols. (Paris: Leroux, 1894–1906) (hereafter cited as *Hosp.*); *Regesta Regni Hiersolymitani*, ed. Reinhold Röhricht, 2 vols. (Innsbruck: Wagner, 1893–1904; rpt., New York: B. Franklin, 1961) (hereafter cited as *Regesta; Tabulae Ordinis Theutonici*, ed. Ernst Strelkhe (Berlin: Wiedemann, 1869; rpt., Toronto: Univ. of Toronto Press, 1972) (hereafter: *Theut.); and Urkunden zur alteren Handels- und Staatsgeschichte der Republik Venedig*, ed. G. Tafel and G. Thomas (Vienna: Hof- und Staatsdruckerei, 1857; rpt., Amsterdam: Hakker, 1964) (hereafter cited as Tafel-Thomas).

5. The examples I have identified: *terraticum* (*Sépulcre*, nos. 120, and #121), *terragium; (Hosp., no. 399)*, and *terraciis; (Theut., no. 57)*. The term *terraticum* is also found in Norman Sicily; see, for example, *Regesta des actes des ducs normands d' Italie (1046–1127)*, ed. Léon R. Ménager (Bari: Grafica Bigiemme, 1980), 54, 121, 201, 217; see also Donald Matthews, *The Norman Kingdom of Sicily* (New York: Cambridge Univ. Press, 1992), 239.

6. See Cahen, "Notes," 300: "C'est cet impôt proportionnel sur les recoltes qui est designée selon les textes tantôt sous le nom occidental de terrage, tantôt sous le nom original de carragium, c'est á dire kharadj"; and Prawer, *Crusaders' Kingdom*, 375: "Under cover of the Latin name [terraticum], we suspect an earlier Moslem tax, the *kharaj*"; Jonathan Riley-Smith, *The Feudal Nobility and the Kingdom of Jerusalem*, 1174–1277 (London: Macmillan, 1973), 44–45.

7. See the discussion by J. Round and W. Stevenson in "Notes and Documents," *English Historical Review* 4 (1889): 105–10.

8. See, for example, Tafel-Thomas, 371.

9. *Cartulaire général de l'ordre du Temple*, ed. Marquis d'Albon (Paris: Champion, 1913), 183–85.

10. See, for example, the many references, especially no. 684 and no. 901, in the index to *Cartulary of the Knights of St. John of Jerusalem in England, secunda camera*, ed. M. Gervers (Oxford: Oxford Univ. Press, 1982). This fee is also called *portagium* (see Prawer, *Crusaders' Kingdom*, 376). Other examples can be found in a document dated 1164–76 from Dublin in *British Borough Charters*, ed. A Ballard (Cambridge: Cambridge Univ. Press, 1913), 184; and in Normandy during the reign of Henry II in a confirmation of exemption to the abbey of Saint-

Evroul "ab omnibus consuetudinibus et theloneis et tailliis et auxiliis et carragiis, muragiis, et es-cuagiis, avenagiis, et fossatis, et omnibus aliis districtionibus," *Recueil des actes de Henri II,* ed. L. Delisle and E. Berger, (Paris: Imprimerie Nationale, 1920), 71.

11. *Hosp.,* no. 1097. The text of this charter is lost; it is summarized in an inventory com-piled by Raybaud, "Inventaire de pièces de Terre Sainte de l'ordre de l'Hôpital," ed. J. Delaville Le Roulx, *Revue de l'Orient latin* 3 (1895): 36–106.

12. Riley-Smith, "Survival," 9–22. *Hosp.,* no. 941. The Latin: "in casalibus et redditibus ab eisdem exeuntibus, caraggiis, pactis."

13. *Hosp.,* no. 2199. "Preterea cum antedicti magister et fratres, pro vicesima de caragiis casalis ejusdem, quinque tantum bizantios exvolant eidem, et rationem illorum, qui recipiunt, ad majorem solutionem ei prestande vicesime teneantur secundum quantitatem receptorum, ex-hiberi sibi postulavit eandem."

14. *Hosp.,* no. 3018.

15. *Hosp.,* no. 94.

16. Tafel-Thomas, 371.

17. See the references to *Rotuli Chartarum,* 2a, 15b, and 47b, cited in *English Historical Review* 4 (1889); 108–10.

18. *Hosp.,* no. 129.

19. See P. Monet, *Inventaire des langues française et latine* (Geneva: Slatkin, 1973).

20. Riley-Smith, *The Feudal Nobility,* 44 and 252, n. 58. "Fragment d'un cartulaire de l'or-dre de Saint-Lazare, en Terre Sainte," ed. A. de Marsay, *Archives de l'Orient latin* 2 (1884): no. 9, 129–30.

21. See n. 39, below, and the text to which the note refers.

22. A recent Arabic edition is *Rihlat Ibn Jubayr,* ed. R. Hayn-Nassar (Cairo: Maktabat Misr, 1992), 383. Cf. J. Riley-Smith, "Some Lesser Officials in Latin Syria," *English Historical Review* 87 (1972); 13, n. 1. A passage from 'Imad al-Din, given a translation by D. S. Richards different from that found in *Recueil des historiens des Croisades,* tends to support the view that the daily lives of the Muslim inhabitants changed little under crusader rule: "The villagers of the Nablus area and the majority of its inhabitants were Muslims and had accommodated them-selves to living as subjects of the Franks (litt. were strung or threaded onto the thread of the sub-ject people with the Franks) who annually collected from them a tax levy (*qarar*), and changed not a single law or cult practice of theirs." Richards notes that, *qarar* as "tribute, levy" has no direct evidence, but the verb form *qarrara* is common in the sense of "impose a levy." In any case, there is here no mention of *kharaj* or *jizya* in a specific or general usage. See D. S. Richards, "Notes," *Arabica* 25 (1978): 203–4.

23. See François L. Ganshoff and Adriaan Verhulst, "Medieval Agrarian Society in its Prime: 1. France, The Low Countries, and Western Germany," *Cambridge Economic History of Europe,* 2d. ed., (Cambridge: Cambridge Univ. Press, 1966) 1: 312; and G. Duby, *Rural Econ-omy and Country Life in the Medieval West,* trans. C. Postan (Columbia: Univ. of South Car-olina Press, 1968), 217. Some specific examples may be found in *Cartulaire de l'abbaye de Saint-Victor de Marseille,* ed. M. Guérard, 2 vols. (Paris: Lahure, 1857): no. 163 (d. 817), no. 174 (d. 1001), no. 189 (d. 1030), and no. 160 (d. 1069); and in *Cartulaire de Sainte-Croix d'Or-leans,* ed. J. Thillier and E. Jarry (Paris: Picard, 1906): no. 28 (d. 1171) and no. 153 (d. 1171).

24. M. Le Mené, "Les redevances à part de fruits dans l'ouest de la France au Moyen Age," *Les Revenus de la Terre* (Flaran, 7) (Auch: Comité departmental du tourisme du Gers, 1985), 13.

25. Le Mené, "Les redevances," 18.

26. For European practice of the tithe, see B. H. Slicher van Bath, *The Agrarian History of Western Europe, A.D. 500–1850,* trans. Olive Ordish (London: Arnold, 1963), as well as the works cited below in n. 43.

27. *Cartulaire de St. Thomas de Trinquetaille,* ed. P. A. Amargier (Gap: Centre d'études des sociétés méditerranéennes, 1972), 119, 175, 179, 180.

28. G. and M. Sicard, "Redevances à part de fruits et métayage dans le sud-ouest del la France au moyen âge," *Les Revenus de la Terre,* 63–67; see also R. Grand, *Le contrat de complant depuis les origines jusqu'à nos jours* (Paris: Tenin, 1917).

29. G. Sivéry, "Les tenures à part de fruits et le métayage dans le nord de la France et les Pays-Bas (jusqu'au début du XVIᵉ siècle)," *Les Revenus de la Terre,* 30.

30. K-H. Spiess, "Teilpacht (métayage) et teilbauverträge (baux à part de fruits) en Allemagne occidentale au moyen âge et aux temps modernes," *Les Revenus de la Terre,* 124.

31. Spiess, "Teilpacht," 136.

32. Andrew M. Watson has characterized the Muslim doctrine of state ownership of land as a "fiction" to which legal and religious authorities sometimes paid "lip service." Such doctrine, he continues, "had almost no practical application." See A. Watson, *Agricultural Innovation in the Early Islamic World* (Cambridge: Cambridge Univ. Press, 1984), 112.

33. See Hans E. Mayer, *The Crusades,* trans. J. Gillingham, 2d. ed. (New York: Oxford Univ. Press, 1988), 165.

34. Claude Cahen, "La Féodalité et les institutions politiques de l'orient latin," *Oriente ed occidente nel Medio Evo* (Rome: Accademia nazionale dei Lincei, 1957), 184.

35. See Chris Wickham, "The Uniqueness of the East," *Journal of Peasant Studies* 12 (1985): 166–96.

36. H. Berktay, "The Feudalism Debate: The Turkish End," *Journal of Peasant Studies* 14 (1987): 291–333; and J. Haldon, *The State and the Tributary Mode of Production* (London: Verso Press, 1993), 75 ff.

37. See J. Richard, *Le Royaume latin de Jérusalem* (Paris: Presses Universitaires de France, 1953); he refers to this tax as *kharaj* (123).

38. John LaMonte, *Feudal Monarchy in the Latin Kingdom of Jerusalem* (Cambridge, Mass.: Medieval Academy of America, 1932), 175.

39. Syrian and Greek Christians, as well as Muslims and Jews, paid poll tax (see Prawer, *Crusaders' Kingdom,* 219).

40. *Josaphat,* nos. 21, 27, 28, 31, and 49.

41. *Chronique d'Ernoul et de Bernard le Trésorier,* ed. L. de Mas Latrie (Paris: Renouard, 1871), 27–30; and *Guillaume de Tyr et ses continuateurs,* ed. M. Paulin (Paris: Renouard, 1879–80), 2: 289–91.

42. *Josaphat,* no. 31.

43. For the history of the tithe in Europe, see P. Viard, *Histoire de la dîme ecclésiastique principalement en France jusqu'au Décret de Gratian* (Dijon: Jobard, 1909), and *Histoire de la dîme ecclésiastique dans le royaume de France aux XIIᵉ et XIIIᵉ siècles* (Paris: Picard, 1912); a more recent but narrowly focused work is Giles Constable, *Monastic Tithes from Their Origins to the Twelfth Century* (Cambridge: Cambridge Univ. Press, 1964). See also n. 26, above.

44. For more discussion of tithe disputes among the crusaders themselves, see Jonathan Riley-Smith, *The Knights of St. John in Jerusalem and Cyprus c. 1050–1310* (London: Macmillan, 1967), 440 ff.

45. See T. Byres, "Historical Perspectives on Sharecropping," in *Sharecropping and Sharecroppers,* ed. T. Byres (London: Cass, 1983), 7–40.

46. See, for example, Tafel-Thomas, 371.

47. See the comments to this effect in Cahen, "La Féodalité," 184.

48. See J. Prawer, "Colonization," 1087–95.

49. See J. Prawer, "Colonization," 1095–1103.

50. The term *medietaria* was often used in a generic sense, referring to the work shared by the tenant and the lord and not necessarily designating a split of one-half to each party. See R. Grand, *L'agriculture au moyen âge: de la fin de l'empire Romain au XVIᵉ siècle* (Paris: Boccard, 1950), 133, n. 2.

51. See Cahen, "Notes," 297.

52. See Ronnie Ellenblum, "Settlement and Society formation in Crusader Palestine," *The Archaeology of Society in the Holy Land,* ed. T. Levy (London: Leicester Univ. Press, 1995), 503–11; see also his "Colonization Activities in the Frankish East: The Example of Castellum Regis," *English Historical Review* 91 (1996): 104–22. His book *Frankish Rural Settlement in the Latin Kingdom of Jerusalem* (Cambridge: Cambridge Univ. Press, 1998) was not available when this paper was written.

53. Duby, *Rural Economy,* 198–204.

54. H. Aubin, "Medieval Agrarian Society in its Prime: ¶VII. The Lands East of the Elbe and German Colonization Eastwards," *Cambridge Economic History of Europe,* 2d. ed. (Cambridge: Cambridge Univ. Press, 1966), 1: 468; J. Blum, "Rise of Serfdom in Eastern Europe," *American Historical Review* 62 (1957): 815.

55. Slicher van Bath, *Agrarian History,* 148.

56. Jonathan Riley-Smith, "History, the Crusades and the Latin East, 1095–1204: A personal view," in *Crusaders and Muslims in Twelfth-Century Syria,* ed. Maya Shatzmiller (New York: Brill, 1993), 1–17.

7. Edward of England and Abagha Ilkhan

1. Reinhold Röhricht, "La croisade du Prince Édouard d'Angleterre (1270–1274)," in his "Études sur les derniers temps du royaume de Jérusalem," *Archives de l'orient latin* 1 (1881): 622–27; René Grousset, *Histoire des croisades et du royaume franc de Jérusalem,* 3 vols. (Paris: Plon, 1934–36), 3: 659–62; Steven Runciman, *A History of the Crusades* (Cambridge: Cambridge Univ. Press, 1954), 3: 336–37; L. Lockhart, "The Relations between Edward I and Edward II of England and the Mongol Il-Khans of Persia," *Iran* 6 (1968): 23–24; Joshua Prawer, *Histoire du royaume latin de Jérusalem,* trans. G. Nahon (Paris: Editions du centre nationale de la recherche scientifique, 1970), 2: 499–505; Jonathan S. C. Riley-Smith, introduction and notes to Ibn al-Furat, *Ayyubids, Mamlukes and Crusaders: Selections from the Tarikh al-Duwal wa'l-Muluk of Ibn al-Furat,* ed. and trans. U. and M. C. Lyons (Cambridge: Cambridge Univ. Press, 1971), 2: 242–43; Michael Prestwich, *Edward I* (Berkeley and Los Angeles: Univ. of California Press, 1988), 66–76.

2. This summary is taken from R. Amitai-Preiss, *Mongols and Mamluks: The Mamluk-Ilkhanid War, 1260–1281* (Cambridge: Cambridge Univ. Press, 1995), 98–99. In general, the present paper is an elaboration of the treatment of this subject in that book *(loc. cit.,* as well as 124–26 and 235). I have, however, modified my ideas a bit and, as will be seen, now attribute the failure of the joint Ilkhanid-Frankish campaign more to the latter than to the former.

3. Röhricht ("Études," 623 n. 35), citing *Liber de Antiquis Legibus,* ed. T. Stapleton (London: Camden Society, 1846), 143. The translation is from Denis Sinor, "On Mongol Strategy," in *Proceedings of the Fourth Altaistic Conference,* ed. Ch'en Ch'ieh-hsien (Tainan, Taiwan: Department of History, National Ch'engkung University, 1975), 224, republished as art. 16 in

Denis Sinor, *Inner Asia and Its Contacts with Medieval Europe* (London: Variorum, 1977). For the possibility that Marco Polo's party had something to do with these negotiations, see John S. Critchley, *Marco Polo's Book* (Aldershot: Ashgate, 1992), 66–67.

4. On Samaghar, see Amitai-Preiss, *Mongols and Mamluks,* index.

5. See the convenient summary in Prestwich, *Edward I,* 76; al-Shaghur is mentioned by Ibn 'Abd al-Zahir, *al-Rawd al-zahir fi sirat al-malik al-zahir,* ed. 'A-'A. al-Khuwaytir (Riyad: n.p., 1396/1976), 390, which is copied by Ibn al-Furat, ed. Lyons and Lyons, 1: 196 (trans. 2: 155; see also the comments of Riley-Smith on II, 242–43).

6. Prestwich, *Edward I,* 77. The original Arabic source for information about this raid is Ibn 'Abd al-Zahir (396–97), who is again copied by Ibn al-Furat, ed. Lyons and Lyons, 1: 197 (trans. 2: 155).

7. Cf. Lockhart, who for some reason refers to this campaign as a success ("Relations," 24).

8. There were other attempts at Ilkhanid-Frankish military cooperation. For the ill-fated "crusade" of James of Aragon, see R. Röhricht, "Der Kreuzzug des Königs Jacob I. von Aragonien (1269)," *Mittheilungen des Instituts für Öesterreichische Geschichtsforschung* (Innsbruck) 11 (1890): 372–95; and Amitai-Preiss, *Mongols and Mamluks,* 97–98. For reports of Genoese sailors in Iraq during the early 1290s (and perhaps earlier), where they were supposedly building ships to be used against Mamluk shipping, see Denis Sinor, "The Mongols and Western Europe," in *A History of the Crusades,* ed. K. M. Setton, 6 vols. (Madison: Univ. of Wisconsin Press, 1961–89), 3: 542. For Frankish activity on the Syrian and Egyptian coast in the aftermath of Ghazan's invasion of the former in 1299–1300, see Sylvia Schein, "*Gesta Dei per Mongolos 1300.* The Genesis of a Non-Event," *The English Historical Review* 94 (1979): 811–12. In none of these episodes, however, can we speak of Mongols and troops from the Frankish West being on the Syrian mainland at the same time.

9. Ibn 'Abd al-Zahir, 395–96; copied by Baybars al-Mansuri, *Zubdat al-fikra fi ta'rikh al-hijra,* MS. British Library Add. 23325, fol. 76a-b; Ibn al-Furat, *Ta'rikh al-duwal wa'l-muluk,* MS. Vienna 814, fol. 202a (this passage is not found in the Lyons edition). The last-mentioned source is the basis of the account in al-Maqrizi, *Kitab al-suluk fi ma'rifat duwal al-muluk,* ed. M. M. Ziyada and S. 'Ashur, (Cairo: s.n., 1934–73), 1: 599–600. This list does not exhaust the sources that repeat this passage.

10. The term *mughul* would seem to refer to "pure" Mongols, as opposed to the more general and common appellation *tatar,* which seems to imply the Mongol soldiery as a whole, and not only those of Turco-Mongolian origin; see the references given in Amitai-Preiss, *Mongols and Mamluks,* 108, n. 8.

11. The various sources mention that this advanced force was under the command of a son (whose name is variously given as Adak, Afak, Aqbal/Iqbal and Aqal) of Baiju Noyan, the famous Mongol general in the Middle East, apparently executed by Hülegü not long after 'Ayn Jalut; see Amitai-Preiss, *Mongols and Mamluks,* 160 n. 13.

12. Al-Yunini, *Dhayl mir'at al-zaman* (Hyderabad: n.p., 1954–61), 2: 467–68; al-Dhahabi, *Ta'rikh al-islam,* MS. Bodleian Laud 279, fol. 9b; Ibn al-Dawadari, *Kanz al-durar wa-jami' al-ghurar,* vol. 8, ed. U. Haarmann (Freiburg and Cairo: Schwartz, 1971), 164–65; Mufaddal ibn Abi 'l-Fada'il, *al-Nahj al-sadid,* in E. Blochet, *Histoire des sultans mamlouks,* published in *Patrologia Orientalis,* vols. 12, 14, and 20 (Paris: Firmin-Didot, 1919–28), 203–4 [of continual pagination]; al-Kutubi, *'Uyun al-tawarikh,* vol. 20, ed. F. Samir and N. Dawud (Baghdad: al-Jumhuriyah al-Iraqiyah, Wizirat al-I'lam, 1980), 417–18. I presume that the original version of this account is found in the lost part of Ibn Shaddad's *Ta'rikh al-malik al-zahir;* the extant part commences only with the later events of A.H. 670. See "L'Estoire des Eracles Empereur,"

RHC Occ. 2: 461, for a short Frankish account of this raid, which states that the Mongols reached as far south as Homs.

13. Ibn 'Abd al-Zahir, 396; al-Yunini, 2: 496–97.

14. Runciman, *History of the Crusades,* 3: 336; Lockhart, "Relations," 24, who for some reason writes the force numbered 10,000 to 12,000 men; Igor de Rachewiltz, *Papal Envoys to the Great Khans* (London: SPCK, 1971), 153; Denis Sinor, "The Mongols and Western Europe," 531; J. A. Boyle, "The Il-khans of Persia and the Princes of Europe," *Central Asiatic Journal* 20 (1976): 30.

15. A. C. M. D'Ohsson, *Histoire des Mongols* (Reprint, Tientsin, China: n.p., 1940; original published at The Hague: Van Cleef, 1834–35), 3: 459–60, who unfortunately does not provide us with information as to his exact source; Grousset, *Histoire,* 661, who, however, mistakenly writes that there were 10,000 troops from Anatolia, *plus* Seljuq auxiliaries (and the smaller force was sent on to north Syria from this large corps).

16. Grousset, *Histoire,* 3: 662; J. Richard, "The Mongols and the Franks," *Journal of Asian History* 3 (1969): 53; Lockhart, "Relations," 24; de Rachewiltz, *Papal Envoys,* 152; Boyle, "Il-khans of Persia," 30–31.

17. See P. Jackson, "Abaqa," *Encyclopaedia Iranica,* 1: 63–64.

18. Röhricht, "La croisade du Prince Édouard," 626 n. 57; Grousset, *Histoire,* 3: 693; Boyle, "Il-khans of Persia," 31.

19. See J. A. Boyle, "The Dynastic and Political History of the Ilkhans," in *Cambridge History of Islam,* ed. J. A. Boyle (Cambridge: Cambridge Univ. Press, 1968), 5: 360–61. Only in 1272–73 was Abagha to send a force to wreak revenge in Transoxania. On the quiet on the border with the Golden Horde, see Amitai-Preiss, *Mongols and Mamluks,* 86–88.

20. On these missions, see Amitai-Preiss, *Mongols and Mamluks,* 94–103, where the relevant literature is cited.

21. There is some contention among scholars about the exact size of the Ilkhanid army, but there is little doubt that it was quite large compared to the armies in neighboring countries. See the discussion in J. M. Smith, Jr., "Mongol Manpower and Persian Population, *Journal of Economic and Social History of the Orient* 18 (1975): 270–99, esp. 278–8 for Hülegü's period, as well as Amitai-Preiss, *Mongols and Mamluks,* 15.

22. R. Amitai-Preiss, "'Ayn Jalut Revisited," *Tarih* 2 (1992): 123–26.

23. Amitai-Preiss, *Mongols and Mamluks,* 171, 219.

24. Paul Meyvaert, "An Unknown Letter of Hulagu, Il-Khan of Persia, to King Louis IX of France," *Viator* 11 (1980): 245–59; Amitai-Preiss, *Mongols and Mamluks,* 94–98.

25. See Riley-Smith's introduction in Ibn al-Furat, ed. Lyons and Lyons, 2: xv-xviii.

26. Lockhart, "Relations," 24.

27. Cited by Baybars's secretary, Ibn 'Abd al-Zahir, *al-Rawd,* 395.

28. This last suggestion, however, may be gratuitous, since we have no evidence for any additional Mongol forces massed on the Mamluk frontier.

29. See the comments in Prestwich, *Edward I,* 82.

30. See P. Jackson, "The Crisis in the Holy Land in 1260," *English Historical Review* 95 (1980): 505–7; and Richard, "Mongols and the Franks," 51–52.

31. Amitai-Preiss, *Mongols and Mamluks,* 129–31. Prestwich, writes: "[Edward, in the summer of 1272] may have hoped that help would be provided by the Mongols, but Baibars soon entered into negotiations with them, and it became clear that they had no intention of a major campaign in the Holy Land" *(Edward I,* 78). There is a misunderstanding here about the nature of the negotiations between Baybars and the Mongols in 1272: these were doomed from the start, as both Baybars and Abagha surely understood. The purpose of this exchange of em-

bassies was probably in the realm of psychological warfare, and to strengthen morale at home (see Amitai-Preiss, *Mongols and Mamluks,* 127–29). By the same token, I disagree with Burkhard Roberg, "Die Tartaren auf dem 2. Konzil von Lyon 1274," *Annuarium Historiae Conciliorum* 5 (1973): 282–83, who attributes much of the blame for the failure of the joint campaign to Abagha, because he believes that the correspondence between Baybars and Abagha in 1272 led to a conclusion of a peace treaty or cease-fire.

32. Röhricht, "La croisade du Prince Édouard," 626.

33. Boyle, "Il-khans of Persia," 30–31; and Prawer, *Histoire,* 2: 502–3. Grousset does not explicitly state this conclusion, but he also blames both sides (*Histoire,* 662).

34. Charles Melville, "Against the Mongols," *Times Literary Supplement,* 2 Feb. 1996, 12.

35. D. Wasserstein, in a review that appeared in *Mediterranean Historical Review* 9 (1994); 276.

36. R. Amitai-Preiss, "Mamluk Perceptions of the Mongol-Frankish Rapprochement," *Mediterranean Historical Review,* 7 (1992): 65. I have to disagree with Prof. Riley-Smith, who has suggested (in the introduction to Ibn al-Furat, ed. Lyons and Lyons, 2: xi-xii), that Baybars's failure to launch a concerted attack against Acre was due to his decision to maintain it as a conduit for trade between his Syrian possessions and the West. Prof. Riley-Smith also suggests that Baybars's preoccupation with the Mongols was an inhibiting factor in his aggression against Acre, a judgment with which I am in complete agreement.

37. Ibn 'Abd al-Zahir, 396. See Amitai-Preiss, "Mamluk Perceptions," 56 n. 23, for a discussion of this passage and other sources that cite it.

8. Crusading for the Messiah: Jews as Instruments of Christian Anti-Islamic Holy War

1. See Jacques de Vitry, *Lettres de Jacques de Vitry (1160/1170–1240) évêque de Saint-Jean-d'Acre,* ed. R. B. C. Huygens (Leiden: Brill, 1960), 141–53; Oliver of Paderborn, *The Capture of Damietta,* trans. John Joseph Gavignan, (Philadelphia: Univ. of Pennsylvania Press, 1948), chap. 55; and Martin Gosman, "La Legende du Prêtre Jean et la Propagande auprès des Croisés devant Damiette (1218–1221)," in *La Croisade, réalités et fictions: actes du colloque d'Amiens, 18–22 mars 1987,* ed. Danielle Buschinger (Göppingen: Kummerle, 1989), 133–42. See also Carlo Conti Rossini, "Il libro dello Pseudo-Clemente e la Crociata di Damietta," *Rivista degli Studi Orientali* 9: nos. 1–2 (1921): 33, and *Directorium ad passagium faciendum,* ed. Charles Kohler, in *RHC Arm.,* 2: 388, which reports that this Muslim fear was still appearing in the fourteenth century.

2. *Gazette* (London), 21 (Jan. 22–25, 1666); 30 (Feb. 22–26, 1666); 33 (Mar. 5–8, 1666); 34 (Mar. 8–12, 1666); also see M. McKeon, "Sabbatai Sevi in England," *AJS Review* [Association for Jewish Studies] 2 (1970): 131–69.

3. See Friedrich Zarncke, "Der Priester Johannes," *Berichte über die Verhandlungen der königlich sachsischen Akademie der Wissenschaften zu Leipzig. Philosophisch-historische Klasse,* 7 (1879): 627–1030, and 8 (1883): 1–186; Vsevolod Slessarev, *Prester John: The Letter and the Legend* (Minneapolis: Univ. of Minnesota Press, 1959); Martin Gosman, ed., *La Lettre du Prêtre Jean: les versions en ancien français et en ancien occitan; textes et commentaires* (Gröningen: Bouma, 1982), 23–31, offers a brief outline and evaluation of these works; Bernard Hamilton, "Prester John and the Three Kings of Cologne," in *Studies in medieval history presented to R. H. C. Davis,* ed. Henry Mayr-Harting and Robert I. Moore (London: Hambledon, 1985), 177–92. Slessarev (*Prester John,* 80–92) notes his own critiques of some of the various theories before positing his own.

4. The story of Jeroboam I and his dominion over the ten tribes of "Israel" in the tenth century B.C.E. is detailed in the Deuteronomic history, 1 Kings 11–12.

5. See Adam Knobler, "Missions, Mythologies and the Search for Non-European Allies in Anti-Islamic Holy War, 1291-c.1540" (Ph.D. diss., University of Cambridge, 1990).

6. See, for example, Robert Chazan, *European Jewry and the First Crusade* (Berkeley: Univ. of California Press, 1987); Yitzhak Baer, *A History of the Jews in Christian Spain*, trans. Louis Schoffman, 2 vols. (Philadelphia: Jewish Publication Society of America, 1971); and Joshua Prawer, *The History of the Jews in the Latin Kingdom of Jerusalem* (Oxford: Clarendon Press, 1988).

7. *Acts of Thomas,* 8.

8. Isa. 11:11; Jer. 31–32.

9. James. 1:1; Rev. 7:4–8.

10. On Eldad, see Adolf Neubauer, "Where are the Ten Tribes?" *Jewish Quarterly Review* 1 (1888/9): 95–114; Carlo Conti Rossini, "Leggende geografiche giudaiche del IX secolo (il Sefer Eldad)," *Bollettino della Reale Società Geografica italiana*, 7th ser. 2; nos. 59–62 (1925): 159–90; and Elena Loewenthal, *Il libro di Eldad il Danita: Viaggio immaginario di un ebreo del medioevo* (Bologna: Fattoadarte, 1993). Eldad's work itself can be found in either *Sipurav ve-hilkhotav be-makhadurot shonot 'al pi kitve-yad u-defusim 'atakim 'im mavo ve-he'arot be-tseruf ma'amar 'al ha-Falashim u-minhagehem/Eldad ha-dani, seine Berichte über die x stame,* ed. Abraham Epstein (Pressburg: Avraham Alkala'i, 1891); or *Die Recensionen und Versionen des Eldad ha-Dâni nach den alten Drucken. . . ,* ed. D. H. Müller (Vienna: Templsky, 1892). An English translation can be found in *Jewish Travelers in the Middle Ages,* ed. Elkan Adler (London: Routledge, 1930; Reprint, New York: Dover, 1987), 4–21.

11. On the Khazars, see D. M. Dunlop, *The History of the Jewish Khazars* (New York: Schocken, 1967). I wish to thank Professor Peter Golden of Rutgers University for his insights into Christian knowledge of Khazar religion.

12. Otto of Freising, *Ottonis episcopi Frisingensis Chronica: sive, Historia de duabus civitatibus,* ed. Adolf Hofmeister, Scriptores rerum germanicarum in usum scholarum (Hanover and Leipzig: Hahn, 1912; reprint, Hanover: Hahn, 1984), 93, For Otto's mention of Prester John, see 364–66.

13. Godfrey of Viterbo, *Pantheon seu universitatis libri, qui chronici appellantur, XX . . . ab O. C.-1186,* ed. B. J. Herold (Basel: Iacobi Parci, 1559), col. 262, quoted in John Kirtland Wright, *The Geographical Lore of the Time of the Crusades* (New York: American Geographical Society, 1925; reprint, New York: Dover, 1965), 471 n. 169.

14. On this, see Gian-Andri Bezzola, *Die Mongolen in abendländischer Sicht,* 34f; Harry Bresslau, "Juden und Mongolen 1241," *Zeitschrift der Geschichte der Juden in Deutchland,* 1 (1887): 99–102. Idem., "Juden und Mongolen: ein Nachtrag," 2 (1888): 382–83.

15. Matthew Paris, *Chronica maiora,* ed. H. R. Luard, Rolls Series, 57 (London, 1872–83), 4: 76–78. The translation here is from *The Journey of William of Rubruck to the Eastern Parts of the World, 1253–55,* ed. and trans. W. W. Rockhill, Hakluyt Society Publications, 2d ser., no. 4 (London: Hakluyt Society, 1900), xiv-xvii.

16. See H. G. Richardson, *English Jewry under Angevin Kings* (London: Methuen, 1960).

17. For a brief summary, see David Morgan, *The Mongols* (Oxford: Blackwell, 1986), 181–82. For a firsthand account of a Western embassy to the Mongols, see Willem van Ruysbroeck, *The Mission of Friar William of Rubruck: His Journey to the Court of the Great Khan Mongke, 1253–1255,* trans. Peter Jackson, ed. Peter Jackson and David O. Morgan, Works issued by the Hakluyt Society, 2d series, no. 173 (London: Hakluyt Society, 1990).

18. On alliance plans between Mongols and the West, see Knobler, "Missions, mytholo-

gies," 22–50; John A. Boyle, "The Il-khans of Persia and the Princes of Europe," *Central Asiatic Journal* 20 (1976): 25–40; Denis Sinor, "The Mongols and Western Europe," in *A History of the Crusades,* ed. Kenneth M. Setton (Madison; Univ. of Wisconsin Press, 1975), 3: 513–44; and Jean Richard, "The Mongols and the Franks," *Journal of Asian History* 3 (1969): 45–57.

19. The Portuguese monarch who most vigorously pursued both these goals was Manuel I (r. 1495–1521). See Charles-Martial de Witte, "Un projet portugais de reconquête de la Terre-Sainte (1505–1507)," in *Congresso internacional de história dos descobrimentos* (Lisbon: Actas Comissao Executiva . . . D. Henrique, 1961), 5: 1, 419–48; and Sanjay Subrahmanyam and Luis Filipe F. R. Thomaz, "Evolution of Empire: The Portuguese in the Indian Ocean during the Sixteenth Century," in *The Political Economy of Merchant Empires,* ed. James D. Tracy (Cambridge: Cambridge Univ. Press, 1991), 298–331.

20. See Charles-Martial De Witte, "Les bulles pontificales et l'expansion portugaise au XVe siècle," *Revue d'histoire ecclésiastique* 48 (1953/54): 683–718; 49 (1954/55): 438–61; 51 (1956/57): 413–53, 809–36; 52 (1957/58): 5–46, 443–71; and Gomes Eanes de Zurara, *Cronica dos feitos de Guiné,* ed. Torquato de Sousa Soares, 2 vols. (Lisbon: Academia Portuguesa da História, 1978–81), chap. 7.

21. George Schurhammer, "Three Letters of Mar Iacob, Bishop of Malabar 1503–1550," *Gregorianum* 14 (1933): 62–86; and Leslie Brown, *The Indian Christians of Saint Thomas: An Account of the Ancient Syrian Church of Malabar,* rev. ed. (Cambridge: Cambridge Univ. Press, 1982).

22. On earlier contacts, see Tadesse Tamrat, *Church and State in Ethiopia, 1270–1527* (Oxford: Clarendon Press, 1972), chap. 7; and Knobler, "Missions, mythologies," 155–71. For the period of Portuguese contact, see Merid Wolde Aregay and Germa Beshah, *The Question of the Union of the Churches in Luso-Ethiopian Relations (1500–1632)* (Lisbon: Junta de Investigaçoes Ultramar, 1964); and Asa J. Davis, "Background to the Zaga ZaAb Embassy: An Ethiopian Diplomatic Mission to Portugal (1529–1539)," *Studia* 32 (1971): 211–302.

23. On Portuguese activity in the Red Sea as early as 1502, see Jean-Louis Bacque-Grammont and Anne Kroell, *Mamlouks, Ottomans et Portugais en Mer Rouge: L'affaire de Djedda en 1517* (Cairo: Institut Français, 1988), chap. 1; and Jean Aubin, "L'Ambassade de Prêtre Jean à D. Manuel," *Mare Luso-Indicum* 3 (1976): 1–56.

24. Jean Aubin, "Le prêtre Jean devant la censure portugaise," *Bulletin des études portugaises et brésiliennes* 41 (1980): 33–57.

25. Conflict between Portuguese clerics and the Ethiopians resulted in Bishop Andre de Oviedo publishing a manifesto (Feb. 2, 1559), forbidding any close association between Latin Catholics and Ethiopian Orthodox. See Manuel de Almeida, *Historia de Ethiopia a Alta ou Abassia. Imperio do Abexim cujo rey vulgarmente he chamado Preste Joam. Historia Aethiopiae, liber I-IV,* ed. Cesare Beccari, Rerum Aethiopicarum Scriptores Occidentales Inediti a saeculo XVI ad XIX, 5 (Rome: C. de Luigi, 1907) 4.9.

26. A text attributed to Reuveni and outlining his travels (both real and possibly feigned) has been published in many editions. The most recent and authoritative is *Sipur David ha-Reuveni 'al-pi kitav-yad Oksford bi-tzaruf kitavim ve 'adviot mi-beni ha-dor' 'im mavo' ve-k-'arot,* ed. A. Z. Aescoly (Jerusalem: Byalik, 1993). An incomplete (and, at times, inaccurate) English translation may be found in *Jewish Travelers in the Middle Ages,* 251–328.

27. On this debate, see Lea Sestieri, *David Reubeni: un ebreo d'Arabia in missione segreta nell'Europa dell '500* (Genoa: Marietti, 1991), 48–49; and Moshe Idel, introduction to *Sipur David ha-Reuveni,* xix-xxvi.

28. Many works have been written on the dialogue between Jews and Christian philo-Semites, chiliasts, and millenarians in the mid-seventeenth century. See David S. Katz, *Philo-*

Semitism and the Readmission of the Jews to England, 1603–1655 (Oxford: Clarendon Press, 1982); *Sceptics, Millenarians and Jews,* ed. David S. Katz and Jonathan I. Israel (Leiden: Brill, 1990); and *Jewish Christians and Christian Jews: From the Renaissance to the Enlightenment,* ed. Richard H. Popkin and Gordon W. Weiner (Dordrecht/Boston: Kluwer, 1994).

29. *The last letters, to the London-merchants and faithful ministers concerning the further proceedings of the conversion and restauration of the Jews* (London: Cotton, 1665), 1.

30. R. R., *A new letter from Aberdeen in Scotland sent to a person of quality* (London: A. Maxwell, 1665), 2–3.

31. "Copia di lettera di Vienna sino il 18 Decembre 65," in Gershom Scholem, "Notes from Italy on the Sabbatean Movement in 1666" (in Hebrew), *Zion* 10 (1942): 55–66.

32. Sir George Rawdon to Viscount Conway, Sept. 5, 1665, in *Calendar of State Papers, Ireland,* 639.

33. Thomas Nunnes, *An Almanack, or Ephemerides for the year of our Lord 1666* (London, 1666), sig. C8^v; John Tanner, *Angelus Britannicus: an ephemeris for the year of our redemption 1666* (London: Horton, 1666), sig. C7 verso.

34. The most complete study of Sabbatai Sevi and Sabbateanism can be found in Gershom Scholem, *Sabbatai Sevi: The Mystical Messiah* (Princeton: Princeton Univ. Press, 1973). For a briefer treatment, see Jonathan I. Israel, *European Jewry in the Age of Mercantilism, 1550–1750,* 2d ed. (Oxford: Clarendon Press, 1989), 209–16.

35. Scholem, *Sabbatai Sevi,* 333–36 ff.; and Petrus Serrarius, *God's love to his people* (London, 1666), reprinted in Mordechi Wilenski, "Four English Pamphlets on the Sabbatian Movement" (in Hebrew, English summary), *Zion* 17 (1952): 169–72. On Serrarius, see Ernestine G. E. van der Wall, "De mystieke chiliast Petrus Serrarius (1600–1669) en zijn wereld," (Ph.D. diss., University of Leiden, 1987).

36. See Michael McKeon, "Sabbatai Sevi in England," *AJS* [Association of Jewish Studies] *Review* 2 (1970): 131–69.

37. *Gazette* (London) 21 (Jan. 22–25, 1666).

38. *Gazette* (London) 30 (Feb. 22–26, 1666); 33 (Mar. 5–8, 1666); 34 (Mar. 8–12, 1666).

39. On the apostasy, see Scholem, *Sabbatai Sevi,* chap. 6. Some Christian commentators had a field day with the event, see John Evelyn, *The History of the three late famous impostors* (London: Herrington, 1669).

40. Mary W. Helms, *Ulysses' Sail: An Ethnographic Odyssey of Power, Knowledge, and Geographical Distance* (Princeton: Princeton Univ. Press, 1988)

41. See Lee Huddleston, *Origins of the American Indians: European Concepts, 1492–1729* (Austin: Univ. of Texas Press, 1967).

9. Images of Tolerance and Intolerance in Cypriot Historical Writings Between the Thirteenth and Sixteenth Centuries

1. Annemarie Weyl Carr and Laurence J. Morrocco, *A Byzantine Masterpiece Recovered: The Thirteenth-Century Murals of Lysi, Cyprus* (Austin: Univ. of Texas Press, 1991), 85–86.

2. Philip M. Holt, *The Age of the Crusades: The Near East from the Eleventh Century to 1517* (London: Longman, 1986), 36–37; Rainer C. Schwinges, *Kreuzzugsideologie und Toleranz: Studien zu Wilhelm von Tyrus, Monographien zur Geschichte des Mittelalters* (Stuttgart: Hiersemann, 1997), 295.

3. Theodore Papadopoullos, "Frontier Status and Frontier Processes in Cyprus," in *The Sweet Land of Cyprus,* papers given at the Twenty-Fifth Jubilee Spring Symposium of Byzantine

Studies, Birmingham, March 1991, ed. A. A. M. Bryer and G. S. Georghallides (Nicosia: Cyprus Research Centre, 1993), 15.

4. This is Leontios Machairas's typical way of mentioning the Mamluk ruler; see *Recital Concerning the Sweet Land of Cyprus Entitled "Chronicle,"* ed. and trans. R. M. Dawkins, 2 vols. (Oxford: Clarendon Press, 1932; reprint, New York: AMS Press, 1980) (hereafter cited as *Machairas)*. For the chronicle itself, see below.

5. Jean Richard, "Culture et population à Chypre au XIIIᵉ siècle," in *The 17th International Byzantine Congress: Abstracts of Short Papers* (Washington: Dumbarton Oaks, 1986), 292; "Le droit et les institutions franques dans le royaume de Chypre," in *Croisés, missionnaires et voyageurs: Les perspectives orientales du monde latin médiéval* (London, Variorum Reprints, 1983), no. 9: 4–5.

6. W. H. Rudt de Collenberg, "Le déclin de la société franque de Chypre entre 1350 et 1450," *Kupriakai Spoudai,* 46 (1982): 73 and passim; Jean Richard, "Le peuplement latin et syrien en Chypre au XIIIᵉ siècle," *Byzantinische Forschungen,* 7 (1979): 173.

7. Peter W. Edbury, "Cypriot Society under Lusignan Rule," *in Caterina Cornaro, Queen of Cyprus,* ed. D. and I. Hunt (London: Trigraph, 1989), 34.

8. For what follows see my "Crusading Images in Cypriot History Writing," in *Cyprus and the Crusades,* papers of a conference held in Nicosia, September 6–9, 1994, ed. Nicholas Coureas (Nicosia: Cyprus Research Centre, 1996), and *"Francus contra Graecum?* Some Notes on Identity in Cypriot History Writing during the Thirteenth Century," in *Visitors, Immigrants, and Invaders in Cyprus,* ed. Paul W. Wallace (Albany, N.Y.: Institute of Cypriot Studies, SUNY Albany, 1995), 114–24.

9. M. R. Morgan, *The Chronicle of Ernoul and the Continuations of William of Tyre* (London: Oxford University Press, 1973), 45, 80, 98, 115, 188.

10. M. R. Morgan, ed., *La Continuation de Guillaume de Tyr (1184–1197),* Documents relatifs à l'histoire des Croisades, 14 (Paris: Geuthner, 1982), 10, 13, 14.

11. C. Galatariotou, "Leontios Machairas' 'Exegesis of the Sweet Land of Cyprus': Towards a Re-appraisal of the Text and its Critics," in *Sweet Land of Cyprus* (see above, n. 3), 412.

12. Morgan, ed., *La Continuation de Guillaume de Tyr,* 46.

13. "Les Gestes des Chiprois," in *RHC Arm.,* 2: 711–15; "Chronique d'Amadi," in *Chroniques d'Amadi et de Strambaldi,* ed. R. de Mas Latrie, 2 vols. (Paris: Imprimerie Nationale, 1891–93), 1: 134, 163 (hereafter cited as *Amadi);* Florio Bustron, *Historia overo commentarii de Cipro,* ed. R. de Mas Latrie in *Mélanges historiques, Choix de documents,* Collection de documents inédits sur l'histoire de France, 5 (Paris: Imprimerie Nationale, 1886), 91 (hereafter: *Bustron).*

14. S. V. Bliznyuk, "Torgovo-ekonomi . . . eskie otnos enija Kipra s gosudarstvami Sredizemnomor'ja v 1192–1373 gg" (Trade and Economic Relations between Cyprus and Countries of the Mediterranean in 1192–1373), in *Vizantija, Sredizemnomor'je, slavjanskij mir: K XVIII Meñdunarodnomu kongressu vizantinistov (Byzantium, the Mediterranean, the Slavic World: To the 18th International Congress of Byzantine Studies)* (Moscow: not available, 1991), 60.

15. *Machairas,* § 499.

16. *Machairas,* § § 153, 329, 336; cf. *Bustron,* 290–91.

17. *Machairas,* § § 416–17 and f. 170 r; cf. *Bustron,* 310.

18. *Machairas,* § § 440–43 and f. 182 v; *Amadi,* 413–14; *Bustron,* 261, 289.

19. *The Chronicle of George Boustronios,* 1456–1489, § 199, trans. R. M. Dawkins, University of Melbourne Cyprus Expedition 2 (Melbourne: Bookroom, University of Melbourne, 1964), 6. See also § 276.

20. *Machairas,* § 22. See also ms. d of the 'L'estoire de Eracles empereur et la conqueste de la Terre d'Outremer,' in *RHC Occ.,* 2: 188.

21. *Machairas,* §§ 23–25.

22. *Machairas,* §§ 230–31 and f. 116v ; Diomede Strambaldi, *Chronica del regno di Cypro, in Chroniques d'Amadi et de Strambaldi,* 2: 92 (see above, n. 13). There is nothing of this nature in *Amadi* and *Bustron.*

23. *Machairas,* § 307; passed over in *Amadi,* 429, and *Bustron,* 279–80.

24. *Machairas,* § 646; not in *Amadi* and *Bustron.*

25. *Machairas,* § 660; cf. *Amadi,* p. 502; and *Bustron,* 359.

26. The story is also briefly narrated by *Amadi,* 502–4, and *Bustron,* 359–61, and quite differently by Monstrelet, as in *Supplementary Excerpts on Cyprus, or Further Materials for a History of Cyprus,* trans. Th. A. H. Mogabgab, 3 pts. (Nicosia, 1941–45), 2: 60–61.

27. *Machairas,* § 667 and f. 311r.

28. *Machairas,* § 692; cf. *Amadi,* p. 509 and *Bustron,* p. 366.

29. *Machairas,* § 695; cf. *Amadi,* p. 512 and *Bustron,* p. 368.

30. *Machairas,* § 489.

10. The Frankish Encounter with the Greek Orthodox in the Crusader States

1. E.g., Donald M. Nicol, "The Byzantine View of Western Europe," *Greek, Roman and Byzantine Studies* 8 (1967), 315–39, and "The Papal Scandal," in Derek Baker, ed. *The Orthodox Churches and the West,* Studies in Church History, 13 (Oxford: Blackwell, 1976), 141–68, Charles M. Brand, *Byzantium Confronts the West* (Cambridge, Mass..: Harvard Univ. Press, 1968); and Aidan Nicols, *Rome and the Eastern Churches: A Study in Schism* (Edinburgh: T. and T. Clark, 1992).

2. J. Darrouzès, "Les documents byzantins du XIIᵉ siècle sur la primauté romaine," *Revue des Etudes Byzantines* 23 (1965): 42–88.

3. For example, the letter of Paschal II of 1112 and response of Nicholas Seides, the dialogues of Anselm of Havelburg with Niketas of Nicomedia, the letter of Basil of Thessaloniki to Hadrian IV in 1156, or the debate of Manuel Komnenos with the Roman cardinals (1166/69); for all these, see Darrouzès, "Les documents byzantins," 42–88.

4. The use of Orthodox monks as suffragan bishops within the Latin episcopal hierarchy is an example of such cooperation; see Bernard Hamilton, *The Latin Church in the Crusader States: The Secular Church* (London: Variorum, 1980), 183–84.

5. Hamilton, *Latin Church,* 18, for general Latin policy toward the Orthodox, and 159–88.

6. *Lettres de Jacques de Vitry,* ed. Robert B. C. Huygens (Leiden: Brill, 1960), 83–84.

7. Leo Tuscus, one of the Pisan brothers at Manuel Komnenos's court in the 1160s, listed twelve causes for schism between the Churches, some of which related to political events, others to theological interpretations. They were quoted by Humbert of Romans in his *Opus Tripartitum* and reproduced by J. Mansi, *Sacrorum conciliorum . . . nova collectio* (Venice, 1780), 24, cols. 126–27.

8. *Patrologia Graeca,* ed. J. P. Migne 102, cols. 721–41 (hereafter cited as *PG*). For Byzantine treatises discussing the historical sources of hostility, see J. Hergenröther, *Monumenta graeca ad Photium ejusque historiam pertinenda* (Ratisbon: Manz, 1869), 154–81.

9. *PG,* 120, cols. 781–96, and, for Peter's reply, cols. 796–816.

10. A. Papadopoulos-Kerameos, *Hierosolomitike Vivliotheke* (St Petersburg: Kirspaoum, 1891, reprint Brussels: Culture et Civilisation, 1963), 20 (Greek Orthodox patriarchate,

Jerusalem, Holy Sepulchre MS 39), 186–92; (Holy Sepulchre MS 108), 485 and (St. Sabas MS 366).

11. J. Darrouzès, "Le mémoire de Constantin Stilbès contre les latins," *Revue des Etudes Byzantines* 21 (1963):, 50–100, for an edition of one such thirteenth-century example and general discussion of the genre.

12. V. Grumel, ed., *Les regestes des actes du patriarcat de Constantinople* (Paris: Institut français d'études byzantines, 1972), 1123.

13. *Regesta Regni Hierosolymitani, Additamentum,* ed. R. Röhricht (Innsbruck: Wagner, 1904), no. 422a, 25–26, for the confirmation by King Amalric in 1166; however, Denys Pringle, *The Churches of the Crusader Kingdom of Jerusalem: A Corpus,* 1, A–K (Cambridge: Cambridge Univ. Press, 1993), 31, suggests an earlier date for the canons' acquisition of the church.

14. R. J. Loenertz, "L'épitre de Théorien le philosophe aux prêtres d'Oreiné," *Memorial Louis Petit: mélanges d'histoire et d'archéologie byzantines (Archives de l'Orient latin,* 1), (Bucharest: Institut français d'études byzantines, 1948), 317–35, with an edition of the letter on pp. 326–33. Reasons for supposing Oreine to be Beth Zechariah ('Ain Karim), near Jerusalem, are discussed on p. 321. In a later edition of the same essay, published in his *Byzantina et Franco-Graeca,* Storia e Letteratura, 118 (Rome: Storia e letteratura, 1970), 45–70, Loenertz revised this opinion and identified Oreine as Oria in Apulia, though without indicating why this was to be preferred to his earlier identification. I continue to support Beth Zechariah, but on grounds not originally advanced by Loenertz, namely, that the Greek pilgrim John Phocas refers to the area as *Oreine* ("hilly"); John Wilkinson, ed., *Jerusalem Pilgrimage 1099–1187* (London: Hakluyt Society, 1988), 332.

15. Cf. Innocent III's concern over shared churches in Calabria, witnessed in his letter of 1201 instructing the archbishop of Cosenza to end a dispute between Latin and Orthodox clergy over the use of altars, *Acta Innocentii papae III,* Fontes, ser. 3, vol. 2. no. 21, 212. For a full recent survey of the question of *azymes* (unleavened bread) in the Holy Land, see Johannes Pahlitzsch, "Die Bedeutung der Azymenfrage für die Beziehungen zwischen griechisch-orthodoxer und lateinischer Kirche in den Kreuzfahrerstaaten," in *Die Folgen der Kreuzzüge für die orientalischen Religionsgemeinschaften,* ed. Walter Beltz (Halle-Saale: Martin-Luther Universität, 1996), 75–93.

16. Benjamin Z. Kedar, "Gerard of Nazareth, A Neglected Twelfth-Century Writer of the Latin East: A contribution to the Intellectual History of the Crusader States," *Dumbarton Oaks Papers* 37 (1983): 55–77. For discussion of Gerard's work on hermits, see Andrew Jotischky, *The Perfection of Solitude: Hermits and Monks in the Crusader States* (University Park, Pa.: Penn State Univ. Press, 1995), 20–23.

17. Kedar, "Gerard of Nazareth," 62. Hamilton (*Latin Church*) 403, assumes that Gerard died in 1161.

18. Kedar ("Gerard of Nazareth," 75–76), published these portions, from Matthias Flacius Illyricus et al., *Ecclesiasticae Historiae, integram ecclesiae Christi . . . secunda centurias perspicuo ordine complectens,* 7 vols. (Basel: Oporinum, 1562–74), 6 [*Duodecima Centuria*], 8, cols. 1230–33.

19. Gregory the Great, *Homiliarum in Evangelia* 2, 25, *Patralogia Latina,* 76, col. 1189: "Maria Magdalena, quae fuerat in civitate peccatrix" (hereafter cited as: *PL*).

20. Bede, *Exegetica genuina in Lucae evangelium expositio* 3, *PL* 92, cols. 423–24.

21. H. M. Garth, *Saint Mary Magdalene in Mediaeval Literature,* Johns Hopkins Univ. Studies in Historical and Political Science 67 (Baltimore: Johns Hopkins University Press, 1950), 21. The standard work on the Magdalene in the West is V̇. Saxer, *Le Culte de Marie Madeleine en Occident des origines à la fin du moyen âge* (Auxerre: Société des fouilles archéologiques et

des monuments historiques de l'Yonne, 1959). See also Susan Haskins, *Mary Magdalen* (London: Harper Collins, 1993), and Giles Constable, "The Interpretation of Mary and Martha," *Three Studies in Medieval Religious and Social Thought* (Cambridge: Cambridge Univ. Press, 1995), 3–143.

22. Victor Saxer, "Les saintes Marie Madeleine et Marie de Bethanie dans la tradition liturgique et homiletique orientale," *Revue des Sciences Religieuses* 32 (1958): 1–37, provides a thorough survey of the Eastern Christian tradition. Saxer suggests that the conflation of Marys in the West may have arisen from the proximity of their liturgical commemorations in the Eastern tradition: Mary of Bethany was celebrated on June 4, and Mary Magdalene on July 22.

23. For the development of the legend, see Haskins, *Mary Magdalen,* 98–113. The representation of the Magdalen in medieval art is catalogued by Louis Réau, *Iconographie de l'Art chrétien* (Paris: Presses Universitaires de France, 1958–59), 3, pt. 2: 846–59.

24. M. M. Edmunds, "La Sainte-Baume and the Iconography of Mary Magdalene," *Gazette des Beaux-Arts* 114 (1989): 16.

25. Edmunds, "La Sainte-Baume," 17.

26. *Itinerarium Egeriae* 29, 19, ed. P. Geyer, Corpus Christianorum Series Latina, 175 (Turnhout: Brepols, 1965), 76 (hereafter cited as *CCSL*).

27. *Itinerarium Antonini Placentini* 16, *CCSL,* 175: 137.

28. Adamnan, *De locis sanctis* 1, 23, *CCSL,* 175: 202.

29. "On the Site of Jerusalem," in Wilkinson, *Jerusalem Pilgrimage,* 179.

30. For an architectural survey of the site, see Pringle, *Churches of the Crusader Kingdom,* 125–35.

31. For the history of the convent at Bethany and discussion of its status and organization, see Hans E. Mayer, *Bistümer, Klöster und Stifte im Königreich Jerusalem,* MGH Schriften 26 (Stuttgart: MGH, 1977), 372–402, and "Fontevrault und Bethanien. Kirchliches Leben in Anjou und Jerusalem im 12 Jahrhundert," *Zeitschrift für Kirchengeschichte* 102 (1991): 14–44. Pringle's architectural survey, *Churches of the Crusader Kingdom,* 135–37, refutes Mayer's thesis of a double convent for men and women.

32. William of Tyre, *Chronicon,* bk. 15, chap. 26, ed. Robert B. C. Huygens, Corpus Christianum Continuatio Medievalis, 63 (Turnhout: Brepols, 1986), 709 (hereafter cited as *CCCM*).

33. William of Tyre, bk. 15, chap. 26, pp. 709–10, "The Life and Journey of Daniel, Abbot of the Russian Land," trans. W. F. Ryan in Wilkinson, *Jerusalem Pilgrimage,* 133. Having established the reason for founding the convent, William then paradoxically states that Queen Melisende placed a "venerable woman" over it as mother superior.

34. This subject has been admirably explored by Joshua Prawer, "Jerusalem in the Christian and Jewish perspectives of the Early Middle Ages," in *Gli Ebrei nell'alto medioevo,* Settimane di studi del centro italiano di studi sull'alto medioevo, 26 (1980), 739–85. See also, in general, Robert L. Wilken, *The Land Called Holy: Palestine in Christian History and Thought* (New Haven: Yale Univ. Press, 1992).

35. *John of Würzburg,* ed. R. B. C. Huygens, *Peregrinationes tres,* CCCM, 139 (Turnhout: Brepols, 1994), 110.

36. *John of Würzburg,* 111.

37. *John of Würzburg,* 111. On the Jacobite monastery of St. Mary Magdalene and its history under the crusaders, see A. Palmer, "The History of the Syrian Orthodox in Jerusalem," part 1, *Oriens Christianus* 75 (1991): 16–43, part 2, *Oriens Christianus* 76 (1992): 74–94, and Johannes Pahlitzsch, "St Maria Magdalena, St Thomas und St Markus. Tradition und Geschichte dreier syrisch-orthodoxer Kirchen in Jerusalem," *Oriens Christianus* 81 (1997): 1–12.

38. The Jerusalem Jacobites seem to have departed from the original tradition of the Eastern Churches in conflating Mary Magdalene with the sinner who anointed Jesus with ointment. The Jacobite synaxarion in use among Copts celebrated Mary Magdalene only as the woman from whom Jesus had expelled demons and who subsequently witnessed the Crucifixion; see *Le synaxaire arabe-jacobite (redaction copte),* trans. R. Basset, *Patrologia Orientalis,* 17, fasc. 3 (Paris: Firmin-Didot, 1923), 693–94. The only anointing incident celebrated in the Jacobite synaxarion was that performed by Mary of Bethany; see *Patrologia Orientalis,* 16, fasc. 2, 244–45.

39. *John of Würzburg,* 112.

40. *John of Würzburg,* 112.

41. Greek Orthodox monks in the Holy Land certainly continued to reproduce the traditional Orthodox accounts of the Magdalene's life in the twelfth century; for example, an early twelfth-century synaxarion for June-August from the monastery of St. Sabas, now Jerusalem Greek Orthodox Patriarchate MS 17, described by Papadopoulos-Kerameos, in *Hierosolomitike Vivliotheke,* 1: 73.

42. Kedar, "Gerard of Nazareth," 75.

43. *Duodecima Centuria,* col. 1233.

44. *Duodecima Centuria,* col. 923.

45. *Duodecima Centuria,* col. 1380.

46. The name Sala is a puzzle. Bernard Hamilton has stated, in private correspondence, that he can find no parallel for it in the Latin East, but surmises that Sala was probably an Arabic-speaking Greek Orthodox who could read both Latin and Greek.

47. Kedar, "Gerard of Nazareth," 63.

48. For the rights of burial of the laity enjoyed by the Templars and Hospitallers in the Latin East, and the problems this caused with diocesans, see Alan Forey, *The Military Orders: From the Twelfth Century to the Early Fourteenth Century* (Basingstoke: Macmillan Education, 1992), 122–23, J. S. C. Riley-Smith, *The Knights of St John of Jerusalem and Cyprus* (London: Macmillan, 1967), 376.

49. Oxford, Bodleian Library MS E Museo 86, f. 202r-v. For discussion of the manuscript, which is concerned with the Carmelite order's reconstruction of its history, see J. P. H. Clark, "A Defence of the Carmelite Order by John Hornby, O. Carm., A.D. 1374," *Carmelus* 32 (1985): 73–106.

50. Kedar, "Gerard of Nazareth," 76.

51. Such as the commune of Antioch's proclamation of an Orthodox patriarch in 1205–6. But this was a case of political opportunism in a struggle over the rulership of the principality that had embroiled the papal legate and Latin patriarch; see Hamilton, *Latin Church,* 216–18.

52. The need for new cemeteries for the Orthodox may suggest that their population was growing.

53. Hamilton, *Latin Church,* 45–46.

54. Odo of Deuil, *De profectione Ludovici VII in orientem,* ed and trans. V. G. Berry (New York: Columbia Univ. Press, 1948), 68. The Treaty of Devol stipulated that the patriarchate of Antioch should be returned to Orthodox control.

55. On Hugo, see A. Dondaine, "Hugues Etherien et Léon Toscan," *Archives d'histoire doctrinale et littéraire du Moyen Age* 27 (1952): 67–134; P. Classen, "Reichersberger Exzerpt aus einem Bericht des Hugo Etherianus über das Konzil von Konstantinopel 1166," *Byzantinische Zeitschrift* 48 (1955): 364–68.

56. *PL,* 202, cols. 229–32.

57. Röhricht, *Regesta Regni Hierosolymitani 1097–1291,* no. 366.

58. William of Tyre, bk. 18, chap. 6 (817–8), bk. 18, chap. 8 (820–22). The bishops found the pope unsympathetic, and the delegation from Outremer to the Third Lateran Council in 1179 had to repeat the complaint.

59. *Innocenti III Regesta,* vol. 2, ep. 212, *PL,* 214, col. 772.

60. *Innocenti III Regesta,* vol. 7, ep. 121, *PL,* 215, col. 407. The letter is directed to an unknown source, but the content makes it clear that it must have been either Outremer or Cyprus. Constantinople might be a possibility, but the letter is dated the nones of August 1204, whereas the letters from the crusaders announcing the sack of the city did not reach the pope until November. Such problems as these brief examples reveal were evidently liable to occur whenever Latins came into contact with an indigenous Orthodox population. In 1368, Urban V complained to the king of Cyprus about the number of Latin women attending Greek churches; see George F. Hill, *A History of Cyprus,* 4 vols. (Cambridge: Cambridge Univ. Press, 1940–52), 3: 1082–83.

11. Tolerance and Intolerance in the Medieval Canon Lawyers

1. Robert I. Moore, *Formation of a Persecuting Society* (Oxford; Blackwell, 1987) and *The Origins of European Dissent* (Oxford: Blackwell, 1985). For a less critical perspective, see Jeffrey Burton Russell, *Dissent and Order in the Middle Ages* (New York: Twayne, 1992).

2. On the relation between the reform movement and the development of canon law, see Stanley Chodorow, *Christian Political Theory and Church Politics in the Mid-twelfth Century: The Ecclesiology of Gratian's 'Decretum'* (Berkeley: Univ. of California Press, 1972).

3. James Muldoon. *Popes, Lawyers, and Infidels: The Church and the Non-Christian World, 1250–1550* (Philadelphia: Univ. of Pennsylvania Press, 1979), 10–11.

4. Benjamin Z. Kedar, *Crusade and Mission: European Approaches toward the Muslims* (Princeton: Princeton Univ. Press, 1984), 76–83.

5. Kedar, *Crusade and Mission,* 46–48.

6. For a survey of Christian-Muslim relations in this period, see *Muslims under Latin Rule, 1100–1300,* ed. James M. Powell (Princeton: Princeton Univ. Press, 1990). The early colonists in Virginia showed a similar disinterest in doing physical labor; see Edmund S. Morgan, "The Labor Problem at Jamestown, 1607–18," *American Historical Review* 76 (1971): 595–611. Generally speaking, Europeans who went on crusade or who later participated in the sixteenth- and seventeenth-century wave of overseas expansion expected to be a new ruling class employing the labor of those who already lived in the lands the Europeans acquired.

7. Muldoon, *Popes, Lawyers and Infidels,* 50–52.

8. James A. Brundage, *Law, Sex, and Christian Society in Medieval Europe* (Chicago: Univ. of Chicago Press, 1987), 379–80.

9. James Powell, "The Papacy and the Muslim Frontier," in *Muslims Under Latin Rule,* 175–203 at 190–91, 198–99.

10. There is a curious parallel in the seventeenth and eighteenth centuries: English settlers were believed to be attracted to the Indian way of life so there were strong pressures not "to go native" in English colonies. See James Axtell, "The White Indians of Colonial America," *William and Mary Quarterly* 32 (1975): 55–88; reprinted in James Axtell, *The European and the Indian* (Oxford: Oxford Univ. Press, 1981), 168–206.

11. See, for example, the Charter of Expulsion that Ferdinand and Isabella issued in 1492: Edward Peters, "Jewish History and Gentile Memory," *Jewish History* 9 (1995): 9–34, esp. 23–28.

12. Brundage, *Law, Sex, and Christian Society,* 243–44.

13. The convert was identified as a husband.

14. Kedar points out that there were occasional stories about the possible conversion of a Muslim ruler living outside Christendom (*Crusade and Mission,* 144), but these came to nothing. The story of Clovis's conversion continued to play an important role in Christian thought.

15. Innocent IV, *Commentaria doctissima in Quinque Libros Decretalium* (Turin: Apud haeredes Nicolai Beuilaquae, 1581), at 3.34.8.

12. William of Tyre, the Muslim Enemy, and the Problem of Tolerance

1. *Willelmi Tyrensis Archiepiscopi Chronicon,* ed. Robert B. C. Huygens, Corpus Christianorum Continuatio Mediaevalis, 63, 63 A (Turnhout: Brepols, 1986), (hereafter cited as WTyr).

2. For William, see Hans Prutz, "Studien über Wilhelm von Tyrus," *Neues Archiv* 8 (1883): 93–132; August Charles Krey, "William of Tyre, the Making of an Historian in the Middle Ages," *Speculum,* 16 (1941): 149–166; D. W. T. C. Vessey, "William of Tyre and the Art of Historiography," *Medieval Studies* 35 (1973): 433–55; Ralph H. C. Davis, "William of Tyre," in *Relations between East and West in the Middle Ages,* ed. Derek Baker (Edinburgh: University Press, 1973), 64–76; Rainer C. Schwinges, *Kreuzzugsideologie und Toleranz: Studien zu Wilhelm von Tyrus,* Monographien zur Geschichte des Mittelalters, 15 (Stuttgart: Hiersemann, 1977); Rudolf Hiestand, "Zum Leben und zur Laufbahn Wilhelms von Tyrus," *Deutsches Archiv* 34 (1978): 345–80; Wolfgang Giese, "Stadt- und Herrscherbeschreibungen bei Wilhelm von Tyrus," *Deutsches Archiv* 34 (1978): 381–410; Robert B. C. Huygens, "Editing William of Tyre," *Sacris Erudiri* 27 (1984): 461–73, and Introduction to *Willelmi Tyrensis Archiepiscopi Chronicon,* 1–95; Peter W. Edbury and John G. Rowe, *William of Tyre: Historian of the Latin East,* Cambridge Studies in Medieval Life and Thought, 4th ser., no. 8 (Cambridge: Cambridge Univ. Press, 1988); Thomas Rödig, *Zur politischen Ideenwelt Wilhelms von Tyrus,* Europäische Hochschulschriften, ser. 3, 429 (Frankfurt/Berne/New York: Peter Lang, 1990). For further contributions, see Hans Eberhard Mayer and Joyce McLellan, "Select Bibliography of the Crusades," in *A History of the Crusades,* (Madison: Univ. of Wisconsin Press, 1989), 6: 524–25.

3. See, for example, Marianne Plocher, *Studien zum Kreuzzugsgedanken im 12. und 13. Jahrhundert* (Ph.D. diss., University of Freiburg in Breisgau, 1950), a less known but still important work; Hans-Dietrich Kahl, *Slawen und Deutsche in der brandenburgischen Geschichte des 12. Jahrhunderts,* Mitteldeutsche Forschungen, 30, 1–2 (Cologne and Vienna: Böhlau, 1964), 225–35, passim; *Heidenmission und Kreuzzugsgedanke in der deutschen Ostpolitik des Mittelalters,* ed. Helmut Beumann (Darmstadt: Wissenschaftliche Buchgesellschaft, 1973), esp. the contributions of Hans-Dietrich Kahl; Norman Daniel, *Islam and the West: The Making of an Image* (Edinburgh: University Press, 1960); Richard W. Southern, *Western Views of Islam in the Middle Ages* (Cambridge, Mass.: Harvard Univ. Press, 1962); Bernard Richard, "L'Islam et les Musulmans chez les chroniqueurs Castillans du milieu du moyen âge," *Hespéris-Tamuda* 12 (1971): 107–32; Paul Sénac, *L'image de l'autre: L'occident médiéval face à l'Islam* (Paris: Flammarion, 1983); Benjamin Z. Kedar, *Crusade and Mission: European Approaches toward the Muslims* (Princeton: Princeton Univ. Press, 1984), 42–96; and Ron Barkai, *Christianos y Musulmanes en la España Medieval* (Madrid: Rialp, 1991), 219–26.

4. Steven Runciman, *The Families of Outremer: The Feudal Nobility of the Crusader Kingdom of Jerusalem, 1099–1291* (London: Athlone, 1960), 22–24; Raymond C. Smail, *Crusading Warfare (1097–1193): A Contribution to Medieval Military History* (Cambridge: Cambridge Univ. Press, 1967), 40 ff.; Nicolas Zbinden, *Abendländische Ritter, Griechen und Türken im ersten Kreuzzug,* Texte und Forschungen zur byzantinisch-neugriechischen Philologie, 48

(Athens: Verlag der Byzantinisch-neugreichischen Jahrbücher, 1975), 23–25, 68–70, 78–79; Schwinges, *Kreuzzugsideologie*, 158 ff., passim; Jonathan Riley-Smith, "Peace Never Established: The Case of the Kingdom of Jerusalem," *Transactions of the Royal Historical Society*, 5th ser., 28 (1978), 87–102, 95–102. See also Rudolf Hiestand, "Der Kreuzfahrer und sein islamisches Gegenüber," *Das Ritterbild in Mittelalter und Renaissance*, Studia humaniora 1 (Düsseldorf: Droste, 1985), 51–68.

5. Hans Eberhard Mayer, "Guillaume de Tyr à l'Ecole," *Mémoires de l'Académie des sciences, arts et belles-lettres de Dijon* 127 (1985/86), 257–65; WTyr, bk. 19, chap. 12, pp. 879–882; Robert B. C. Huygens, "Guillaume de Tyr étudiant. Un chapitre (XIX, 12) de son 'Histoire' retrouvé," *Latomus* 21 (1962): 811–29; Schwinges, *Kreuzzugsideologie*, 19–45; Edbury and Rowe, *William of Tyre*, 13–15, 44–46.

6. Schwinges, *Kreuzzugsideologie*, 21 n. 10, 234–40. See also Verena Epp, "Das Entstehen eines 'Nationalbewußtseins' in den Kreuzfahrerstaaten im 12. Jahrhundert," *Deutsches Archiv* 45 (1989): 596–604.

7. *L'Estoire de Eracles Empereur et la Conqueste de la Terre d'Outremer, RHC Occ.*, vol. 1, 1–2 (Paris: Imprimerie royale, 1844; reprint, Farnsborough: Gregg, 1967), 1: 1–2 here published together with William's Latin text. For a discussion, see Schwinges, *Kreuzzugsideologie*, 44–45, 322 (Register); Franz Ost, *Die altfranzösische übersetzung der Geschichte der Kreuzzüge Wilhelms von Tyrus* (Ph.D. diss., University of Halle, 1899). See also John Pryor, "The Eracles and William of Tyre: An Interim Report," in *The Horns of Hattin*, ed. Benjamin Z. Kedar (Jerusalem: Israel Exploration Society; London: Variorum, 1992), 270–93.

8. WTyr, Prologue, 100; 1: 1, 105–06; 1: 3, 109; 10: 17, 472.

9. For a summary of these interpretations, see Schwinges, *Kreuzzugsideologie*, 68–104; and Kedar, *Crusade and Mission*, 85 ff.

10. Schwinges, *Kreuzzugsideologie*, 90–92, 121–34.

11. WTyr, 1, 4, p. 110: "qui vero Egyptiorum traditiones preferunt appellantur Ssiha, qui nostre fidei magis consentire videntur." For comment, see Schwinges, *Kreuzzugsideologie*, 111–14.

12. Schwinges, *Kreuzzugsideologie*, 266, 274, 279; *Extrait du voyage d'Ibn Djobeir, RHC Or.* (Paris: Imprimerie Royale, 1884; reprint, Farnsborough: Gregg, 1969), 3: 451–52, 454. See also Hans Eberhard Mayer, "Latins, Muslims and Greeks in the Latin Kingdom of Jerusalem," *History* 63 (1978): 175–92, esp. 186; Benjamin Z. Kedar, "The Subjected Muslims of the Frankish Levant," in *Muslims under Latin Rule, 1100–1300*, ed. James M. Powell (Princeton: Princeton Univ. Press, 1990), 135–74, esp. 167–68.

13. See Plocher, *Kreuzzugsgedanken*, 5–88, esp. 10–20.

14. For these and other personal descriptions, see Schwinges, *Kreuzzugsideologie*, 125–26, 155–214, esp. the schedules (160–61, 172–73).

15. WTyr, 20, 31, p. 956: "Noradinus maximus nominis et fidei christianae persecutor, princeps *tamen* justus, vafer et providus, et secundum gentis suae traditiones religiosus." [Italics mine] See also Wtyr, bk. 16, chap. 7, 723. For comments, see Schwinges, *Kreuzzugsideologie*, 187–99; and Kedar, *Crusade and Mission*, 89.

16. Acts 10: 35.

17. Schwinges, *Kreuzzugsideologie*, 214–67. For the difficulties between theory and practice, see Riley-Smith "Peace Never Established," 87–102. For the problems of contracts and real solutions, see Michael A. Köhler, *Allianzen und Verträge zwischen fränkischen und islamischen Herrschern im Vorderen Orient: Eine Studie über das zwischenstaatliche Zusammenleben vom 12. bis ins 13. Jahrhundert* (Berlin: Walter de Gruyter, 1991); see also Pedro T. Zwahlen, *Normative Grundlagen des Rechtsverkehrs zwischen lateinisch-christlicher und islamischer Welt:*

Eine vergleichende Studie zur vormodernen Völkerrechtsgeschichte im Mittelmeerraum (Lic. phil. diss., University of Berne, 1996).

18. WTyr, 13, 18, p. 609: *"Illi vero* [the Franks] *stricto gladio hostibus incumbentes, regem quoad possunt strenue nimis imitari nituntur, et fidei zelum habentes divinam simul et suas ulcisci nituntur iniurias. At vero Doldequinus suos nichilominus dictis animat et ad pugnam promissis incendit, asserens eos justum bellum gerere pro uxoribus et liberis, et pro libertate, quod majus est, proque solo patrio cum praedonibus decertare* [italics mine].

19. For the just war doctrine, see: Gustave Hubrecht, "La 'juste guerre' dans la doctrine chrétienne des origines au milieu du XVIᵉ siècle," *Recueils de la Société Jean Bodin* 15: La Paix, vol. 2 (Brussels: Société Jean Bodin, 1961), 107–23; Anna Morisi, *La guerra nel pensiero cristiano dalle origini alle crociate* (Florence: Sansoni, 1963); Frederick H. Russell, *The Just War in the Middle Ages* (Cambridge: Cambridge Univ. Press, 1975); Ernst-Dieter Hehl, *Kirche und Krieg im 12. Jahrhundert: Studien zu kanonischem Recht und politischer Wirklichkeit*, Monographien zur Geschichte des Mittelalters, 19 (Stuttgart: Hiersemann, 1980); Paulus Engelhardt, "Die Lehre vom 'gerechten Krieg' in der vorreformatorischen und katholischen Tradition: Herkunft-Wandlungen-Krise," *Der gerechte Krieg. Christentum, Islam, Marxismus,* Friedensanalysen, 12, ed. Reiner Steinweg (Frankfurt am Main: Suhrkamp, 1980), 72–124, esp. 72–87; James T. Johnson, *Just War Tradition and the Restraint of War: A Moral and Historical Inquiry* (Princeton: Princeton Univ. Press, 1981); Josef Rief, "Die bellum-iustum-Theorie historisch," *Frieden in Sicherheit: Zur Weiterentwicklung der katholischen Friedensethik,* Festschrift für M. Gritz, ed. Norbert Glatzel and Ernst J. Nagel (Freiburg/Basel/Vienna: Herder, 1982), 15–40; Gerhart Beestermöller, *Der Gerechte Krieg bei Thomas von Aquin: Friedensethik im theologischen Kontext der Summa Theologiae,* Theologie und Frieden, 4 (Cologne: J. Bachem, 1989); Schwinges, *Kreuzzugsideologie,* 221–30, and "Kreuzzug als Heiliger Krieg," in *Glaubenskriege in Vergangenheit und Gegenwart,* ed. Peter Herrmann, Veröffentlichungen der Joachim Jungius-Gesellschaft der Wissenschaften Hamburg, 83 (Göttingen: Vandenhoeck & Ruprecht, 1996), 93–108.

20. Schwinges, *Kreuzzugsideologie,* 229–30, 283. See Zwahlen, *Normative Grundlagen,* 124–29.

21. WTyr, bl. 13, chap. 18, p. 610: *"tandem opitulante divina clementia et intercedente pro eis doctore gentium egregio hostes in fugam versi sunt."* See Schwinges, *Kreuzzugsideologie,* 244–45.

22. WTyr, bk. 1, chap. 3, p. 109; bk. 19, chap. 21, p. 892. For a discussion of the possible Arabic sources and the tenor, see Prutz, "Studien," 107–14; Schwinges, *Kreuzzugsideologie,* 41–43; and Hannes Möhring, "Zur Geschichte der orientalischen Herrscher des Wilhelm von Tyrus: Die Frage der Quellenabhängigkeiten," *Mittellateinisches Jahrbuch* 19 (1984): 170–83. See also Davis "Relations," 71–73; and Edbury and Rowe, *William of Tyre,* 23–24.

23. Charles J. Halperin, "The Ideology of Silence: Prejudice and Pragmatism at the Medieval Religious Frontier," *Comparative Studies in Society and History* 26 (1984): 442–66, which refers to William of Tyre. See also Rainer C. Schwinges, "Die Wahrnehmung der Anderen. Muslime und christliche Geschichtsschreibung im Zeitalter der Kreuzzüge," *Interkulturell. Forum für Interkulturelle Kommunikation, Erziehung und Beratung,* 4 (1996): 64–75.

24. *L'Estoire de Eracles,* 11, 24, 494: *"por la foi premierement, apres por leur vies, por leur fames et por leur enfanz."*

25. WTyr, bk. 13, chap. 16, p. 606; Schwinges, *Kreuzzugsideologie,* 237–38. Remarkably, William's ideas of the hate in religious wars were concerned with the *bellum iustum* of both Baldwin II of Jerusalem and of Tughtigin of Damascus in which the apostle Paul interceded with God to save the Muslims from a complete defeat; see nn. 18 and 21, above.

26. See Emmanuel Sivan, *L'Islam et la croisade. Idéologie et propaganda dans les réactions Musulmanes aux croisades* (Paris: Maisonneuve, 1968), esp. 93–96.

27. Schwinges, *Kreuzzugsideologie,* 64–67.

28. For the development of tolerance in European thought since patristic times, see the basic articles by Klaus Schreiner: "Toleranz," *Geschichtliche Grundbegriffe. Historisches Lexikon zur politisch-sozialen Sprache in Deutschland,* vol. 6, ed. Otto Brunner, Werner Conze, and Reinhart Koselleck (Stuttgart: Klett-Cotta, 1990), 445–94, esp. 446–66; and "Duldsamkeit (tolerantia) oder Schrecken (terror)," *Religiöse Devianz. Untersuchungen zu sozialen, rechtlichen und theologischen Reaktionen auf religiöse Abweichung im westlichen und ostlichen Mittelalter,* ed. Dieter Simon (Frankfurt am Main: V. Klostermann, 1990), 159–210.

29. WTyr, bk. 19, chap. 5, p. 871.

30. Schwinges, *Kreuzzugsideologie,* 160–61, and 172–73 (schedules). For the classical use, see Schreiner "Toleranz," 448–51. See also Christoph Schäublin, "Christliche Humanitas–christliche Toleranz," *Museum Helveticum. Schweizerische Zeitschrift für klassische Altertumswissenschaft* 32 (1975): 209–20; Peter Garnsey, "Religious Toleration in Classical Antiquity," in *Persecution and Tolerance,* ed. W. J. Sheils, Studies in Church History, 21 (Oxford: Blackwell, 1984), 89–98.

31. Huygens, "Editing of *William of Tyre,*" 469.

Selected Bibliography

The following list is composed of books that have been consulted by the authors and should prove worthwhile for further study on the topic. Those who desire to pursue these topics further should consult the endnotes to each essay or one of the numerous recent bibliographies, such as those found in *Crusaders and Muslims in Twelfth Century Syria*. Ed. Maya Shatzmiller (Leiden: Brill 1993), 216–31, or *The Second Crusade and the Cistercians*. Ed. Michael Gervers (New York: St. Martin's, 1992), 211–53. Each of these is more generally useful than the title might suggest.

Amitai, R. *Mongols and Mamluks: The Mamluk-Ilkhanid War, 1260–1281*. Cambridge: Cambridge Univ. Press, 1995.

Aregay, Merid Wolde, and Germa Beshah. *The Question of the Union of Churches in Luso-Ethiopian Relations 1500–1632*. Lisbon: Junta de Investigaçoes Ultramar, 1964.

Arpee, Leon. *History of Armenian Christianity, From the Beginning to Our Own Times*. New York: Armenian Missionary Association, 1946.

Ashtor, E. *A Social and Economic History of the Near East in the Middle Ages*. London: Collins, 1976.

Atiya, Aziz S. *History of Eastern Christianity*. Notre Dame, Ind.: Univ. of Notre Dame Press, 1968.

Bacque-Grammont, Jean-Louis, and Anne Kroell. *Mamlouks, Ottomans et Portugais en Mer Rouge: L'affaire de Djedda en 1517*. Cairo: Institut français, 1988.

Baer, Yitzhak. *A History of the Jews in Christian Spain*. Translated by Louis Schoffman. 2 vols. Philadelphia: Jewish Publication Society of America, 1971.

Barkai, Ron. *Christianos y Musulmanes en la España medieval*. 2d ed. Madrid: Rialp, 1991.

Beeler, John. *Warfare in Feudal Europe, 730–1200*. Ithaca: Cornell Univ. Press, 1971.

Bennet, H. *Life on the English Manor*. Cambridge: Cambridge Univ. Press, 1937.

Ben Sasson, M. *The Emergence of the Local Jewish Community in the Muslim World: Qayrawan, 800–1057* (in Hebrew). Jerusalem: Magnes, 1996.

Bisson, T. N. *The Medieval Crown of Aragon: A Short History*. New York: Oxford Univ. Press, 1986.

Brand, Charles M. *Byzantium Confronts the West*. Cambridge, Mass.: Harvard Univ. Press, 1968.

Brodman, James W. *Ransoming Captives in Crusader Spain: The Order of Merced on the Christian-Islamic Frontier*. Philadelphia: Univ. of Pennsylvania Press, 1986.

Brown, L. *The Indian Christians of Saint Thomas: An Account of the Syrian Church of Malabar*. Rev. ed. Cambridge: Cambridge Univ. Press, 1982.

Brundage, James A. *Law, Sex, and Christian Society in Medieval Europe*. Chicago: Univ. of Chicago Press, 1987.

———. *Medieval Canon Law and the Crusader*. Madison: Univ. of Wisconsin Press, 1969.

Burns, Robert I., S.J. *The Crusader Kingdom of Valencia: Reconstruction on a Thirteenth-Century Frontier*. 2 vols. Cambridge, Mass.: Harvard Univ. Press, 1967.

———. *Islam under the Crusaders: Colonial Survival in the Thirteenth-Century Kingdom of Valencia*. Princeton: Princeton Univ. Press, 1973.

Canard, M. *Histoire de la dynastie des Hamdanides de Jazira et la Syrie*. Paris: Presses Universitaires de France, 1953.

Carr, Annemarie Weyl, and L. J. Morrocco. *A Byzantine Masterpiece Recovered: The Thirteenth-Century Murals of Lysi, Cyprus*. Austin: Univ. of Texas Press, 1991.

Chahin, M. *The Kingdom of Armenia*. New York: Dorset, 1991.

Chazan, Robert. *European Jewry and the First Crusade*. Berkeley: Univ. of California Press, 1987.

Chodorow, Stanley. *Christian Political Theory and Church Politics in the Mid-twelfth Century: The Ecclesiology of Gratian's "Decretum."* Berkeley: Univ. of California Press, 1972.

Cipollone, G. *Cristianità-Islam: Cattività e Liberazione in nome di Dio: Il tempo di Innocenzo III dopo "il 1187."* Rome: Università gregoriana, 1992.

Cole, Penny. *The Preaching of the Crusades to the Holy Land, 1095–1270*. Cambridge, Mass.: Medieval Academy of America, 1991.

Constable, Olivia Remie. *Trade and Traders in Muslim Spain: The Commercial Realignment of the Iberian Peninsula, 900–1500*. New York: Cambridge Univ. Press, 1994.

Constantelos, D. J. *Byzantine Philanthropy and Social Welfare*. New Brunswick, N.J.: Rutgers Univ. Press, 1968.

Contamine, Philippe. *War in the Middle Ages,* Translated by Michael Jones Oxford: Blackwell, 1984.

Critchley, J. *Marco Polo's Book*. Aldershot: Variorum, 1992..

Crone, P. *Roman, Provincial, and Islamic Law*. Cambridge: Cambridge Univ. Press, 1987.

Daniel, Norman. *Islam and the West: The Making of an Image*. Edinburgh: Univ. Press, 1960.

De Rachewiltz, Igor. *Papal Envoys to the Great Khans*. Stanford: Stanford Univ. Press, 1971.

D'Ohsson, A. C. M. *Histoire des Mongols*. Reprint, Tientsin, China, 1940; original edition published at The Hague: Van Cleef, 1834–35.

Donner, F. M. *The Early Islamic Conquests.* Princeton: Princeton Univ. Press, 1981.

Duby, G. *Rural Economy and Country Life in the Medieval West.* Translated by C. Postan. Columbia: Univ. of South Carolina Press, 1968.

Dufourcq, Charles-Emmanual. *L'Espagne catalane et le Maghrib aux XIIIe et XIVe siècles.* Paris: Presses Universitaires de France, 1966.

Dunlop, D. M. *The History of the Jewish Khazars.* New York: Schocken, 1997.

Edbury, Peter W., and John G. Rowe. *William of Tyre: Historian of the Latin East,* Cambridge Studies in Medieval Life and Thought, 4th ser., no. 8. Cambridge: Cambridge Univ. Press, 1988.

Fattal, A. *Le statut légal des non-musulmans en pays d'Islam.* Beirut: Imprimerie catholique, 1988.

Finucane, Ronald C. *Soldiers of the Faith: Crusaders and Muslims at War.* London: Dent, 1983.

Fortescue, Adrian. *The Lesser Eastern Churches.* London: Catholic Truth Society, 1913.

France, John. *Victory in the East: A Military History of the First Crusade:* Cambridge: Cambridge Univ. Press, 1994.

Friedman, E. G. *Spanish Captives in North Africa in the Early Modern Age.* Madison: Univ. of Wisconsin Press, 1968.

Friedman, M. A. *Jewish Polygyny in the Middle Ages: New Documents from the Cairo Geniza.* Jerusalem: Universität Tel Aviv, 1986.

Garth, H. M. *Saint Mary Magdalene in Mediaeval Literature.* Baltimore: Johns Hopkins Univ. Press, 1950.

Geremek, Bronislaw. *Poverty: A History.* Translated by Agnieszka Kolakowska. Cambridge, Mass.: Harvard Univ. Press, 1994.

Goitein, S. D. *A Mediterranean Society.* 2 vols. Berkeley: Univ. of California Press, 1967–71.

———. *Palestinian Jewry in the Early Islamic and Crusader Times.* (in Hebrew). Jerusalem: Yad Izhak Ben Zvi, 1980.

Grousset, R. *Histoire des croisades et du royaume franc de Jérusalem.* Paris: Plon, 1934–36.

Grousset, Rene. *The Empire of the Steppes.* Translated by N. Walford. New Brunswick, N.J.: Rutgers Univ. Press, 1970.

Halm, H. *The Empire of the Mahdi: The Rise of the Fatimids.* Translated by M. Bonner. Leiden: Brill, 1996.

Hamidullah, Muhammed. *Muslim Conduct of State.* Hyderabad: Government Central Press, 1954.

Hamilton, Bernard. *The Latin Church in the Crusader States: The Secular Church.* London: Variorum, 1980.

Haskins, Susan. *Mary Magdalen.* London: Harper Collins, 1993.

Hehl, Ernst-Dieter. *Kirche und Krieg im 12. Jahrhundert: Studien zu kanonischen Recht und politischer Wirklichkeit.* Monographien zur Geschichte des Mittelalters, 19. Stuttgart: Hiersemann, 1980.

Helms, Mary. *Ulysses' Sail: An Ethnographic Odyssey of Power, Knowledge, and Geographical Distance.* Princeton:, Princeton Univ. Press, 1988.

Hill, Sir George. *A History of Cyprus.* 4 vols. Cambridge: Cambridge Univ. Press, 1940–52.

Housley, Norman. *The Avignon Papacy and the Crusades, 1305–1378.* New York: Oxford Univ. Press, 1986.

Huddleston, Lee. *Origins of the American Indians: European Concepts, 1492–1729.* Austin: Univ. of Texas Press, 1967.

Israel, Jonathan. *European Jewry in the Age of Mercantilism, 1550–1750.* 2d ed. Oxford: Clarendon Press, 1989.

Johnson, James T. *Just War Tradition and the Restraint of War: A Moral and Historical Inquiry.* Princeton: Princeton Univ. Press, 1981.

Jones, Terry, and Alan Ereira. *The Crusades.* New York: Facts on File, 1995.

Jotischky, Andrew. *The Perfection of Solitude: Hermits and Monks in the Crusader States.* Univ. Park, Pa.: Penn State Univ. Press, 1995.

Kahl, Hans-Dietrich. *Slawen und Deutsche in der brandenburgischen Geschichte des 12. Jahrhunderts,* Mitteldeutsche Forschungen, 30 1–2. Cologne and Vienna: BÖhlau, 1964.

Katz, David S. *Philo-Semitism and the Readmission of Jews to England, 1603–1655.* Oxford: Clarendon Press, 1982.

Kedar, Benjamin Z. *Crusade and Mission: European Approaches toward the Muslims.* Princeton: Princeton Univ. Press, 1984.

Köhler, Michael A. *Allianzen und Verträge zwischen fränkischen und islamischen Herrschern im Vorderen Orient: Eine Studie über das zwischenstaatliche Zusammenleben vom 12. bis ins 13. Jahrhundert.* Berlin: de Gruyter, 1991.

Kraemer, J. L. *Humanism in the Renaissance of Islam.* Leiden: Brill, 1986.

Le Strange, G. *Palestine under the Muslims.* London: Palestine Exploration Fund, 1890.

Lilie, Ralph-Johannes. *Byzantium and the Crusader States.* Translated by J. Morris and J. Ridings. Oxford: Clarendon Press, 1993.

Little, Lester K. *Religious Poverty and the Profit Economy in Medieval Europe.* Ithaca: Cornell Univ. Press, 1978..

Loenertz, R. *La Société des frères pérégrinants.* Rome: Ad S. Sabinae, 1937.

Loewenthal, Elena. *Il libro di Eldad il Danita: Viaggio immaginario di un ebreo del medioevo.* Bologna: Fattoadarte, 1993.

Lokkegaard, F. *Islamic Taxation in the Classic Period.* Copenhagen: Branner & Korch, 1950.

Lomax, Derek W. *The Reconquest of Spain.* London: Longman, 1978.

Lyons, C., and D. E. P. Jackson. *Saladin: The Politics of the Holy War.* Cambridge: Cambridge Univ. Press, 1982.

MacKay, Angus. *Spain in the Middle Ages: From Frontier to Empire, 1000–1500.* New York: St. Martin's, 1977.

MacKenzie, N. D. *Ayyubid Cairo: A Topographical Study.* Cairo: American Univ. of Cairo Press, 1992.

Mann, J. *The Jews in Egypt and Palestine under the Fatimid Caliphs*. Oxford: Oxford Univ. Press, 1969.

Mayer, Hans Eberhard. *Bistümer, Kloster und Stifte im Königreich Jerusalem*. Stuttgart: MGH, 1977.

McGeer, E. *Sowing the Dragon's Teeth: Byzantine Warfare in the Tenth Century*. Washington, D.C.: Dumbarton Oaks, 1995.

Mollat, Michel. *The Poor in the Middle Ages: An Essay in Social History*. Translated by Arthur Goldhammer. New Haven: Yale Univ. Press, 1986.

Morisi, Anna. *La guerra nel pensiero cristiano dalle origini alle crociate*. Florence: Sansoni, 1963.

Moore, R. I. *Formation of a Persecuting Society*. Oxford: Blackwell, 1987.

———. *The Origins of European Dissent*. Oxford: Blackwell, 1985.

Morony, M. G. *Iraq after the Muslim Conquest*. Princeton: Princeton Univ. Press, 1984.

Moule, Arthur C. *Christians in China Before the Year 1500*. New York: Macmillan, 1926.

Mouton, Jean-Michel, *Damas et sa principauté sous les saljouquides et les bourides, 468–549/1076–1154*. Cairo: Institut français, 1994.

Muldoon, James. *Popes, Lawyers, and Infidels: The Church and the Non-Christian World, 1250–1550*. Philadelphia: Univ. of Pennsylvania Press, 1979.

Ormanian, Malachi'a. *The Church of Armenia*. London: Mowbray, 1955.

Ostrogorsky, George. *History of the Byzantine State*. Translated by J. Hussey. Rev. ed. New Brunswick, N.J.: Rutgers Univ. Press, 1969.

Pluckett, T. *The Medieval Bailiff*. London: Athlone, 1954.

Popovic, A. *La révolte des esclaves en Iraq au IIIe/IXe siècles*. Paris: Geuthner, 1976.

Potthast, A. *Regesta pontificum romanorum inde ab anno post Christum natum MCCCIV*. 2 vols. Berlin: Decker, 1874–5.

Powell, James M. ed. *Muslims under Latin Rule, 1100–1300*. Princeton: Princeton Univ. Press, 1992.

Powers, James F. *A Society Organized for War: The Iberian Municipal Militias in the Central Middle Ages, 1000–1284*. Berkeley and Los Angeles: Univ. of California Press, 1988.

Prawer, Joshua. *The Crusaders' Kingdom: European Colonialism in the Middle Ages*. New York: Praeger, 1972.

———. *Histoire du royaume latin de Jérusalem*. Translated by G. Nahon. Paris: Centre de recherche scientifique, 1970.

Prestwich, Michael. *Edward I*. Berkeley and Los Angeles: Univ. of California Press, 1988.

Pringle, Denys. *The Churches of the Crusader Kingdom of Jerusalem: A Corpus*. Vol. 1: A–K. Cambridge: Cambridge Univ. Press, 1993.

Rabbat, N. O., *The Citadel of Cairo*. Leiden: Brill, 1995.

Reilly, Bernard F. *The Conquest of Christian and Muslim Spain*. Cambridge, Mass., 1992.

———. *The Medieval Spains*. Cambridge: Cambridge Univ. Press, 1993.

Ribera, Manuel Mariano. *Centuria primera del real y militar orden de Nuestra Señora de la Merced redempción de cautivos cristianos.* Barcelona: Campins, 1726.

Riley-Smith, Jonathan. *The Feudal Nobility and the Kingdom of Jerusalem, 1174–1277.* London: Macmillan, 1973.

———. *The First Crusaders, 1095–1131.* Cambridge: Cambridge Univ. Press, 1997.

Roberg, B. *Die Union zwischen der greichischen und der lateinischen Kirche auf dem II. Konzil von Lyon.* Bonn: Röhrscheid, 1964.

Robinson, I. S. *Authority and Resistance in the Investiture Controversy: The Polemical Literature of the Late Eleventh Century.* Manchester: Univ. of Manchester Press, 1978,.

Roca, Josep Maria. *L'hospital migeval de Sant Macià.* Barcelona: n.p., 1926.

Rödig, Thomas, *Zur politischen Ideenwelt Wilhelms von Tyrus,* Europäische Hochschulschriften, ser. 3, 429. Frankfurt/Berne/New York: Peter Lang, 1990.

Rogers, Randall. *Latin Siege Warfare in the Twelfth Century.* Oxford: Clarendon Press, 1992.

Runciman, Steven. *The Families of Outremer: The Feudal Nobility of the Crusader Kingdom of Jerusalem, 1099–1291.* London: Athlone, 1960.

———. *A History of the Crusades.* 3 vols. Cambridge: Cambridge Univ. Press, 1951–54; reprint, 1965.

Russell, Frederick H. *The Just War in the Middle Ages.* Cambridge: Cambridge Univ. Press, 1975.

Russell, Jeffrey Burton. *Dissent and Order in the Middle Ages.* New York: Maxwell Macmillan, 1992.

Salavert y Roca, Vicente. *Cerdeña y la expansión mediterránea de la Corona de Aragón, 1297–1314.* Madrid: Consejo superior de Investigaciones Científicas, Escuela de Estudios Medievales, 1956.

Saxer, V. *Le Culte de Marie Madeleine en occident des origines à la fin du moyen âge.* Auxerre: Société des fouilles archéologiques et des monuments historiques de l_Yonne, 1959.

Scarcia Amoretti, B. *Tolleranza e guerra santa nell'Islam.* Florence: Sansoni, 1978.

Scholem, Gershom. *Sabbatai Sevi: The Mystical Messiah.* Princeton: Princeton Univ. Press, 1973.

Schwinges, Rainer Christoph. *Kreuzzugsideologie und Toleranz: Studien zu Wilhelm von Tyrus. Monographien zur Geschichte des Mittelalters,no. 15.* Stuttgart: Hiersemann, 1977.

Sénac, Paul. *L'image de l'autre: l'occident médiéval face à l'Islam.* Paris: Flammarion, 1983.

Sestieri, Lea. *David Reubeni: Un ebreo d'Arabia in missione segreta nell'Europa dell'1500.* Genoa: Marietti, 1991.

Setton, Kenneth M., ed. *A History of the Crusades.* 6 vols. Madison: Univ. of Wisconsin Press, 1969–89.

———. *The Papacy and the Levant, 1204–1571.* 4 vols. Philadelphia: American Philosophical Society, 1976–84.

Siberry, E. *Criticism of Crusading, 1095–1274.* Oxford: Oxford Univ. Press, 1985.

Sivan, Emmanuel. *L'Islam et la croisade: Idéologie et propagande dans les réactions musulmanes aux croisades.* Paris: Librairie d'Amerique et d'Orient, 1968.

Slessarev, Vsevolod. *Prester John: The Letter and the Legend.* Minneapolis: Univ. of Minnesota Press, 1959.

Smail, Raymond C. *Crusading Warfare 1097–1193: A Contribution to Medieval Military History,* 2d ed. Cambridge: Cambridge Univ. Press, 1967.

Soldevila, Ferran. *Història de Catalunya.* 3 vols. Barcelona: Editorial Alpha, 1962.

Southern, Richard W. *Western Views of Islam in the Middle Ages.* Cambridge, Mass.: Harvard Univ. Press, 1962.

Strickland, Matthew. *War and Chivalry: The Conduct and Perception of War in England and Normandy, 1066–1217.* Cambridge: Cambridge Univ. Press, 1996.

Tamrat, T. *Church and State in Ethiopia, 1270–1527.* Oxford: Clarendon Press, 1972.

Tierney, Brian. *Medieval Poor Law: A Sketch of Canonical Theory and Its Application in England.* Berkeley and Los Angeles: Univ. of California Press, 1959.

Tournebize, Fr. Henri François. *Histoire politique et religieuse de l'Arménie.* Paris: Picard, 1910.

Tyan, E. *Histoire de l'organisation judiciaire en pays d'islam.* 2d ed., rev. Leiden: Brill, 1960.

Verbruggen, J. F. *The Art of Warfare in Western Europe during the Middle Ages: From the Eighth Century to 1340.* Translated by Sumner Willard and S. C. M. Southern. New York: North Holland, 1977,.

Watson, A. *Agricultural Innovation in the Early Islamic World.* Cambridge: Cambridge Univ. Press, 1984.

Zbinden, Nicolas. *Abendländische Ritter, Griechen und Türken im ersten Kreuzzug, Texte und Forschungen zur byzantinisch-neugriechischen Philologie.* 48 Athens: Verlag der Byzantisch-neugriechischen Jahrbrücher, 1975, also PhD. diss. Univ. of Zürich, 1975.

Index

DATE DUE
